The Life-Changing Art of Self-Brain Surgery is a brilliant synthesis of neuroscience and practical wisdom, grounded in Dr. Warren's decades of experience as a brain surgeon. This book makes the revolutionary principles of neuroplasticity accessible, showing readers how to enhance their mental health by becoming, in effect, their own brain surgeons. This important resource can bring lasting hope and healing for anyone seeking freedom from negative thinking. It offers readers powerful tools to reshape their thoughts and transform their lives.

JEFFREY M. SCHWARTZ, MD, author of *Brain Lock* and coauthor of *You Are Not Your Brain* and *The Mind and the Brain*

As a brain surgeon, Dr. Lee Warren has spent decades transforming lives in the operating room. Now, in *The Life-Changing Art of Self-Brain Surgery*, he hands the scalpel to you. Combining cutting-edge neuroscience with practical tools, Dr. Warren shows how to rewire your thinking, overcome toxic patterns, and build a healthier, more abundant life.

DR. JOSH AXE, *New York Times* bestselling author of *Think This, Not That* and cofounder of Ancient Nutrition

I've been waiting for a book like this! The perfect blend of science, therapy, and faith. In these days of mental anguish, my good friend Dr. Lee Warren is perfectly suited as a neurosurgeon and a man of faith to help us manage our minds. Practical and powerful, *The Life-Changing Art of Self-Brain Surgery* is a gift!

MAX LUCADO, pastor and *New York Times* bestselling author of *What Happens Next* and *Tame Your Thoughts*

What Dr. Lee Warren has done to equip us for change in *The Life-Changing Art of Self-Brain Surgery* cannot be overstated. His wisdom and insights are thorough yet accessible, thought-provoking yet practical, physical yet spiritual. If I'd had these tools much earlier in life, I could have saved myself and my family a lot of heartache. But you do have them. Don't ignore them. Use them. Again and again.

JONATHON M. SEIDL, author of *Confessions of a Christian Alcoholic*

Dr. Warren is a brilliant neurosurgeon who treats *structural* problems of the brain like tumors, aneurysms, and traumatic brain injuries every day. But in this book he has woven not only his professional but also his personal and spiritual experiences into a masterpiece Rx on how to perform "self–brain surgery" to overcome the epidemic of *functional* problems of the brain like anxiety, depression, loneliness, and grief. A must-read "prescription" for us all!

JOSEPH C. MAROON, MD, professor of neurosurgery, Heindl Scholar in Neuroscience, University of Pittsburgh Medical Center; consultant neurosurgeon for the Pittsburgh Steelers

In *The Life-Changing Art of Self-Brain Surgery*, Dr. Warren hands us back our power, showing us how to harness the incredible plasticity of our brains to lead happier, healthier, and more joyful lives. Dr. Warren gives us the ultimate gift: the practical tools to operate on our own brains and come out the other side the best and most whole versions of ourselves.

ANNIE GRACE, author of *This Naked Mind*

The human mind is nothing short of miraculous, and I can't think of anyone more qualified to help you tap its potential than Dr. Lee Warren. This book will stretch your thinking about thinking and help you change your mind, which is the quintessence of repentance. With so many people struggling with mental health, this is the right book at the right time.

MARK BATTERSON, *New York Times* bestselling author of *The Circle Maker*

Dr. Lee Warren combines scriptural truth, neuroscience, and practical advice to help you transform your life by changing the way you think. No one can do this for you. If you need some revelatory insights on how to frame and practice a healing perspective, take the time to work through these pages. It will change your life.

SUSIE LARSON, bestselling author, national speaker, and talk radio host

We are more than simply bodies and brains. We are *soulish* creatures who actively use our *minds* to navigate, understand, and respond to the world around us. In his book, Dr. Warren describes the power you have to change the way you see yourself and chart your future. As a believer and a neurosurgeon, Dr. Warren is perfectly suited to help you "be transformed by the renewal of your mind" (Romans 12:2, ESV).

J. WARNER WALLACE, *Dateline* featured cold-case detective, senior fellow at the Colson Center for Christian Worldview, adjunct professor of apologetics at Talbot School of Theology, and author of *Cold-Case Christianity* and *The Truth in True Crime*

I lost count of the number of *aha!* moments I experienced while reading this extraordinary book. Written by one of the most trusted global voices at the intersection of neuroscience and faith, *The Life-Changing Art of Self-Brain Surgery* connects the latest scientific discoveries about the brain's neuroplasticity with ancient wisdom about the power of prayer and the methodologies of spiritual formation. I believe it will help you find the answers, the strategies, and the life you've longed to find.

PETE GREIG, 24-7 Prayer International

The Life-Changing Art of Self-Brain Surgery is a step-by-step guide to healing from the inside out that is practical, hopeful, and genuinely life-changing.

CAROLINE BEIDLER, MSW, author of *When You Love Someone in Recovery*

Lee Warren makes the neuroscience of change accessible, actionable, and deeply human. If you're facing something that feels impossible, this book won't give you platitudes. It will give you process, presence, and a path forward.

STEVE MESLER, executive and performance coach, Hall of Fame Olympic gold medalist, and founder of Classroom Champions

Only Lee Warren could write this book. A world-class neurosurgeon with a pastor's heart, he fuses brain science, personal tragedy, and deep faith into a gripping, no-fluff guide to real transformation. *The Life-Changing Art of Self-Brain Surgery* isn't just smart—it's raw, wise, and bursting with hard-won hope. You won't just read it. You'll feel it.

IAN MORGAN CRON, author of *The Road Back to You*

Dr. Lee Warren delivers an incisive master class, merging neuroscience, faith, and clinical precision to help readers reclaim agency over their thought lives. *The Life-Changing Art of Self-Brain Surgery* doesn't offer fluff or pop-psych slogans. It's a rigorous, hope-filled invitation to become a steward of your own mind. Rooted in science, anchored in Scripture, and loaded with practical tools, this book is a game changer for anyone ready to heal from the inside out.

CHRISTOPHER COOK, author of *Healing What You Can't Erase* and podcast host of *Win Today: Your Roadmap to Wholeness*

We desperately need the strength and healing Dr. Warren prescribes so powerfully and so clearly. He brings together neuroscience, practical wisdom, and faith in God as a remedy for all that is crippling our souls. He explains why we need to take action to heal ourselves, how to use science to do it, and how to ask God for his grace to heal us. Dr. Warren shows us the truth that will set us free.

MICHAEL EGNOR, MD, professor of neurological surgery, Stony Brook University, and author of *The Immortal Mind*

Dr. Warren invites us into the fascinating world of neurosurgery to demonstrate how scientific breakthroughs in neuroplasticity align with what God has revealed about the power of our thoughts to transform our lives, physically altering our brains in much the same way a neurosurgeon uses a scalpel. I have personally experienced what Dr. Warren teaches about being a self–brain surgeon and how it can lead you from a very stuck, hopeless place to a new season of joy.

JOHN BURKE, *New York Times* bestselling author of *Imagine Heaven*

Packed with neurosurgical and spiritual insight as well as practical strategies, *The Life-Changing Art of Self-Brain Surgery* highlights the steps we can take toward our own growth and recovery. Dr. Warren doesn't simply offer us the theory; he leads by example, showing how this approach was pivotal when he was walking his own road of deep pain and loss.

    DR. SHARON DIRCKX, speaker, broadcaster, and author of *Broken Planet* and *Am I Just My Brain?*

Since reading this book, I'm proud to say I've officially begun my amateur (but deeply personal) pursuit of becoming my own brain surgeon. If you're like me—excessively curious about how science strengthens our faith in a God who fearfully and wonderfully makes human beings—this book is for you. It's spiritual nourishment with a heaping side of neuroscience. Get ready to indulge . . . in the best way.

    ALISA KEETON, founder of Revelation Wellness and author of *The Body Revelation*

Self-brain surgery is not another self-help prescription. It is an invitation for lasting change from a neurosurgeon who has the skills, experience, and empathy, not just to lead you out of self-defeating thinking but also to equip you to fight for the true mental freedom that can be yours.

    MATTIE JACKSON, bestselling author of *Lemons on Friday*

This unputdownable book is a stunning, faith-filled guide to rewiring your mind with conviction, clarity, and hope. It's a brilliant manual rich in personal courage, clinical wisdom, and theological insight with transformative power for all who are ready to change their thoughts—and their life.

    ANN VOSKAMP, *New York Times* bestselling author of *One Thousand Gifts*, *WayMaker*, and *Loved to Life*

Dr. Lee Warren's credentials as an accomplished neurosurgeon with strong Christian convictions are extraordinarily unique. His life makes a compelling case for the compatibility of faith and science and the power of self-brain surgery. You'll be captivated by his latest work!

    LEE STROBEL, *New York Times* bestselling author of *The Case for Christ* and *Seeing the Supernatural*

FOREWORD BY DANIEL G. AMEN, MD
W. LEE WARREN, MD

The Life-Changing Art of Self-Brain Surgery®

Connecting Neuroscience and Faith to Radically Transform Your Life

TYNDALE REFRESH™

Think Well. Live Well. Be Well.

Visit Tyndale online at tyndale.com.

Visit Dr. W. Lee Warren at drleewarren.com.

Tyndale, Tyndale's quill logo, *Tyndale Refresh*, and the Tyndale Refresh logo are trademarks of Tyndale House Ministries, registered in the USA, and common law trademarks in various other jurisdictions around the world. All rights reserved. See tyndale.com for a full list of trademarks owned by Tyndale House Ministries. Tyndale Refresh is a nonfiction imprint of Tyndale House Publishers, Carol Stream, Illinois.

Self-Brain Surgery is a registered trademark of W. Lee Warren, MD.

The Life-Changing Art of Self-Brain Surgery: Connecting Neuroscience and Faith to Radically Transform Your Life

Copyright © 2026 by W. Lee Warren, MD. All rights reserved.

Cover and interior illustration of brain engraving copyright © Hannu Viitanen/Depositphotos. All rights reserved.

Author photograph copyright © 2025 by Maci Kay Photography. All rights reserved.

Cover design by Libby Dykstra

Interior design by Laura Cruise

Published in association with the literary agency of Helmers Literary Services.

All Scripture quotations, unless otherwise indicated, are taken from the Holy Bible, *New International Version*,® *NIV*.® Copyright © 1973, 1978, 1984, 2011 by Biblica, Inc.® Used by permission. All rights reserved worldwide. Scripture quotations marked EASY are from the EasyEnglish Bible Copyright © MissionAssist 2018, 2024 – UK Charitable Incorporated Organisation 1162807. Used by permission. All rights reserved. Scripture quotations marked ESV are from The ESV® Bible (The Holy Bible, English Standard Version®), copyright © 2001 by Crossway, a publishing ministry of Good News Publishers. Used by permission. All rights reserved. Scripture quotations marked NASB are taken from the (NASB®) New American Standard Bible,® copyright © 1960, 1971, 1977, 1995, 2020 by The Lockman Foundation. Used by permission. All rights reserved. www.lockman.org. Scripture quotations marked NKJV are taken from the New King James Version,® copyright © 1982 by Thomas Nelson. Used by permission. All rights reserved. Scripture quotations marked NLT are taken from the *Holy Bible*, New Living Translation, copyright © 1996, 2004, 2015 by Tyndale House Foundation. Used by permission of Tyndale House Publishers, Carol Stream, Illinois 60188. All rights reserved. Scripture quotations marked The Voice are taken from The Voice,™ copyright © 2012 by Ecclesia Bible Society. Used by permission. All rights reserved.

The URLs in this book were verified prior to publication. The publisher is not responsible for content in the links, links that have expired, or websites that have changed ownership after that time.

While the medical stories in this book are based on actual events, pseudonyms have been used and identifying details have been changed to protect the privacy of individuals. The names and details of characters applying the principles of self-brain surgery are fictional composites based on hundreds of people the author has met or interacted with over the years. Any resemblance to real people is coincidental.

For information about special discounts for bulk purchases, please contact Tyndale House Publishers at csresponse@tyndale.com, or call 1-855-277-9400.

Library of Congress Cataloging-in-Publication Data

A catalog record for this book is available from the Library of Congress.

ISBN 979-8-4005-0988-9

Printed in the United States of America

32	31	30	29	28	27	26
7	6	5	4	3	2	

For everyone with a brain, who wonders how to operate it more effectively.
For everyone who is searching for the Truth that changes everything.
To my girls: Caity, Kimber, Kalyn, and Amber. I'm so proud of you.
And to Lisa, always.

Medical Disclaimer

Self–brain surgery is one tool you can use to responsibly operate your own mind-brain-body interface and better manage your life. Please note, though, that the information in this book is of a general nature and is not intended to replace the advice of your health care provider or mental health professional. Do not forget that medical problems can create or complicate mental health issues. They can also cause physiological symptoms that you may misinterpret as anxiety or other mental struggles. There may be a problem with your thyroid gland or some other medical issue going on. You may need therapy, medication, or some other treatment that you cannot provide for yourself. So if you're having trouble getting better or making progress in some area, *check in with your doctor or seek professional help.*

Self–brain surgery puts you in the position of the specialist whose primary job is to make sure your patient (you) gets better. Part of that job is to know when to call in a consultant. When I, as a trained and empowered neurosurgeon, encounter a problem with my patient that is outside of my area of expertise, I consult a colleague with the training and knowledge to assist me. Getting that help is part of my responsibility to my patient. Your therapist or provider will welcome you taking this level of control over your own progress and will encourage you to stay involved in your own care.

One other note: While the medical stories in this book are based on actual events, I've used pseudonyms and changed identifying details to protect the privacy of individuals.

Contents

Foreword by Daniel G. Amen, MD xv

INTRODUCTION:
How Self-Brain Surgery Will Change—and Maybe Save—Your Life 1

PART 1: THE WAITING ROOM
1 Out of Options? 7
2 New Patient Paperwork 15

PART 2: THE OFFICE
3 But What If I Don't Want to Have Surgery? 23
4 Why Good Surgeons Change Approaches 29
5 **APPROACH #1**
Nothing Can Help Me 41
6 **APPROACH #2**
Maybe *Something* Can Help Me 51
7 **APPROACH #3**
Maybe Science Can Help Me 63
8 **APPROACH #4**
Maybe God Can Help Me 77
9 Your Role in Rewiring Your Brain 89

PART 3: THE TEN COMMANDMENTS OF SELF-BRAIN SURGERY
10 Why We Need Guiding Principles 105
11 **THE FIRST COMMANDMENT**
I Must Relentlessly Refuse to Participate in My Own Demise 111
12 **THE SECOND COMMANDMENT**
I Must Believe That Feelings Are Not Facts;
They Are Chemical Events in My Brain 115
13 **THE THIRD COMMANDMENT**
I Must Believe That Most of My Automatic Thoughts Are Untrue 123
14 **THE FOURTH COMMANDMENT**
I Must Believe That My Mind Is in Charge of My Brain 131

15 THE FIFTH COMMANDMENT
I Must Believe That Self–Brain Surgery Is Not a Metaphor;
It Is the Mechanism of Transforming My Life ... 139

16 THE SIXTH COMMANDMENT
I Must Love Tomorrow More Than I Hate How I Feel Right Now ... 145

17 THE SEVENTH COMMANDMENT
I Must Stop Making an Operation Out of Everything ... 149

18 THE EIGHTH COMMANDMENT
I Must Not Perpetuate—or Start—Harmful Generational Thought or
Behavioral Issues in My Life or Family ... 153

19 THE NINTH COMMANDMENT
I Must Believe That I'm Getting Better at What I'm Doing ... 159

20 THE TENTH COMMANDMENT
I Must Understand That Thoughts Become Things ... 165

PART 4: THE OPERATING ROOM

21 Operating Your Mind as a Self–Brain Surgery Specialist ... 173
22 The Whole-System Scan ... 179
23 The Thought Biopsy ... 187
24 Basic Self–Brain Surgery ... 195
25 Completing the Training Program ... 209

PART 5: THE PRACTICE

26 Rewiring for Radical Transformation ... 215

EPILOGUE:
How Self–Brain Surgery Saved My Life ... 231

APPENDICES

APPENDIX A
Tactical Self–Brain Surgery Procedures for Specific Problems ... 237

1. When You Feel Sad or Depressed ... 238
2. When You Have a Chronic Illness ... 241
3. When You're Chronically Stressed or Anxious ... 243
4. When You Feel Stuck ... 246
5. When You're Tired of Settling ... 248
6. When You Have Chronic Pain ... 252
7. When You Struggle with Negative Self-Talk and Self-Doubt ... 256
8. When the Biopsy Shows "I" Trouble ... 258
9. When You Focus on the Worst-Case Scenario ... 260

10. When You Feel Lonely or Isolated	264
11. When You're Suffering	266
12. When You're Falling into Old Habits	269
13. When You're Grieving	275
14. When You're Having a Panic or Anxiety Attack	279
15. When You're Offended	281

APPENDIX B
Progress Notes and Reports … 286

APPENDIX C
Pediatric Self-Brain Surgery … 290

APPENDIX D
Guiding Others in Self-Brain Surgery … 293

APPENDIX E
The Self-Brain Surgery Library … 297

APPENDIX F
Self-Brain Surgery in the Bible … 300

Gratitude and Praises … 303

Notes … 305

About the Author … 317

Foreword

Daniel G. Amen, MD
Author of *Change Your Brain Every Day*

In over forty years of studying, treating, and scanning brains, I've learned a vital truth: Your brain is the most complex, miraculous, and misunderstood organ in the universe. When it works right, you work right. When it is troubled, every area of your life suffers.

Yet as powerful as this organ is, its function is not fixed. Your brain responds to how you live, what you think, and how you interact with the world. And the most exciting revelation? You can intentionally guide this process, creating lasting change. That's what makes Dr. W. Lee Warren's *The Life-Changing Art of Self-Brain Surgery* so groundbreaking.

This book is not just a collection of techniques; it's a call to action. Dr. Warren boldly declares that we are all surgeons of our own brains, capable of reshaping neural pathways and creating healthier, more vibrant lives. As someone who has examined over three hundred thousand brain scans and authored books on topics ranging from memory to emotional health, I am thrilled to endorse his scientifically grounded yet deeply human approach.

Dr. Warren invites readers to embrace what I've long championed in my own work: the integration of faith, science, and self-discipline. The power to heal, grow, and transform lies in your hands—and your thoughts. Through neuroscience, he shows us that faith and science are not in conflict but are complementary forces, capable of enhancing our capacity for love, resilience, and purpose.

In this era of skepticism and division, many people feel forced to choose between science and faith. Dr. Warren rejects this false dichotomy. He demonstrates how prayer, gratitude, and aligning one's mind with God's design are not only spiritually enriching but also scientifically valid practices for improving brain health. Modern neuroscience validates what Scripture has taught for centuries: "Be transformed by the renewing of your mind" (Romans 12:2).

The Power of Self-Brain Surgery

I was captivated by Dr. Warren's concept of self-brain surgery, which moves beyond metaphor to a literal application of neuroplasticity. This process—the brain's ability to reorganize itself by forming new neural connections—is the foundation of the techniques he presents in this book. Self-brain surgery isn't a catchy phrase or a fleeting idea; it's a concrete, evidence-based strategy for making intentional changes in your thoughts to alter the physical structure and function of your brain.

Dr. Warren provides practical tools to take charge of this process. His ten commandments of self-brain surgery are not just a road map for mental health—they're a manifesto for a life well-lived. By rejecting harmful habits, embracing healthier patterns, and relentlessly pursuing the truth about ourselves, we can rewire our brains for peace, clarity, and purpose.

Empowering Change

As someone who has seen patients overcome immense adversity through brain-directed strategies, I can confirm that Dr. Warren's techniques are more than theoretical. From battling trauma to managing chronic stress, the steps outlined in this book have the potential to change lives. One of the book's most powerful ideas is what Dr. Warren calls the patient-to-doctor switch: the transformation from passively waiting for someone else to fix you to actively taking charge of your own healing.

This switch is crucial in a world where too many people feel stuck. Whether it's depression, anxiety, or generational trauma, we often believe our circumstances or biology are unchangeable. Dr. Warren reminds us that while therapy and medication have their place, the ultimate power to change rests within each of us. When you understand that every thought you entertain is either helping or hurting your brain, you'll realize the urgency of becoming an intentional "surgeon" of your own mind.

A Unique Contribution to the Field

But what makes this book especially unique is its spiritual dimension. In a world increasingly divided between faith and science, Dr. Warren builds a bridge. He argues—persuasively—that aligning our minds with God's design is not only rational but transformative. Neuroscience validates the benefits of prayer, gratitude, and purpose. Dr. Warren elegantly integrates these truths into his method.

As a psychiatrist who has spent decades advocating for a brain health revolution, I resonate deeply with Dr. Warren's approach. Like my own efforts to redefine mental health as brain health, he challenges outdated paradigms and encourages a proactive, hopeful approach to personal growth. This book empowers readers to take control of their mental, emotional, and spiritual lives.

For readers who are struggling—whether with depression, anxiety, chronic illness, or simply the weight of daily life—this book is a lifeline. It doesn't promise quick fixes or give superficial advice. Instead, it offers a deep understanding of how your thoughts shape your brain and, by extension, your world.

Practical, Actionable, and Life-Changing

The beauty of Dr. Warren's work lies in its practicality. He doesn't leave readers with abstract concepts or lofty goals. Instead, he equips you with clear, actionable steps that you can start applying today. His analogies, like the idea of treating your mind as both the patient and the surgeon, make the material accessible and empowering.

Whether you're learning how to overcome chronic pain, silence the negative self-talk that keeps you stuck, or recover from grief, the techniques in this book are designed to address real-life struggles. By combining cutting-edge neuroscience with timeless spiritual principles, Dr. Warren provides a framework that works for everyone, regardless of their starting point.

A Call to Action

This book is also a call to action for clinicians, coaches, and educators. The insights and techniques presented here are not only transformative for individuals but also invaluable for professionals helping others unlock their potential. As someone who has trained hundreds of therapists and reviewed tens of thousands of cases, I see tremendous value in incorporating these principles into practice.

For anyone who doubts their ability to change, I leave you with this: Science has shown us that the brain is a dynamic organ, capable of remarkable transformation at any age. Change is possible, no matter how stuck you feel. As Dr. Warren has told me, "Self–brain surgery is not optional—it's just a question of whether you'll direct the process for your good or let the default mode run the show." Those words resonate deeply with me because I've seen the profound impact of intentional brain care. I hope, as you read this book, you'll feel the same spark of possibility.

It's an honor to write this foreword. Dr. Warren's wisdom, compassion, and expertise shine through every page. His story, both personal and professional, is a testament to the resilience of the human spirit and the power of faith-infused science. *The Life-Changing Art of Self-Brain Surgery* is a masterwork of empowerment, and I can't wait to see the lives it transforms.

So turn the page. Start the journey. And remember: Your brain is always listening. Let's make sure it hears the right message.

INTRODUCTION

How Self-Brain Surgery Will Change— and Maybe Save—Your Life

If you're like most people, you find life to be more difficult than you want it to be, and you'd love to discover a way to make it better. Something is keeping you sad, sick, stressed, stuck, or constantly settling, and you want to get past it. But so far nothing has given you a reason to believe that things can be significantly better, especially if you struggle with anxiety, depression, grief, ongoing relationship issues, dissatisfaction at work, chronic pain, or a nagging sense of meaninglessness.

I hope to convince you that, while you can't control everything that happens to you, you have a lot more power over how you experience your circumstances than you might think. And often you can begin changing your situation once you learn how to use your mind to alter your brain. Doing so can radically transform your life.

I'm going to show you how, through a process called self–brain surgery.

It's not as crazy as it sounds; it's something you are already doing, every second of every day. Rather than the painful, delicate procedures neurosurgeons like me perform in operating rooms, self–brain surgery happens inside your head with every thought you think, whether or not you are aware of or consciously directing it.

Modern brain imaging and neuroscience have revealed that your brain is constantly breaking and remaking connections between its estimated eighty to one hundred billion neurons. Incredibly, a growing body of research demonstrates that you can control most of those connections when you determine what you pay attention to and how you deliberate about those things. It turns out that you can direct structural changes in your brain by thinking different thoughts, and those brain changes can benefit your body through improved physiology, reduced stress hormone production, and even alterations in the ways your genes are expressed.

Some of these changes can be passed on to the next generation through a process called epigenetics. This stunning truth raises the stakes because when you decide to practice self–brain surgery and command your brain in ways that improve your life, you may also boost your future children's baseline resilience, happiness, and ability to feel comfortable in their own skin. Self–brain surgery is never just about us. This is what I call the two-patient rule: When we change our minds, it has an immediate and future impact on others.

This lies in stark contrast to the message you've likely heard in school, in the media, and in society. Most of us have believed, at least to some extent, the ubiquitous idea that we are the product of the genes we inherit, the family in which we were raised, and the circumstances we face. This reflects a school of thought called determinism (closely related to materialism and reductionism). This theory, which stretches back to seventeenth-century physicist and mathematician Isaac Newton, teaches that once you understand the stuff from which something is made, you can predict how that thing— including you—will behave. In the determinist worldview, then, every decision you'll ever make is determined by undirected biological processes. I call that theory "brain-out" because it says that everything about "you" happens between neurons apart from any agency on your part. The belief that you are just your brain, your genes, or your trauma creates frustration, helplessness, and a feeling that you require outside help to feel better, perform at a higher level, or find hope in your suffering.

It is my intention in the coming pages to teach you how to command the power of self–brain surgery to take mind-down (or top-down) control of your brain. Once you recognize that your mind is separate from your brain and has the creative, restorative power to change and direct the structure and function of your brain, you can use self–brain surgery to help manage chronic pain, heal old emotional wounds, and change how you respond to any challenge. I will show you how to follow a rational, scientific approach to discover the truth of how your mind and brain are designed to function optimally, and how to operate them to your advantage.

Finally, I will explain how modern neuroscience is revealing the surprising role that faith plays in achieving an almost superpower level of emotional resilience and stability no matter what you face. You'll see how this lines up with concepts written about in the Bible thousands of years ago. Rather than science and faith being enemies, then, I will illustrate how they complement each other to help you become the version of yourself that has always felt out of reach.

What Difference Does It Make?

Why did I, a neurosurgeon who addresses acute brain and spinal injuries and diseases in the operating room, become interested in learning how to address the desperation, dread, and defeat that cannot be solved with a scalpel? As intriguing as I found the neuroscience, it took what I've referred to elsewhere as The Massive Thing to test the limits of my capacity to navigate tragedy and overcome the toxic thinking it produced in my life. When our son Mitchell died horrifically in 2013, my wife Lisa and I were plunged into despair. I tell the story more fully in a previous book, *I've Seen the End of You*.[1] As we battled daily bouts of desperation, I slowly realized that my brain and body offered a lot of input and chatter, but I didn't have to accept or act on all of it. Instead, I could take control of my thoughts and outlook. While our Christian faith and loved ones provided lifegiving support, only I could change my mind. In my book *Hope Is the First Dose*[2] I explain how Lisa and I learned to live expectantly again by transforming the way we think—lessons that I now try to pass on to others.

Once I saw how neuroscience, life experience, and faith align, I found my specific calling and purpose. Before I put all of this together, I thought my only job was to perform neurosurgery. Now I see more clearly that I am here to help people figure out what's hurting them and how self–brain surgery can enable them to overcome the thoughts, attitudes, and habits that are holding them back.

If that sounds outlandish, scary, or impossible, consider this: Since we now know that people can change their brains by changing their minds, you are already a surgeon. The only question is whether you will take charge of your thoughts or allow your brain to repeat old, unhelpful scripts. If you take a passive approach, defaulting to reinforcing limiting beliefs and negative stories about your capabilities, you will continue to feel stuck. There is a better way, and I intend to help you see that learning to use your mind to enhance your brain's function, gene expression, and physical health is a type of surgical practice as real as the one I perform in the OR with scalpels and other instruments!

To be clear: You can benefit from self–brain surgery whether you feel that your life so far is relatively normal with no major hardship or you come to this book beaten, bloodied, or bullied by a life full of trauma, drama, tragedy, or other massive things. We are all constantly bombarded by thoughts and feelings that lead to moods, decisions, and actions that we didn't ask for and wouldn't have chosen. The problem comes when we assume we're helpless and give up.

Furthermore, self–brain surgery is a viable option whether you believe that science alone can answer life's questions—even if it hasn't answered all of yours yet—or you draw hope from your faith despite the fact that life right now looks anything but flourishing.

In the early twentieth century, physicists wanted to understand the fundamental particles that make up everything in the universe—including our own bodies. This research led to breakthroughs that changed history, from the atomic bomb and nuclear reactors to an astonishing array of technologies we rely on today. But the true power hidden within atoms could not be fully unleashed until they were accelerated to nearly the speed of light and made to collide. These high-energy collisions forced atoms to reveal their deepest secrets—the subatomic forces and interactions that shape reality—and in doing so, they released incredible energy that transformed the world.

In the same way, when we smash together psychology, neuroscience, neurosurgery, theology, and quantum physics—rather than studying them in isolation—the energy that is released is seismic and transformational. As I'll show you, when taken together, these disciplines reveal how we gain the power to change literally any aspect of our lives by first changing our minds. This book reveals how these disciplines are converging at exactly the right moment in history to bring hope in an era of crisis. Despite the abundance of mental health resources, therapies, medications, and providers, rates of depression, anxiety, suicide, and identity struggles are at all-time highs. People around the world are searching for an answer. The time has come to unlock the full power of how we were designed to think, heal, and flourish.

I'm inviting you into a lifelong practice that will provide you with that answer. Self–brain surgery is not another self-help program or a new take on positivity bias training. It's not a buffet of available techniques to pick and choose from when you want to tweak some aspect of your life. It's not therapy, although many therapists are teaching it to their clients around the world. It's not brain surgery as I perform in the operating room.

Once you master self–brain surgery, everything changes. You will gain profound mental clarity and power for your life and develop a resilience you never knew you had that will equip you for whatever challenges lie ahead. The hope-oriented journey we will take to get from *here* to *there* starts in Antarctica and winds its way through Oklahoma, Iraq, and other places. But it's not just a trip; it's a transformation. Self–brain surgery is not a metaphor; it's the mechanism of personal change. And it just might save your life.

To begin showing you how, let me introduce you to a man who saved his.

PART 1

The Waiting Room

*The problem is not so much to see
what nobody has yet seen,
as to think what nobody has yet thought
concerning that which everybody sees.*

ARTHUR SCHOPENHAUER

1
Out of Options?

> As long as you remain unaware of what your brain is doing or believe that there is no way to alter how your brain functions, you are essentially powerless.
>
> **JEFFREY M. SCHWARTZ AND REBECCA GLADDING**
> You Are Not Your Brain

The pain had become unbearable.

On April 30, 1961, Leonid Rogozov was the only physician on the sixth Soviet Antarctic expedition, and he had an immense problem. His abdominal discomfort had been steadily worsening for a few days, and the young surgeon had grown convinced that he was suffering from acute appendicitis.

Rogozov was in trouble, and he knew it. A dark winter was closing in on the southern hemisphere, the ocean was full of treacherous ice, and the ship he'd journeyed on had already left his team of a dozen explorers alone in Antarctica and could not return for months. The weather made it impossible to fly Rogozov away for help, and he seemingly had no options.

No one was coming to save him. If his appendix burst, he would almost certainly die.

Faced with an impossible situation, Rogozov decided his only chance to live was to perform surgery on himself. It sounded absurd, even to him. But the alternative was death, his life fading away in the polar winter, and he would never see his family or home again.

Rogozov's diary entries from those days make his internal struggle clear. At first he perceived himself to be a sick and potentially dying man, and from that position his situation could have become overwhelmingly hopeless. When you read his words, the desperation is palpable: "An oppressive feeling of foreboding hangs over me. . . . This is it."[1]

But that's not the end of the story because Rogozov did not allow perception to become reality. Faced with this impossible and absurd scenario, he chose to broaden his perspective. When he did, he realized that he was not completely unprepared. He had the knowledge to diagnose the problem and the training to repair it. The only thing he had to do was shift his thinking from that of a sick and scared man alone in the most desperate circumstances imaginable to that of a skilled and compassionate physician who could step in and take action.

"I have to think through the only possible way out—to operate on myself. . . . It's almost impossible . . . but I can't just fold my arms and give up."[2]

If he was going to survive, Rogozov had to stop contemplating and start operating. So, assisted by a meteorologist and a driver whom the surgeon-turned-patient had trained to revive him if he passed out during the surgery, Leonid Rogozov removed his own appendix, saving his life. He had learned the technical skills to perform the procedure from professors and honed those techniques through practice, but don't miss the most important part of the story: Long before the actual surgery, Dr. Rogozov had changed his mind. Before he could even conceive the notion of performing major abdominal surgery on his own body, he first had to become a self–brain surgeon.[3]

And the same is true for you, my friend.

The Tools Are Already in Your Hands

You'll almost certainly never be in the same situation Rogozov was—forced to remove your own inflamed organ on a frozen polar base. But perhaps, if your perception of life presents you with similarly desperate thoughts—*I'm sad, I'm stressed, I'm sick, I'm stuck, I'm out of options*—you need to realize that while perception immobilizes, perspective empowers you to see and respond to your situation from a different point of view.

> Perception immobilizes, but perspective empowers you to see and respond to your situation from a different point of view.

Like an inflamed appendix, disordered thoughts, feelings, and beliefs can cause trouble in several ways.

- You react to them as if they are always trustworthy, when in fact often they are not. Research shows that a huge percentage of our automatic feelings and thoughts are false.
- You pay excessive attention to them or believe that you are obligated to allow them to direct your decisions rather than inform them.
- You have to spend time and energy redirecting your feelings if you later discover them to have been untrue.

Whether or not you're doing so deliberately, you are practicing self–brain surgery every moment. The good news is that your brain wants to heal, change, and grow. It is designed to operate in a way that helps and doesn't hurt you, but that process requires a specific kind of attention and mental direction.

Rogozov's professors taught him how to be a surgeon, and this book will train you to be intentional in the practice of what I call self–brain surgery. In some sense, then, I want to walk alongside you, just as I would do with patients *and* medical students. Here in part 1, you're in "The Waiting Room." It's important that as you begin, you acknowledge the two roles you play in your physical and mental well-being—that of patient and doctor. This is also the place to answer the question, "Why am I here?" Finally, it is the place to begin filling out paperwork, which includes listing the symptoms that are bothering you.

It's crucial to keep track of where you start and how you change by diligent record-keeping. That's why—after you've learned to identify what brought you here—I'll teach you a simple but powerful tool that most medical students and health care providers use to document patient encounters. Writing down what you're thinking, feeling, and believing as you go along helps build hope so you can measure and share your improvement. If you don't write it down, then you can convince yourself that nothing is changing. (As one of my professors in medical school said, "What didn't get documented didn't happen.") Finally, just as medical students start by learning foundational procedures like making an incision and inserting an IV, I'll offer you basic tips on learning to notice and reframe your thinking in this first part.

In part 2, "The Office," you will learn the scientific, philosophical, and even theological principles of what happens in your brain when you use your mind to pay attention to the right things in the right way. This is how you take charge of those mental processes that are supposed to help but can badly hurt you if you let them run amok like the infection in Leonid Rogozov's appendix. We'll look at what neuroscience research reveals about how your brain is constantly undergoing structural changes and your role in determining whether you direct those changes or simply allow them to happen, perpetuating a sense of helplessness and hopelessness.

The answer will largely depend on how deliberately you select your approach. In the second part, I'm going to teach you several ways you can use your mind and your brain to improve (and maybe save) your life. The first three approaches don't require you to believe anything other than the science, while the fourth approach dares you to face the big questions about meaning and purpose.

Once you understand the neuroscience behind and possible approaches to self–brain surgery, you'll be introduced in part 3 to the guiding principles, or what I call "The Ten Commandments of Self–Brain Surgery," which will serve as guardrails as you begin to practice managing your mind as a lifestyle. These are truths about how your mind, brain, and life are designed to work best, as well as how they can fail to do so because of disordered thinking.

In part 4, "The Operating Room," you'll learn some specific ways to assess how your body and brain interact with your mind. Here you'll master the basic self–brain surgery operation to handle troubles brought on either by your life experiences or the way you've been taught to see the world.

Part 5, "The Practice," is a guide to moving out of training and into the regular habit of performing self–brain surgery. Here you are no longer a sick and scared patient; now you are a skilled and compassionate physician who operates from a renewed perspective—informed by what you've been taught, able to see things more accurately, and ready to adapt to whatever life throws at you.

While the basic self–brain surgery procedure is designed as an all-purpose technique to correct distorted thinking, appendix A contains tactical self–brain surgery operations you can use for fifteen common and specific issues. This is the part you'll come back to whenever you want to address a particular problem. When you struggle with, say, anxiety, grief, depression, or even just a lousy attitude, you'll find operations to help you overcome those troubles. Just as I choose different instruments to help me accomplish specific goals in surgery, these operations—such as journaling, breath work, and grounding—employ therapeutic techniques that are proven to help overcome particular problems you may face.

In the back of the book, I've provided some other tools you can use as you become skilled in self–brain surgery. Appendix B includes templates and examples of how to document your progress. Because improving the way you use your mind never stops with you, appendices C and D will show you how to take the skills you learn to help other people—from children to seniors—think and operate like self–brain surgeons too. The final two appendices include the books and Scriptures I recommend you read if you want to learn more about how science and faith go together beautifully.

First Things First

Taking mind-down control begins by answering one of the first and most important questions your medical team asks you: "Why are you here?" They are listening for what they call the chief complaint—a one-sentence summary of what the patient thinks is wrong, like, "My back hurts" or "My arm is weak." It's not a diagnosis; it is a statement of *what feels wrong and what the patient hopes to achieve by seeing the doctor.*

You're reading this book because something isn't working. What's going on in your life that led you to read a book about self–brain surgery? Here are some possibilities:

- You are struggling with your emotional health, and you want to feel better. Your chief complaint might be, "I feel sad, and I want to become happier."

- You are dealing with chronic pain or an irreversible situation, and you want to learn better ways to handle it. You may say, "I feel sick, but I can't change the underlying issue. I want to learn a healthier way to process it and feel better."

- You are under a lot of pressure in some parts of your life, so you might report, "I always feel stressed, and I need some new ways to manage my anxiety."

- You have gone through something difficult that you're having trouble moving past. You might explain, "I feel stuck since this happened, and I want some tools to help me get moving again."

- You have developed some habits that are holding you back, and you want to overcome them. You might say, "I am repeating some things that are not serving me well, and I want to become healthier."

- You feel a lack of purpose or meaning in your life. You could write, "I need to understand why I'm here and where I'm going."

- You can't seem to break through to a higher level of performance, so you report, "I am tired of settling for less than I believe my life is supposed to be."

- You've never been a believer, but now life is making you ask deeper questions. You could write, "I keep feeling like there's something missing in my life, and I need to find out what it is."

- You have gone through something that has made you question your beliefs or doubt God's love or care for you. You might write, "I'm not sure what I believe anymore, and I need to find hope and faith again."

Identifying your chief complaint is the first step in your transition from patient to doctor. You no longer see yourself as a passive, powerless patient who must wait for someone to come along and "fix you." Like Leonid Rogozov, you realize that while you are a patient who needs something to be addressed, you are *also* a surgeon who is capable of operating on yourself. This attention and perspective shift allows you to take a sober look at your situation so you can begin to draw on the resources that are already inside you.

You can't fix something until you know what's broken! Before you can perform self-brain surgery, you need to identify your chief complaint—the problem or mindset that brought you to this book and that you hope to address. In the next chapter, you'll be invited to document it; for now, just begin to consider what it is.

It's Up to You

Recent discoveries in neuroscience make it clear that you don't need to remain stuck. Your brain is undergoing structural changes every second of your life, and you can direct most of those changes by changing how you think.

The problem is that if you do not learn to direct those changes purposefully, they will still happen. And in most cases, passive processes simply direct the brain to continue operating in the same way. Default often leads to decline, building the perception that things can never change. The result of this passive perpetuation of sameness is that we begin to believe, *This is just how I am.*

If what you've been doing has left you searching for a path forward, remember Leonid Rogozov.

He realized that the ship was gone and wasn't coming back anytime soon.

He realized that the weather was too poor for anyone to fly him away for help.

He knew that he was sick and getting sicker, and that he was out of options.

He knew the diagnosis, and he knew the treatment.

All that was left for him to realize was that he wasn't just the patient; he was also the surgeon. And to do that, he had to change his mind.

Once he changed his mind, he had to stop contemplating and start operating.

You're reading this book because something hurts, something doesn't feel right, or you realize that what got you *here* won't get you *there*—"there" being the place your heart is telling you will finally close the gap between the life you're living and the one you're supposed to be living.[4]

You can't just fold your arms and give up.

It's time to change your mind. It's time to change your life.

Surgery starts soon, and you're the surgeon. You're not alone, though, because I'm going to help. By the time you're finished with this book, you will have the knowledge to diagnose and understand the problems you're facing, and the training to repair them.

I've never been to Antarctica, and I've never removed my own appendix. But I've been desperately lost in disordered thinking, in despair over the hard things I'd experienced and asking myself whether life could ever feel okay again. Self-brain surgery saved my life, just like it saved Leonid Rogozov's by revealing that his path to healing would come when he changed his perspective from patient to doctor.

The pages ahead hold hope and healing if you're ready to reorder your mind, rewire your brain, and radically transform your life.

You're in the waiting room, and it's almost your turn.

It's time to stop contemplating and prepare to start operating.

2
New Patient Paperwork

One must never forget that in the drama of existence we are ourselves both actors and spectators.

NIELS BOHR

In my fourth year of medical school, I spent a month in western Oklahoma learning about rural medicine. During my drive to the small-town medical center where I'd been assigned, I listened to music and snacked on fruit-flavored hard candies. My short road trip took a painful turn when I bit down on a sour apple candy and felt a stabbing sensation in my mouth, like one of my teeth had shattered. I choked on something that went down the back of my throat, and with my tongue I could feel a gaping hole in one of my molars. I managed to keep driving, but by the time I reached my destination, I was in intense pain.

When I pulled up to the clinic, I realized that the hospital, doctors' offices, and dental clinic were all in the same building. As I walked in through the front door, I noticed a sign that said, "Emergency, Primary Care, Obstetrics & Gynecology, and General Dentistry."

It was early, and I was alone in the room other than the receptionist behind the desk. She looked up from her monitor and said, "Hello, what can I do for you?"

That's when I probably became the only person ever to introduce myself to her as both a patient and a student-doctor. "Hi, I'm a medical student, and I'm supposed to start my clerkship today. But I also broke a tooth on the drive here, and I really need to see a dentist."

The receptionist made a phone call and then told me that the dentist was on his way, but I'd need to wait a while.

For the next hour, I sat in the waiting room of the multipurpose clinic, filling out registration paperwork both to see the dentist and to work in the facility that month. A few other patients trickled into the waiting area, checked in with the receptionist, and took seats around the room while my jaw throbbed and I continued filling out the forms.

The family doctor I was there to study under came out to meet me, and he gave me a short booklet that explained my role and what was expected of me. On the last page was a template of how I was to document patient visits so that my reports would be consistent with the way he liked information recorded in the chart. The booklet said that I was to write a progress note on each patient using the SOAP format.[1] This was comforting to me since I'd been writing these notes for over a year in medical school.

SOAP stands for subjective, objective, assessment, and plan. It follows the chief complaint, the succinct summary of the patient's problem that we looked at in the last chapter. Now let's unpack each of the following elements of the progress note.

Subjective: This is a record of the words the patient uses to describe how they feel or the symptoms they're experiencing. At this point, no attempt is made to line up the patient's feelings and thoughts with reality. We simply document what the patient says.

The subjective section is important because we need to know what the patient thinks and feels about their problem. Wise and compassionate doctors start where the patient is and try to understand the problem from the patient's perspective. We take into account their perceptions, beliefs, and history, and we see them from a whole-person, trauma-informed frame of mind.

For our purposes, the chief complaint and subjective entries in our progress note tell us why the patient is seeking help so that we can begin to build a diagnostic and therapeutic plan to help them overcome their problem.

Recall that while Rogozov saved his life with his own hands, he had to break through a mental barrier first. He wasn't a superhero; he was just a man in a difficult situation who could either wallow in the realities of the problem and watch his fears come true, or work toward a different reality by changing his mind. Like any patient, he began by cataloguing how he felt. From there, he could begin assessing the situation objectively.

Likewise, after we've gotten into the patient's head to understand what they think, feel, and believe about their situation, it's time to switch perspectives. The progress note isn't just a diary; it's also a place for facts, data, and a plan of action. That brings us to the objective, assessment, and plan parts of the progress note.

Objective: This section is for data. We write down what we can measure, test, or observe directly—details that a different, unbiased person could determine as well. This is where we add science and reason to the subjective notes, and it's where we can begin to change perceptions by shifting our perspective from how we feel to what we can know.

Rogozov felt and thought several things subjectively, but once he switched from the role of patient to doctor, he began to look at his situation differently. Remember that the objective section is filled with information that any wise and compassionate observer could independently determine.

Assessment: This is an unemotional and clear summarization—after all the talking and data collection—of where we stand when we've contemplated our situation long enough to know that it's time to do something. As a physician, Rogozov knew what infection was behind his symptoms—and the dire consequences if he didn't act.

Plan: This is what we intend to do about the problem. At some point, what we think, feel, believe, and observe aren't going to save us, unless we take action. We must stop contemplating and start operating. This is the moment when Rogozov determined to remove his own appendix.

Here's an example of a SOAP progress note, using Leonid Rogozov as both patient and doctor.

Patient Information:

Name: Leonid Rogozov   **Date:** April 30, 1961

Chief Complaint:

Abdominal pain and fever

Subjective:

I feel terrible. My abdomen hurts, I'm nauseated, I have a fever, and I'm scared. I feel hopeless because there is no one here to help me. I'm alone, and I'm afraid I will die.

Objective:

Abdomen is very tender and swollen. Patient has fever, vomiting, loss of appetite; blood pressure is low, and heart rate is elevated.

Assessment:

Acute appendicitis, likely rupture and death without immediate surgery

Plan:

Perform emergency laparotomy with me as both patient and surgeon

How Doctor and Patient Work Together

A year before I began my rural assignment, I saw a classmate standing in the hallway of our medical school one day. He was holding a paper while staring out a window with his shoulders slumped and posture sagging. "What's wrong, Brad?" I asked.

Without words, he held out the paper. It was a graded assignment from our general surgery professor. He'd asked us to fill in the SOAP sections on a progress note for a patient. There was a big red "C" at the top of the page, and at the bottom the professor had written, "Chief complaint, subjective, and objective sections are shoddy, incomplete, and hopelessly mixed up. But the assessment and plan were especially weak."

I share that story to say this: We all have to start somewhere, and documenting our progress is something we learn, not something we're born knowing how to do. It takes practice and courage to tell the truth to yourself about where you stand and how far you have come or have yet to go—but it's worth it. Brad kept trying, and now he's a successful internal medicine subspecialist who has saved countless lives. But even he had to learn how to write SOAP notes.

Like Brad, I had suffered a bit from red markings by professors as I learned how to parse out what my patients said and felt from what I could measure and test, but I was getting better at it through practice.

You're now ready to fill in the chief complaint and subjective parts of your own SOAP progress note. Remember that the subjective section differs from the chief complaint in that it reflects your feelings and beliefs about your problem. You might compare the chief complaint to the subjective section of the sample progress note on page 17 before recording your chief complaint and subjective notes on the progress note template on page 286.

As I looked around the waiting room in the rural Oklahoma clinic, I had a strange and novel set of feelings. I was surrounded by people with their own lives, there to see someone about their troubles. I didn't know them or their stories, but it was such a small town that I figured there was a good chance I'd be seeing some of them as a provider over the course of the month I'd be there. None of them knew me either. They didn't know that I was only a few weeks away from being a doctor, or that I was also a patient with my own pains and problems, like the broken tooth I'd soon have fixed.

Eventually, the receptionist called my name, and I went through the door into the dental clinic to have my tooth repaired. Later that day, with my face still numb and my speech a little slurred, I met my first patient for the month. Sure enough, it was one of those folks who had been in the waiting room with me while I'd been filling out forms to both receive and give care in that small hospital.

That day, I sat in two different chairs just as Rogozov had: I'd been both a patient and a student-doctor in the waiting room. I was first treated by the dentist, and then I helped treat other patients a few hours later.

And here we are as well, my friend. We're both patients. And we're also both self–brain surgeons. We have our own set of pains and problems, and we both need to learn the art of changing chairs—of separating subjective things from objective ones so that we will no longer try to document our progress in a way that seems shoddy, incomplete, and hopelessly mixed up.

It's time to go into the office. Let's walk through the door together, but first let's record our progress.

Learning New Practices

As you now know, learning to write effective progress notes takes time and practice. It's important to note that in medical school, students start learning this process by focusing only on the chief complaint and subjective sections. They first have to learn how to distill everything the patient says into a succinct reason for the visit (in other words, record why the patient thinks they're here) and accurately document the words the patient uses to describe what they feel and think about their own problems. Students are primarily data-gatherers at first, so early on you should focus on clearly describing what you are thinking and feeling. Learning to think about what you are thinking about[2] is a great first step as you train to practice self–brain surgery. Of course, you are not coming to this book as a medical student. But because you have a mind and a brain, you are already a practicing self–brain surgeon.

You are already a practicing self–brain surgeon.

Did you ever have one of those dreams where you showed up to class and found out that you were supposed to take the final exam, only you'd somehow slept through the entire semester, and you were hopelessly unprepared for the test? That sense of disorientation is similar to what you may feel once you realize that your brain's behavior is significantly under your own control. It dawns on you that the thoughts you allowed your brain to accept and reinforce kept you feeling stuck, even though you had the ability to allow your mind to change your brain all along. The freedom you've always dreamed of to change your life is available, and all you need is some training.

The good news is, once you know the truth that you've never actually been stuck and that changing your perspective will reliably alter that perception, all you need to do is decide to practice differently than you have before.

Our general surgery professor wrote that Brad's progress note had an especially weak assessment and plan. That's because Brad (and all of us at that early point in medical school) *lacked the training to discern between the subjective things his patient thought, felt, and believed and the objective things he could measure and test.*

Don't worry if it feels awkward to you, too, the first few times you write down these notes and mentally "switch chairs" between patient and doctor. All students struggle with keeping the subjective and objective categories appropriately separate at first, because how we feel and think seem perfectly objective to us.

Before we move on to "The Office," I encourage you to begin filling in the chief complaint and subjective portions of the SOAP progress note. You'll find the template on page 286. As you go along, you'll likely want to add comments or more specifics to the note. Once you get to "The Operating Room," I'll give you detailed instructions on how to fill out the final sections of the note before performing self–brain surgery. Beginning in the next chapter, you'll join me not as a student but as a colleague, someone already practicing who simply needs to add new techniques and approaches to your skill set in order to operate more effectively—and to find the hope and healing you long for.

PART 2

The Office

Attention changes the world.
How you attend to it changes what it is you find there.
What you find then governs the kind of attention
you will think it appropriate to pay in the future.

IAIN MCGILCHRIST
The Matter with Things

3

But What If I Don't Want to Have Surgery?

A personal belief in the power of one's mental intentions to affect one's physical future is the rational foundation of our lives.

HENRY P. STAPP
Quantum Theory and Free Will

It happens at least once a week in my office. A patient is referred to see me, waits six weeks for an appointment, and then sits in the exam room for fifteen minutes before I enter.

We shake hands, and I ask them questions about why they're there. They explain what hurts and everything they've already tried. They may have done physical therapy, injections, or surgery, yet they're at my practice, perhaps contorted by pain, low on hope, and worried that nothing can help them feel better.

I examine them, study the imaging, and find something that's not been addressed before. Then I say the magic words: "I can fix it, but you'll need surgery."

Instantly it's like someone sucked the oxygen out of the room. The patient's mouth drops open, and they shake their head. "Oh my," they might say. "I didn't come here to get surgery. I'm not having surgery."

Often, if someone came to the appointment with them, my patient makes eye contact with that person. This family member or friend nods and speaks for the first time. "Yup. I've had three back surgeries, and none of them worked. I wouldn't do that again."

I turn back to the patient and ask the questions again. "You tried physical therapy, right?"

They look down. "Yes. Eight weeks, and it didn't help at all."

"And steroid shots?"

Another nod. "Made it worse."

We go back through any previous surgeries, and then I explain what I saw on their new imaging that may finally reveal what needs to be addressed and why I believe surgery will offer them hope of recovery and pain control.

"No," they insist. "I am not going to have surgery. It's too scary and hurts too much. Everybody I know has had a similar experience. Surgery never helps."

I look into my patient's eyes and ask the final question. "What exactly were you hoping I could do for you if you'd already decided against surgery before you came?"

They shrug their shoulders and say something like, "I don't know. Maybe a prescription. I thought you might recommend some new treatment I hadn't heard of. My cousin had stem cell injections, and my aunt bought a copper back brace she read about in a magazine ad, so I wondered about that stuff."

"Did those things work for them?" I ask.

"No, but I was just hoping . . ."

This is when the tears often come. The dying embers of hope fade to black in their eyes as they realize I do not have an instantaneous cure that will eliminate their suffering; instead they must either accept what I'm offering or continue living with the pain.

It's frustrating when I know what will help my patient, but their past experiences and others' influence have created a barrier they're afraid to cross. The gap between hurting and healing seems too wide to bridge.

No Opt-Out Clause

Now let's put you in my patient's place. Imagine yourself on the exam table in my office and think of why you might be there.

Remember your chief complaint, the reason you've picked up this book. Something isn't clicking, and you're looking for a higher level of performance or success. Or something hurts, and you've been unable to move through it and get back to "normal." You've identified a problem, and what you've tried hasn't worked. Your family and friends have shared similar frustrations and told you nothing has helped them make progress either.

My patients who refuse surgery are unable to choose the one thing that would help them because they've come to my office with a limiting story that has convinced them that change isn't possible. The real problem is their mindset: They view surgery as some sort of Hail Mary pass or last resort when it's really what they've needed all along. What's keeping these patients from the healing and pain relief they so badly want is their perception that what I'm offering them—surgery—will make their problem worse, is too dangerous, or won't help them.

And the truth of the matter is that I can't force someone to have surgery if they don't want it. Except in emergencies, people must give consent before doctors can operate.

Not so for you, my friend.

You are already undergoing self–brain surgery by default. Every second of your life your brain is making new connections, or synapses, between neurons— a process called neuroplasticity. Unlike the surgery I perform in a hospital, you cannot opt out of this process.

Your brain has been making new neurons and breaking and recreating synapses between them even while you've been reading this chapter. That fact from neuroscience leads to a startling and life-changing reality: Neuroplasticity does not require your consent, but it can (and should) come under your control.

> **Neuroplasticity does not require your consent, but it can (and should) come under your control.**

Neuroscientist Iain McGilchrist wrote that, "Things change according to the stance we adopt towards them, the type of attention we pay to them, the disposition we hold in relation to them."[1] We now know that we can direct our minds to take charge of a stunningly large percentage of the structural changes our brains make. This gives our thoughts tremendous power to improve our own lives, the lives of those around us, and even those who come after us; but how we wield the power to choose what we think about determines whether we make such improvements or not.[2]

That day in the waiting room of the Oklahoma clinic, I could have skipped my appointment with the dentist. I could have declined treatment because I was scared of the drill. I might have decided that the pain was bearable and maybe even that I somehow deserved a broken tooth. After all, I'm the dummy who decided to bite into that hard candy and rip the filling out of my molar, right? If search engines had been readily available then, I could have found an online forum of people who didn't believe in modern dentistry, and I could have downloaded some home remedies for broken teeth.

Had I done any of those things, however, my tooth would have remained fractured, and I would have probably come down with an infection and needed an even bigger dental procedure.

Why? Because I could choose whether to go to the dentist and follow his advice. I had agency and the free will to either get help or refuse it.

The entire point of this chapter is to get you to accept one premise: You are undergoing self–brain surgery whether you like it or not. The neuroplastic changes your brain makes by default rarely help you and often keep you stuck in an endless loop of doing what you've been doing and getting what you've always been getting.

Now that you know that your brain is changing all the time and that you can direct many of those changes in ways that will help you, look for places where you've let past failures or other people convince you that change is impossible. Those false and limiting beliefs can be fixed through self–brain surgery!

But you're not a hopeless patient anymore; you are an empowered self–brain surgeon. It's time to make the compassionate mental shift from patient to doctor and take control of your brain, body, and life by learning that your mind gives you top-down control over everything you previously thought was beyond your ability to change. In fact, every decision is a choice for either the status quo or for change.

So without shame or stress, just admit to yourself that you can either continue making choices that have led to your current circumstances, or you can make other decisions, from an empowered perspective, that will lead to a different outcome (or, even if the situation doesn't change, your role in it and feelings about it can).

Foundational Principles of Self-Brain Surgery

Your brain's continual formation of neural connections is a little like breathing; you do both all the time, probably without noticing or understanding how these systems work. Self–brain surgery, when used in a way that brings healing, is simply the practice of intentionally and carefully directing the process of how your brain behaves with the goal of making those processes work for you and not against you. Before learning the techniques, it's important that you understand the principles behind the procedure.

1. Your mind and your brain are not the same. Psychiatrists Jeffrey Schwartz and Rebecca Gladding explain the distinction: "The brain receives inputs and generates the *passive* side of experience, whereas the mind is *active*, focusing attention and making decisions."[3]

2. Your mind controls your brain and body from a top-down (mind-down) perspective, but it listens to information from both.

3. Learning to distinguish inputs from your brain—which sound like thoughts and are usually in your own voice—from mind-generated actual thoughts is the starting point of the self–brain surgery practice. (In "The Operating Room," you will learn the Thought Biopsy procedure to distinguish between them.)

4. Your nervous system constantly tries to automate tasks that are frequently performed (including repetitive thoughts, behaviors, and attitudes) so that they require less mind-down control. These responses start to feel unchangeable over time. (More about this when we get to "The Ten Commandments of Self–Brain Surgery.")

5. You are practicing self–brain surgery whether or not you do so intentionally. However, the structural changes your brain makes as it creates new neurons and connections (synapses) can be directed to a stunning degree by changing how and what you pay attention to and think about.

6. Allowing this rewiring process to occur passively or by default is what keeps you stuck or limited.

Maybe you're desperate for change or you simply feel stuck, believing you've tried everything possible to find relief. Perhaps this whole self–brain surgery idea seems like a last-ditch effort.

For the patient I described at the start of this chapter, surgery was not a last resort; it was always the one and only solution to their problem. Self–brain surgery has never been your final recourse because you've already been using it. All you need is the training to perform it in a way that helps you.

Now that you realize you actually have a lot of control over your thoughts, we'll look at four ways people think about the possibility of change in their lives. These four approaches parallel the way we train surgeons to think about solving problems in the operating room, and they will form the basis of the work we're doing to become healthier, feel better, and be happier. They are perspectives and tools we use to bring attention to our thoughts and lives whenever we're faced with a challenge or an opportunity.

4

Why Good Surgeons Change Approaches

Thus emboldened, you will embark on the voyage of your life, let your light shine, so to speak, on the heavenly hill, and pursue your rightful destiny.
JORDAN PETERSON
12 Rules for Life

"Tumor is out," Dr. Takanori Fukushima said.

He held an almond-sized piece of reddish-tan tissue in a pair of forceps. "Show them the craniotomy size, Lee." I picked up an instrument off the scrub tech's stand and used it to grasp a dime that Dr. Fukushima had sterilized. This was always his final demonstration to the half dozen or so neurosurgeons who had flown to Pittsburgh from all over the world to watch him operate. I held the dime over the hole we'd made in the patient's skull, using the surgical microscope to cast the image onto large television monitors that hung on the operating room wall.

This was my favorite part of the long cases we did under Dr. Fukushima's guidance, because it was the only part I, as a mid-level resident, was allowed to perform. When I positioned the dime over the skull opening, eclipsing the hole we'd made to remove the tumor, the visiting surgeons gasped. They could see that Dr. Fukushima had performed this incredibly delicate operation—removing a skull base brain tumor—through a hole in the skull that was literally the size of a dime. In those days, it was typical to make massive skull openings, which led to all kinds of complications and trouble for patients after surgery. Dr. Fukushima was one of the first surgeons in the world to pioneer the minimally invasive surgeries that most patients now expect, but it was groundbreaking work in the late 1990s.

The visitors looked at each other and excitedly nodded and murmured, then broke into gentle golf-clapping applause, as if Dr. Fukushima—with me as his caddy—had just sunk a putt to win the Masters. Dr. Fukushima gave me a little wink before leading the surgeons out of the room so he could teach them more about his operation. One by one, the visitors gave me an approving nod as they filed out behind Dr. Fukushima—the only moment of celebrity I would have before I turned to the business of closing the patient's wound and getting them safely out of surgery.

A similar story repeated itself every week in Pittsburgh during my training, as we had a number of world-famous surgeons on our staff who drew neurosurgeons from universities all over the globe.

What is so amazing is that these travelers were not novices in the medical field. They were department chairs, tenured professors, and published researchers. They came from hospitals in Japan, Germany, Brazil, Italy, Canada, Switzerland, and all over the United States. They had written textbooks, which I'd studied to learn how to be a brain surgeon, and they'd lectured and taught others for decades. They were board-certified neurosurgeons who were already performing similar surgeries.

So why, you might ask, would these established and acclaimed experts in their field travel to Pennsylvania to watch surgeons operate when they already had their own practices, reputations, and good techniques?

The answer is that they recognized the need for a new approach.

In surgical training, we learn that simply knowing how to cut, sew, and perform technical procedures is only a small part of being a safe and successful neurosurgeon. We go to medical school to learn the science of how the body works in health and in disease. Then we go into the hospital to practice caring for people by learning how to place IVs, suture lacerations, perform CPR, and deliver babies. After acquiring the basic techniques and skills every physician needs, we spend years in residency learning the specific procedures to care for people whose problems lie in our specialty.

This is where we learn about approaches. Every problem in neurosurgery, such as a brain tumor in the frontal lobe, can be operated on using a number of different approaches. Many of the techniques will be the same from one approach to another. But approach isn't merely technical; it's also philosophical.

Approach encompasses how we place the patient on the table, where we make the skin incision, how much hair we shave, and how big the bone opening needs to be—things we do to *prepare the patient for the operation*. In brain and spine surgery, an approach includes details like whether the patient will sit up or lie on their side, back, or belly, which we call positioning. So approach is partly what we do *before the surgery begins*, but it also includes what *we believe to be possible* for us to accomplish during the surgery. Those beliefs guide us as we make choices during a procedure, including the technologies we employ and how far we're willing to go to try to solve our patient's problem. We'll come back to this idea soon when we look at the approaches we use for self–brain surgery.

I was blessed to have trained in Pittsburgh, where the world-famous neurosurgeon Dr. Joseph Maroon had founded the residency program and assembled a team of famous surgeons to teach us how to perform almost every type of surgery from multiple approaches. We were taught that sometimes one approach would be less invasive or lead to lower risk, which is why learning when and how to apply each approach was just as important as the technical maneuvers we were learning.

More than once, I saw a surgeon reach the middle of a case and decide they would not be able to complete the surgery safely unless they closed the incision and moved the patient into a different position. They would then complete the operation using a different approach. This takes tremendous character because it is not easy to admit that you made the wrong choice, especially when you're faced with the strong inertia of an operation that is already underway.

It might surprise you to hear that neurosurgeons are not typically known for their humility, which is why it's so remarkable that Dr. Fukushima's visiting doctors would come from their successful practices to learn another way to do something they were already doing quite well. In each case, they came because they realized there was something missing in the approaches they knew and had been using.

I experienced firsthand how narrow one's practice would be without that openness to other approaches. About six months before I was to graduate and be a fully trained neurosurgeon, I was the chief resident in my training program. Late one night I was called into the hospital to care for a patient with a ruptured brain aneurysm. As the chief, I was responsible for making the diagnosis, taking the patient to surgery, and getting the operation started.

By this late point in my training, I'd performed over one hundred brain aneurysm surgeries. My department chairman had told me—in front of other professors—that I was the best aneurysm surgeon he'd ever trained, and I was extremely comfortable with the decision I needed to make that night. The patient was a young woman who had collapsed at home after telling her husband that she had the worst headache of her life. By the time the ambulance arrived, she was in a coma and having seizures.

The CT scan showed a subarachnoid hemorrhage, the type of bleeding we see when aneurysms burst in the brain. I sent her for an angiogram, and the interventional radiologist confirmed that she had an aneurysm of the posterior communicating artery, which we referred to as the PCOMM. Ruptured PCOMM aneurysms are often less technically challenging to handle surgically than some other types, and I had clipped many of them during my training. I knew from the approaches I'd learned from Dr. Fukushima and other attendings that there were multiple ways to set up the surgery and safely control the aneurysm to protect the patient from further bleeding and give us a chance to save her life.

It was around midnight when the angiogram confirmed the aneurysm. I notified the operating room staff that we had a case, and soon we were preparing the patient for surgery. I called the attending physician, who had started working there a month or so before. He was on call that night, and it was his job to come in and supervise me, make sure I was doing the right thing for the patient, and serve as a resource if I ran into any trouble with the procedure. I'd only been around him a few times, and this would be the first aneurysm we'd operated on together.

"Are you comfortable getting the case started?" he asked over the phone. "I'll let you get going, and I'll be there shortly."

"Of course," I said. "See you soon."

An hour later, the surgery was well underway. I'd managed to position the patient, shave her head, cover her with sterile drapes, make the skin incision and peel the temporalis muscle away to expose her frontal and temporal bones. I'd used a drill to perform a craniotomy, opened her dura mater to expose the brain, and irrigated all the blood away to clean the brain so I could find the aneurysm. Her brain had been very swollen, so I had inserted a catheter through her frontal lobe into her ventricle to drain off some cerebrospinal fluid, which made the brain softer and allowed me to gently retract it away from the skull base.

I'd brought the surgical microscope into the field and used it to magnify and light the brain. Once I'd used tiny microscissors to gently cut away the arachnoid membrane (it looks like a spider's web), I was staring at the bloody, pulsatile aneurysm. It had bubbled out the side of a critical artery that supplies blood to the brain. I'd navigated safely around the optic nerve and the delicate third cranial nerve (which moves the eye and constricts the pupil) to make sure I could safely apply a clip to the aneurysm without damaging these critical nerves.

Then I selected an appropriately sized titanium aneurysm clip—named after Dr. Fukushima, who'd invented this type of clip—and placed it on the special clip-applier instrument, which was also named Fukushima. I very carefully approached the aneurysm with the clip. This is the tensest moment of all brain surgeries, because sometimes as you close the clip across the neck of the aneurysm, it will tear. If the tissue is so diseased that it is too thin to hold the clip, it will shear off. In that moment, arterial blood sprays everywhere, and we face the desperate situation of regaining control of the artery so we do not lose the patient.

I always say a little prayer at this moment, steady my hands, and apply the clip.

I was literally hovering the clip over the neck of the aneurysm, taking one last look around through the microscope before the point of no return, when I heard a booming voice.

"What in the world are you doing, Lee?" The attending burst into the room, and the power and anger in his voice startled me. I withdrew my hand without firing the clip and looked up to see him storming to the bedside.

For the next half hour, he spouted every swear word I'd ever heard (plus a few new ones), all used to tell me that I was the dumbest resident he'd ever seen. He told me that I'd set up the operation all wrong, that the approach was way off, and that I should probably call my mother and tell her I wasn't cut out to be a brain surgeon.

We moved the table and changed the angle of the patient on the bed. Then we stapled four blue towels around the edges of the wound because the attending said that no brain surgery should ever be performed without being framed by squared-off blue towels. We moved the microscope to a different position, and he asked the nurse to play classical music over the radio because "brain surgery needs to be performed in a relaxed environment."

All the while, the patient's swollen brain pulsed, her aneurysm remained unsecured and ready to rupture again at any moment, and everyone in the room knew I'd been only a second away from clipping it.

When the attending was finally satisfied with the draping and positioning of the patient, he allowed me to proceed. I clipped the aneurysm uneventfully, we closed up the patient, and she ultimately made a good recovery.

But that night, as we were closing, the attending continued to berate me. I finally asked, "So what was wrong with my approach?"

He shook his head and said, "We clip all aneurysms the way I showed you. It's the only way."

"But I learned the approach I was using from Dr. Fukushima and Dr. Jannetta, two of the most famous neurosurgeons in the world, and I've performed it successfully dozens of times," I said.

He laughed. "Good outcomes don't justify bad operations. In my training program, we did them all the same way, and that's how we're going to do it here."

Over the rest of my chief resident year, I operated with that attending on numerous occasions, and he used his approach every time. Even when the angle was bad. Even when it was hard, and I would gently suggest that Dr. Jannetta's approach might be more efficient or safer.

I learned more about the young attending as I continued working with him. I liked him, and we actually got along well after that first night. He told me that his training program had hired only its own graduates for decades, so everyone there had trained under the same chairman. They had one way of doing things, the chairman's way, and there was no variance. It was his way, or you would work somewhere else.

The young attending didn't last long in Pittsburgh; our program valued doing the best thing for the patient in the most efficient and safest way possible. That's why Dr. Maroon had brought in so many different surgeons from all over the world to teach us. All the residents in my program learned multiple approaches to each problem, and all the attendings were willing to change approaches when it was best for the patient.

The attending was a gifted technical surgeon. He had mastered the approach he'd learned for aneurysm surgery, and when it worked, he was as good as anyone I ever saw in the operating room. The problem was not that he didn't have the skills to be a great surgeon; the problem was that he *genuinely believed that no other approach would work.*

If his approach presented some challenge or problem, then it was the anatomy's fault, the anesthesiologist's fault, the aneurysm's fault, or the patient's fault because their blood pressure was too high, their artery was too thin, or they were too overweight. It never seemed to occur to him that the problem might lie in his approach, probably because that would raise questions about his training, philosophy, and entire history as a neurosurgeon.

Charting Your Approach to Life

Are you in a similar situation? Or have you discovered that your attempts to address your presenting problem aren't working? If so, I congratulate you for recognizing that the way you've always thought may not be the optimum or the only way to move forward.

I believe that when we think about our lives, all of us have two pictures in our minds. We envision our ideal life in which everything is working, and we are happy, successful, and fulfilled. But then we consider the life we're actually living. We imagine there's someone out there who's doing it better, making more money, and enjoying a more fulfilling marriage. We have this nagging sense that others are more successful or better looking, or they have more followers than we do—and we can prove it with a few moments of scrolling through Instagram.

We may have been through something hard, some trauma or tragedy, and we feel stuck and as if we'll never be whole again. Teachers or therapists may have taught us that our brains can be broken by these experiences, or that if we were born into the wrong family with the wrong genes or have some form of neurodivergence or permanent disorder, we are out of luck, stuck with the brains we have. No matter our area of struggle, I believe that we all measure our lives against some ideal that we're not hitting. If we could chart such a comparison with others, perhaps the blank graph would look something like this.

Maybe as you plot the level where you fall when it comes to living a happy life, it isn't where you think it should be. If so, especially if you've tried and failed to make progress, perhaps your dissatisfaction is due less to your situation itself and more to your determination that it is permanent and hopeless. Allow me to humbly suggest, as your professor of self–brain surgery, that perhaps all you need is a new approach—a better way to make lasting change in your life.

> If you've tried and failed to make progress, perhaps all you need is a new approach—a better way to make lasting change in your life.

In residency, we learned several approaches to each problem, some of which were favorites and others we didn't like and thought we'd never use. Over the course of my career, however, I've been frequently surprised by how often I have to use an approach I swore I'd never need, and I'm always so thankful that I learned so many ways to get the job done for my patients.

It is important to note that some of the surgeons who visited Pittsburgh worked with partners who chose *not* to learn from the master surgeon. These surgeons stayed put, content with the approaches they were already comfortable with.

You might assume that the surgeons who thought they had nothing to learn were the most skilled, successful, and knowledgeable. You also might assume that the doctors who boarded the plane to Pittsburgh were somehow deficient and needed to augment their practice with more training.

But think about it from the standpoint of their patients. Would you feel more comfortable with a surgeon who was unwilling or unable to learn, grow, and adapt as new knowledge became available? Or would you feel safer in the hands of someone who relentlessly pursued improvement, challenged themselves to be better, and would go anywhere and do anything to make sure you had every opportunity to be made well?

Most people—even neurosurgeons—get into routines and are not aware that they have stopped learning or growing. Some actually believe there could not possibly be anything more for them to learn. It is rare for someone to look at themselves objectively and admit they need help or need to change. You and I are not most people, though, because we're willing to adopt a new approach and do the work to become healthier, feel better, and be happier. As Jesus said, "Small is the gate and narrow the road that leads to life, and only a few find it,"[1] and we're committed to finding it.

It's time to change chairs again, my friend. Think of where you fall on the graph and decide now that you are willing to change approaches if that's what it takes to get unstuck and become more satisfied with life.

A Note About Complications and Abandoned Approaches

Every surgeon who practices long enough will have a few cases that do not go the way they intended. Multiple factors contribute to this, including each patient's condition or history, prior surgeries, scar tissue, or altered anatomy and the surgeon's decision-making and execution during the operation.

But something I've noticed over the years is that often a surgeon will abandon a particular approach—or even an entire type of surgery—based on a single case or a handful of cases that resulted in complications or suboptimal outcomes. A surgeon who lost a patient, for instance, may be too nervous to perform the same type of surgery again or may avoid caring for patients who are at higher risk. The surgeon who has been sued for malpractice may begin to work defensively, narrowing their scope of practice to avoid the pain of accusation and legal troubles. They may send patients to specialists in bigger hospitals, and over time their practice becomes extremely narrow. Eventually, the surgeon provides only a fraction of the procedures they're trained to offer their patients.

A well-trained, formerly exceptional surgeon, now filled with doubt, chooses to avoid pain rather than take further risks. I've even seen surgeons retire or go into entirely different careers because they were wrecked by one bad outcome. They've lost confidence—in themselves, in their techniques, in their approaches.

Self-brain surgeons are prone to this problem as well. It usually progresses in three stages:

1. We encounter some sort of trouble, and the pain of that experience drives us to reduce the scope of our existence—we live smaller, take fewer risks, and thus limit our potential. At some level, we may even decide that we are the problem. Based on that self-diagnosis, we adopt a "treatment plan" in which we try avoiding the situation, which reduces the scope of our lives.

2. Years pass, and we realize that our lives have become progressively more limited. The activities and people that formerly made our days feel abundant and free now seem dangerous. We feel as if something has been stolen from us, and the solid foundation we used to stand on has been destroyed. We spend a lot of time thinking about our lives before the event(s) that got us stuck.

3. If we cannot bear the angst of living in the inescapable smallness of our limited life, we may anesthetize ourselves with our numbing agent of choice—alcohol, shopping, gambling, scrolling, comfort foods—but this just means we will have to face the pain another day, and it often creates new problems.

We feel stuck. That's not so different from some of the surgeons who traveled to observe Dr. Fukushima. I am certain that some of them came because they'd had a problem with a patient. They'd had a poor outcome or a complication, and they realized that something had to change. Rather than retiring or radically reducing their own practices, they got on a plane to learn another approach. They had patients to care for, and they weren't going to let failure or frustration keep them from achieving everything they were called to.

You may have reached a point where the ways you've tried to move forward are simply not working, or you believe the risk of the problem repeating itself is simply too high. That's when you need to follow the example of those surgeons and learn a new approach. If you keep doing what you've been doing, you'll keep getting what you've been getting. If you want to wind up in a different place, you've got to walk a different path.

This, my friend, is the way.

Why? Because a narrow practice, and a narrow life, is boring at best and devastating at worst.

Once again, think about your chief complaint. Consider how it's connected to ways that you've tried to protect yourself, whether through avoidance or numbing. You might add some of your conclusions to the subjective portion of the SOAP progress note that you've started.

Sure, sometimes we narrow our approach to life (and surgery) because it feels safer. As neurosurgeons, we *should* operate that way to an extent, and we generally avoid major complications when we do. The problem is, taking a *completely* safe approach often leaves our patient with a residual tumor, persistent pain, or a partially treated issue that's destined to return. Our "safe surgery" winds up creating more problems later, but if we want to make sure we never make any mistakes, we may accept those complications.

It's true in your life too. Even though you're here to train in self–brain surgery, the pain of failure can keep you stuck. The cognitive dissonance of living a life short of the one you're called to can become unbearable and produce anxiety, depression, rumination, and despair.

Frustrations and problems are a part of every surgical practice—and of every life. But if you've restricted your scope to avoid some issue that has caused you pain or is keeping you stuck, today can be a turning point for you.

Great self–brain surgeons, like all great surgeons, face the challenge of anxiety and unexpected setbacks by following these steps:

1. We honestly evaluate the difficult situation, analyzing it for clues as to what happened.

2. We then discern what factors led to the problem and look for things we can control the next time we face similar circumstances. For example,

   a. If we recognize the problem was technical, we work on the techniques we need to refine for next time.

   b. If we realize the issue was something we could have controlled or done differently, we make necessary adjustments and improve our habits, practices, and discipline.

   c. If the problem was related to choosing the wrong approach, we assess which approach would have worked better. We may seek training in this approach, and we do whatever is needed to master it for our patients' sake.

3. If the problem was completely out of our control, we look for ways to improve how we reacted and formulate a plan, should something similar arise in the future. Such planning does not eliminate the risk of unforeseen complications, but it does prepare our minds to respond to unexpected circumstances more effectively.

In the coming chapters we will examine the four basic approaches people take when considering how to use their mental ability to manage their lives and become healthier, feel better, navigate hardship, perform better, or avoid being stuck.

Remember: Surgeons learn new approaches to take better care of their patients. In self–brain surgery, you are the surgeon *and* the patient.

Your approach matters, and the stakes are high.

5

Approach #1: Nothing Can Help Me

What matters most to us is what we are able to do about our physical future, and how we are able to do it.

HENRY P. STAPP
Quantum Theory and Free Will

"We don't really have a choice, do we?"

It had been almost a month since our son Mitch died, but time felt meaningless. Every day was just another one to survive. Lisa and I sat at the kitchen table on a Tuesday afternoon, staring at an email from our accountant, Gerry—the kind of email that once would have seemed urgent but now felt impossible to care about.

Lisa had been running our office since we started our neurosurgery practice a few years before. Gerry had not only helped with the bookkeeping, but he and his firm also consulted with us on every aspect of our business. He had mentored Lisa in growing our practice into the busiest neurosurgery clinic in Alabama, and he'd become something of a father figure to us both.

One of the things we loved was how blunt he was when something had to be done, and his email that day was very direct: *Guys, the bottom line is that you're not going to make payroll unless you go back to the office soon.*

Private practice is fee-for-service, which means you get paid solely for seeing patients and doing surgery. And since I was the *only* doctor at our practice, the weight of Gerry's email landed on my shoulders, like I was Atlas trying to hold up the world. But I wasn't Atlas. I wasn't some immortal strongman with unshakable strength—I was just a grieving father who could barely drag himself out of bed. Yet my patients still needed a surgeon who wouldn't make a fatal mistake. My family needed someone to provide for them, and my employees needed paychecks. But I had nothing left to give.

Lisa was in the same spot as me, equally broken but just as needed at the office since she called all the shots, set the schedule, paid the bills, managed the staff, and handled customer service issues. We looked into each other's bottomless eyes and knew it was true: We had to go back to work. Lisa emailed our staff and instructed them to schedule a half day of clinic appointments for me the following Monday, which made me feel like I did when I received my orders to go to the Iraq War—anguished, terrified, and out of control.

That Sunday night, I tried desperately to drift off, knowing that even if I did, my sleep would be full of the nightmares I'd been having. We'd watched an online church service that day and heard the pastor mention Psalm 126:5-6: "Those who plant in tears will harvest with shouts of joy. They weep as they go to plant their seed, but they sing as they return with the harvest" (NLT). That passage, as everything I had read in the Bible or heard from the pastor since Mitch died, felt impossible to believe—except for the part about the tears.

I was afraid of *everything*. Afraid of leaving the house and being close to anywhere Mitch had been. Afraid of going to work and trying somehow to muster compassion for someone else's pain without making a mistake that could hurt them more. And afraid of finding out that those words from Scripture that seemed to say that our tearful work would be rewarded someday were as false as they felt right then.

Unsure of what else to do, I just stared into the darkness and tried to chart a path forward through the void. I prayed, but I either felt nothing at all or a deep sense that God didn't want to hear from me—and I couldn't tell which felt worse. I started to reach for Lisa's hand, but I realized she'd finally fallen asleep. I knew that her sleep was as tenuous and hard to come by as mine, so instead, I just held my hand close to her and listened to her breathe. I thought about getting up, but I knew I'd find myself in Mitch's room, overwhelmed again by his absence.

In the end, I just lay there, admitting to myself what I'd finally come to believe: Nothing could help me.

As sad as our story was, it isn't unusual. Most people never stop to think that they *are* using an approach to respond to their pain—especially if that approach happens by default. They wake up in the morning, do what they always do, and progress through their days without any real expectation that things can be different. When they hurt, when unexpected things occur, many folks shrink their lives in response to the pain and never imagine any other possibility.

Life can make us feel like it is what it is. We get into routines, and even when nothing's wrong, we can struggle because nothing feels *right*, either. Left unchallenged, we can find ourselves deep into a life that doesn't seem to be going anywhere, and there is no clear path to make it better.

That leads me to point out two critical distinctions between self–brain surgery and "real" brain surgery. I put the word *real* in quotation marks because by now I hope I've convinced you that self–brain surgery is as real as what I do in the operating room—just without all the bleeding and pain. Nevertheless, there are obvious differences, and one is of prime importance to learning the approaches needed to change your mind and your life. We'll get to the other difference later in this chapter.

> **Life can make us feel like it is what it is. We get into routines, and even when nothing's wrong, we can struggle because nothing feels right, either.**

Self–Brain Surgery vs. "Real" Brain Surgery

#1: Not Choosing an Approach Is an Approach

Neurosurgeons always specifically choose an approach. We do not just wake up in the operating room during a procedure and think, *Holy cow, I'm in the middle of performing a pituitary tumor procedure from an endoscopic transnasal approach! How did this happen?* Rather, we head to surgery with a particular approach in mind, one specifically chosen for its advantages over other approaches, and with a clear understanding of its limitations and potential pitfalls.

Perhaps you've never considered it before, but you, too, are following an approach in the way you conduct your life. As with your thoughts, you may choose your approach or it may happen by default. If you've allowed it to happen passively, I encourage you to learn from the best-prepared surgeons.

Surgeons learn new approaches because they seek new ways to improve patient care. This is a positive step, and surgeons do not feel shame or guilt that they need a new approach. In fact, they learn multiple approaches so they can apply the one that's best for each patient. Sometimes, however, a new approach will challenge something a surgeon believes, and a rigorous scientific standard will require a willingness to address and adjust that belief.

When "real" surgeons forget that there *are* other approaches available, or a certain approach is so ingrained in their minds that it's become a habit, or they're sure that their way is the best way, they may fail to consider other approaches when what they're doing isn't working.

This resistance to any approach other than the one we're using is a common problem among self–brain surgeons as well. And it can happen in at least three different ways:

1. We've tried everything we can think of to make a particular change, only to get the same results over and over. Especially when life has hurt us in some way, we can begin to believe that change is impossible, at least for us. *This produces apathy, which is one of the steps that leads into the basement of hopelessness.*

2. We genuinely believe that the approach we've taken so far is the only option. We are unaware of other ways people have successfully managed the issue we're dealing with, because we're in a culture, organization, family, or church in which everyone thinks like we do about it. This is a dangerous and frustrating position, because as we continue to struggle, we can begin to believe that the problem is *us*. *This is a form of ignorance, a lack of awareness that change is not only possible, but that it is happening in people's lives all around us.*

3. We know that other people are using a different approach, but we truly believe that ours is superior. We're sure that "those people" who are getting results another way are still wrong, and we'll eventually be proven right. We refuse to change our approach, even when an objective observer would point out that we're struggling to manage something that could be much easier and more effective if we'd modify our strategy in some way. *This is a form of arrogance.*

If you believe that your approach has failed you but there is no alternative, or if you believe that all other approaches are illegitimate or inferior to yours, or if you're simply battered by life and you've lost the hope to even try something new, then you may throw up your hands and say, "Nothing can help me."

HOPELESS AND HELPLESS?

The "Nothing can help me" approach is also sometimes practiced by those who live by a brain-out worldview. If you believe that your genetics, brain structure, or evolution has fated you to feel, think, or "be" a certain way and there is nothing you can do about it, this approach can become your default. After all, you may believe that every decision, thought, feeling, and action you make is simply the undirected process of a neuron firing in your brain. Even your concept of "you" is just a neurochemical reaction that is being presented to you by your brain. Thus, "you" have no real meaning or purpose, and when you die, you will simply cease to exist. If this is your view, when some part of your life isn't working, you will sigh, shrug your shoulders, and say, "Nothing can help me; this is just how life is."

Surprisingly, some Christians and other spiritually minded people also adopt this approach. Even though they believe (as I do) that God loves them and that there is a life after this one, when everything will be set right, they've been driven to their knees by *this* life with its trauma and tragedy, or even just its monotony. They can't seem to break through, heal, or overcome their problems, so they throw up their hands and think, *Nothing can help me, so I'll just knuckle down and wait for heaven.*

FOUR APPROACHES TO LIFE

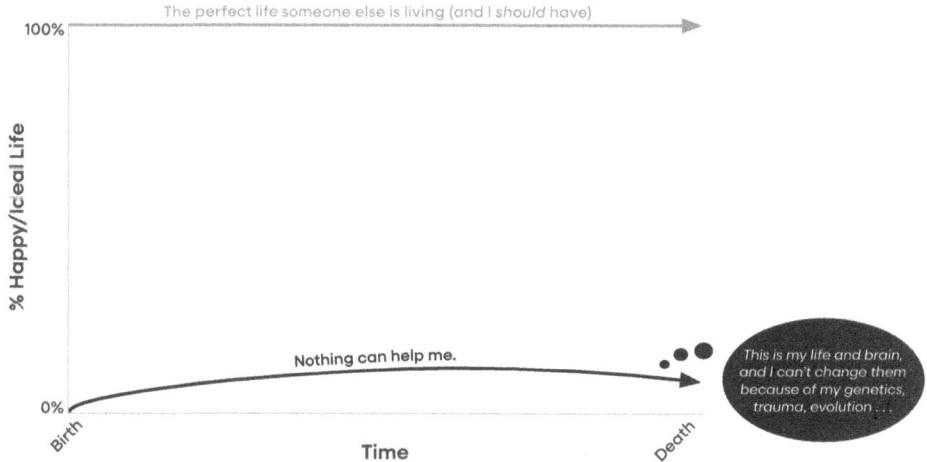

I write about the "Nothing can help me" approach not to criticize you if this is the one and only approach you've taken, but to tell you from personal experience that this outlook will never move you forward. I want to share the realization that finally opened my eyes to another approach. Believe it or not, I found it in a straightforward math equation. Don't worry—you don't have to solve any math problems to understand this, but I do need to explain it to you.

PAIN IS REAL, BUT THE GOOD IS GREATER

The formula looks like this: A > SKD.

That's the equation I stumbled upon at the hardest moment in my life, when I was telling myself that nothing could help me. Following Mitch's death at nineteen, Lisa and I (and our entire family) were grieving. We wondered whether anything we'd previously believed was true.[1] Everything about my approach to life seemed to be in question, and I was filled with doubt.

Even though I work in a profession in which I see tragedy almost daily, I somehow naively failed to consider that such a massive emotional trauma could happen to *my* family. I believed that my faith in God would protect my children, even though I had plenty of personal and professional evidence that bad things *do* happen to good people. Now I wasn't sure what I believed anymore, and the places I used to turn to when I was hurting—my faith in God and his promises—seemed unhelpful and maybe even untrue. I was lost.

One day I was reminded of Jesus' words in John 10:10: "The thief comes only to steal and kill and destroy. I came that they may have life and have it abundantly" (ESV).

At first it seemed ridiculous: Jesus was saying that a thief might steal from us, destroy our lives, and even attempt to kill us (physically or emotionally). Yet Jesus came to earth so that we could have abundance. How could we have rich and meaningful lives in the midst of the objectively awful behaviors of the thief that Jesus described—and the grief we were facing after Mitch's death?

For a long time, I felt certain that my life would always be dark and painful, and that there was no path forward to find hope again. Then something that felt like a miracle happened, and it required the convergence of two seemingly unrelated events for me to see it.

On the day of Mitch's funeral, our first grandchild was born. Our daughter Caity and her husband, Nate, could not be at Mitch's funeral in Alabama, and we were supposed to have been with them in San Antonio for their first child's delivery. Scarlett came into the world while we said goodbye to her Uncle Mitch, whom she would never meet, and it felt awful. But at the same time, Scarlett's arrival brought us joy and enough light to see a glimmer of hope in the darkness.

When we were able to travel to Texas to meet Scarlett, I absorbed the unmistakable light radiating from her precious life as I held her for the first time. In that moment, something cracked open in my mind: *Two things can be true at the same time.* I remembered the verse in which Jesus' promise of abundance bumped up against all that stealing, killing, and destroying business, and I realized it wasn't an either-or situation: *Jesus was saying that both things can happen in the same life at the same time.*[2]

The both-and proposition, for some reason, made sense to me even in the confusion of my traumatized state, probably because it reminded me of superposition, a principle I knew to be true from quantum physics. Simply put, at the atomic level an electron can seem to be in two places at one time, until someone actually measures or observes it, which collapses the uncertainty into one reality. That sounds impossible, but the truth of quantum superposition gave rise in the twentieth century to technologies like atomic bombs, semiconductors, and smartphones.[3] In my bereaved, grieved mind, the darkness around losing my son swirled together with the light of holding my granddaughter, a reflection from the lesson of physics. The idea that hope can coexist with hopelessness suddenly made sense to me.

If you're balking at me mentioning a passage from the Bible, just hang with me for a moment. Even if you don't believe in God, can we just agree that life is hard? Have you encountered some places where it feels like there is something or someone out there acting like a thief who's trying to steal, kill, or destroy your happiness or success? If so, you may feel as hopeless as I did after Mitch died. Even though God's promises didn't *feel true* to me then, I kept returning to them because nothing else felt true either, and I did know that *feelings are not facts*. (We'll look more closely at this in "The Ten Commandments of Self–Brain Surgery.")

Groping around for something to hold on to, I kept reaching for what felt a little hopeful, and over time the *two things can be true at once* truth of John 10:10 felt more and more like a solid place to try to stand up on. I followed my own science-based rules of testing and refining until something proved to be true, and this truth held me up. Let's look at the equation:

A > SKD

Abundance is greater than steal, kill, and destroy.

We're after a livable approach to life, remember? And hammering away with the same strategy when it's keeping us stuck isn't a good practice for self–brain surgeons any more than it is for regular brain surgeons. Yet many of us hold on to our approach even when it isn't working, convinced there's no better way. And that brings us to the other major difference between "real" brain surgery and self–brain surgery.

Self–Brain Surgery vs. "Real" Brain Surgery

#2: Self–Brain Surgery Is an Ongoing Process

I began this chapter by telling you about how I lay in the darkness a few weeks after Mitch died. But what I didn't tell you was this: Remember our trip to San Antonio to meet Scarlett? Well, that happened *a week before* my sleepless night of despair over returning to the office. Although I had just discovered the hope-igniting power that two things can be true at once and A > SKD, within a few days, I plunged back into the depths of "Nothing can help me."

We returned to our home in Alabama, and the light we'd glimpsed while holding Scarlett slowly dimmed as we descended back into grief's clear and present darkness. It wasn't because A > SKD stopped being true, and it wasn't because we forgot about the light and hope we'd seen and held just a few days before. The problem was that I did not yet know that *whatever you're actively doing rewires your brain to make you better at doing it.* It seems so clear to me now, but in those early days after the devastating loss of my son, I could see only the pain. I never stopped to realize that the synaptic surgery I was performing on my brain was reinforcing my growing belief that nothing could help me.

And that's the other major difference between the surgeries I perform in the hospital and the self–brain surgery we're learning here: In the operating room, the procedure I use is intended to be a lasting fix for whatever is troubling my patient. But in the operating room of our minds, we surgically graft change into our brains with every thought we think. And that means that we can never stop operating, unless we want to drift back into a less helpful, default approach like "Nothing can help me."

> *Do you agree that darkness and light (or sorrow and hope) can coexist? If so, how is that playing out in your life right now? And if not, how might challenging the belief that "Nothing can help me" provide a path forward?*

The core promise of this book is that self–brain surgery is not a metaphor but the mechanism you use to transform your life by changing your thinking. But the corollary to that promise is that renewed thinking is not a one-time event. That's one reason the Bible says to take every thought captive.[4] Each thought makes a structural change in your brain and has downstream consequences in your life and the lives of those around you. We do not dabble in self–brain surgery whenever we want a quick fix and then slip back into the abyss of wherever our default thinking takes us. Not if we want to live in the power of A > SKD.

I'm here to tell you that abundance is possible, even amid hardships, the frustrations that keep you stuck, or the dripping faucets of everyday life. And my job, as your attending professor of self–brain surgery, is to convince you that there are other approaches besides the despair of "Nothing can help me." These proactive approaches work for the believer and the doubter, the atheist and the agnostic, and for those who never even ponder spiritual ideas. I'm here to show you that changing to another approach isn't a character flaw; it's a necessity if you want to finally break through to hope and healing.

You don't have to stay paralyzed, thinking that nothing can help. Learning a new approach can give you momentum, get you unstuck, and convince you that the future can look different from the past. Two things can be true at once: You can find the light even when trauma, tragedy, and other massive things make everything seem so dark. Abundance can be found because A > SKD. My job isn't to convince you *which approach* is best for you. My job is to show you that there *are* other scientifically backed approaches.

Have you ever felt stuck, like nothing could help you? Have you wondered if there was a better way somewhere out there that might help you move forward? The question isn't whether change is possible—it's whether you're willing to try a new approach. And that's exactly what we'll explore next.

6

Approach #2: Maybe *Something* Can Help Me

> Peace of mind is an inside job, unrelated to fame,
> fortune, or whether your partner loves you.
>
> **ANNE LAMOTT**
> *Almost Everything*

"Move your legs for me," I said.

"I'm trying! I just can't," the young man replied. His face reddened, and sweat covered his forehead. He was obviously straining to move, but nothing was happening.

He weighed almost five hundred pounds, so at five foot seven, the nineteen-year-old was morbidly obese. His family had called 911 when he lost control of his bladder and was unable to move. He reported that he'd been going numb from the waist down for several days and had tremendous back pain that extended down both legs. His parents hadn't noticed the growing weakness because he had been essentially bedridden for months due to his back pain. They had been bringing him food and helping him to the bathroom, hoping he'd feel better.

But that night when he lost bladder control, his mom finally told him something had to be done. The ambulance crew and four firemen worked for three hours to get him out of his bed, then carried him out of his house and transported him to the emergency department at the hospital. It was after midnight when I was called to see him.

I examined him and confirmed that he was profoundly weak in both legs and numb on both sides, from the groin down to his toes. He had no reflexes, had lost rectal tone, and was leaking stool and urine onto the bed.

The most likely diagnosis was cauda equina syndrome, which happens when a disc ruptures into the spinal canal and compresses the nerves to the legs. From the second lumbar vertebra in your spine down to the tailbone, the nerves that extend out of the end of the spinal cord run inside the spinal sac in a bundle that resembles the tail of a horse, hence the Latin name *cauda* (tail) *equina* (of the horse). Other possible causes included multiple sclerosis, spinal cord stroke, tumor, or infection. To know for sure—and to determine whether surgery could help him—he would need imaging.

I asked the nurse to insert a Foley catheter, which would decompress his bladder and protect the delicate nerves there from permanent injury until we could figure out the problem and develop a plan to fix it. Then I ordered a magnetic resonance imaging (MRI) scan of his lower back to try to nail down the diagnosis.

A few minutes later my phone rang, and I realized the young man's problem had gotten much worse.

It was the on-call radiologist, Sandy, and he had bad news.

"Lee," he said, "we can't do an MRI on this kid. Our machine is only rated for 350 pounds; he won't fit into the tube."

"What about the open MRI across town?" I asked.

"The magnet isn't powerful enough to image someone of that size. You won't be able to see the nerves."

Without a good picture of my patient's spinal cord, there was no way to diagnose or treat the problem. Cauda equina syndrome is a surgical emergency, and if we did not take action quickly, the incontinence and paralysis could become permanent. But going to surgery without a clear plan is malpractice since there is no way to know for sure where or what the issue is. We do not perform exploratory neurosurgery; we have to know what we're doing before we operate.

The only reasonable option seemed to be to fly him to one of the two closest major medical centers, which hopefully would have a wide bore MRI scanner and could help him. That hope faded quickly when we called the Life Flight crew. There were major storms across the area, and no one could safely fly.

Out of other options, we performed a computed tomography (CT) scan of my patient's lumbar spine. It wasn't ideal because CT does not show us the same degree of anatomical detail as an MRI. We would not be able to see the spinal cord clearly enough to rule out multiple sclerosis or other neurological conditions. But we can usually rule out big things like fractures, and sometimes we can see the spinal canal clearly enough to determine if something is pressing on the nerves. In this situation, it was all we had.

Sandy and I looked at the scan together. Because of the young man's size, the pictures were grainy and hard to interpret, but we both quickly saw the problem: One of the discs in his lower back had ruptured, filling his spinal canal with disc material and crushing the tail end of his spinal cord. The scan confirmed the diagnosis of cauda equina syndrome, and he would be permanently paralyzed without emergency surgery.

Since the helicopters could not fly in the thunderstorms, I knew that sending him to a major hospital would take too long and greatly increase the risk that his weakness and incontinence could become irreparable. He would have to have surgery that night, in my hospital, and it was up to me to operate.

I called the anesthesiologist who was on call, and then my team—Nate, my scrub tech,[1] and Zane, my nurse—who began setting up for the surgery. A few minutes later we were in the operating room preparing to put the young man to sleep and position him on the surgical table.

That's when another problem presented itself.

The anesthesiologist had a very difficult time getting the patient intubated due to his size. Once the breathing tube was in place, we tried to get the young man onto his belly so I could get to his back. We had six people in the room working together to safely roll him onto his stomach so I could operate, but every time we got him prone, his oxygen levels would crash. When we flipped him back over, his oxygen would come back up to a safe number. He was so large that being on his belly compressed his chest too much for the breathing machine to overcome.

We tried this several times, and it became clear that the normal approach to the spine was impossible to safely perform. He was either going to die from positioning, or he was going to become a paraplegic because I couldn't safely operate on him.

Nate said, "What are you going to do, Doc?"

Moments like this stand out over the course of my career. Times when everyone in the room is waiting for me to make a decision, and someone's life and future are in my hands. I felt the pressure of the young man's disc pressing on his spinal cord as if it were pressing on mine, and I foresaw years of his life spent in a wheelchair because I couldn't help him. The ventilator hissed, the heart monitor beeped, and the weight of being the one to decide his future felt like it would paralyze me as well.

Decision Time

What do you do when you're under pressure? When the approach you've been using isn't working and you've reached a critical moment?

A decision must be made. It's time to stop contemplating and start operating. The people in your life (or even the person in the mirror) look at you and say, "What are you going to do?"

Before you were aware that your brain changes in response to your thinking, moments like these may have produced despair, the crushing fear of being out of control. Maybe this is when you heard the voice in your head (which sounds like "you") saying that your situation was impossible: *Well,* the voice says, *you've tried everything, and nothing can help you. This time you're really in trouble.*

But now you know that this approach is not your only option—and soon I will teach you how to recognize that voice for what it is—a lie. (We'll break down the neuroscience of deceptive thoughts and feelings in "The Ten Commandments of Self-Brain Surgery" section.)

Part of the process of moving away from your default reaction is deciding on your approach, keeping in mind that even if you're unaware that you're using an approach, you are *still* using one—just as being unaware that you are already performing self-brain surgery doesn't make your neuroplasticity grind to a halt.

Situations in which you feel extreme pressure or stress, times when there's a real crisis that demands some kind of action, reveal the extent to which you've decided to believe that you can do something to help yourself.

Remember that "reordering" your mind doesn't mean that you have a disorder in your thinking, a

> **Situations in which you feel extreme pressure or stress reveal the extent to which you've decided to believe that you can do something to help yourself.**

diagnosis that gives you both an explanation and an excuse to keep reacting in the same way. Mind-down control means that you're changing to the doctor's chair in the situation, deciding that you have the training, the skills, and the tools to steer the problem to a different outcome than the one you're used to achieving. And in order to get there, you have to think about the right things in the right order.

The conclusion that "Nothing can help me" produces despair and chaos. It causes you to hide from its repercussions and choose avoidance or numbing behaviors like using alcohol or other distractions to push your pain into tomorrow, or at least to stop feeling it for a while. The problem is, there's still a patient on the table (you). There's still an urgent situation that needs to be handled, and everyone is waiting on you to take action.

So, in moments of extreme stress, when your brain that sounds like "you" tells you to fall back on "Nothing can help me," it's time to remember that there are other approaches. It's time to remember that abundance is greater than steal, kill, and destroy. It's time to recall Leonid Rogozov, dying for lack of a surgeon and then remembering that *he was* a surgeon.

Getting It Done

My patient was still on the table too. And in the seconds that felt like hours, Nate's question, "What are you going to do?" hung in the air with the beeps and hisses from the operating room equipment.

Then I heard my wise professor's voice in my head. *You know how to do this, Lee*, Dr. Maroon's voice whispered. *You might not like it, but you can get it done.*

By the late 1990s, most spine surgeries were performed with the patient prone on the table, face down like we'd been attempting that night with our young patient. Prone positioning has a host of benefits over the older lateral approach, in which the patient is placed on their side and the surgeon sits on a stool behind them to operate.

With the patient face down, an assistant or trainee can stand across the table from the primary surgeon. If the surgeon is using a surgical microscope, the assistant can see everything the surgeon sees and actively participate in the operation. They are standing straight up, looking down on the patient, and the scope can even be connected to television monitors so that others in the room can see what's happening (like the surgeons who came to watch Dr. Fukushima operate).

Before microscopes were available, most surgeons operated using surgical telescopes attached to eyeglasses, which are called loupes. When wearing loupes, the doctor's field of vision is narrowed, and they can really only see what is directly in their line of sight.

When surgeons first started performing spine surgery, modern technologies such as electrocautery and mechanical suction were not yet invented. Thus, these operations caused a lot of bleeding, and with the patient in the prone position the blood would pool in the wound by gravity, making it very difficult for the surgeons to see what they were doing. This problem was solved nicely by placing the patient on their side, in the lateral position, which allowed the blood to drain out of the wound so the surgeon was able to operate safely. At the time, three of the renowned neurosurgeons I trained under in Pittsburgh—including Dr. Maroon himself—insisted that we perform most types of back surgery using this older method, with the patient in the lateral position.

However, convenience comes at a price.

The surgeon sits on a stool behind the patient, with the table elevated so that the incision is at eye level to the surgeon. They must hold their arms out in front of them to work, which causes neck and shoulder strain, as well as arm fatigue, as the case progresses. If they are using a microscope instead of wearing loupes, the scope is between the surgeon and the patient, which means they are even farther away, stretching their arms out more to reach around the scope, making it essentially impossible for an assistant to help. And as a trainee, it is very difficult to learn anything when you cannot really participate in the procedure since the surgeon's head is directly in the line of the wound and you can't see into the patient.

In training, I hated performing spine surgery from the lateral approach. It was uncomfortable and inconvenient, and it seemed archaic. When the chief resident gave us our work assignments each morning on rounds, my colleagues and I would moan and complain when we were told we had to help one of these three surgeons with a lateral position case.

"Ugh," the unlucky resident would say, "I have to go do that old-timey operation with one of those dinosaurs."

It was Dr. Maroon who took time to explain why he kept using the approach, even when most of his peers had moved on to the more "modern" prone position.

"Lee," he told me, "someone has to teach you that there's more than one way to do almost anything. There will come a time when you'll be grateful for the way we've put this program together."

I remember once telling another resident that story as I was fussing about how much my neck hurt after operating with Dr. Maroon for hours. He said, "Whatever. As soon as I'm out of here, I'm never using that approach again. It's completely useless these days."

Nate snapped me out of my head and back into the operating room with my very ill young patient and the team waiting for my call. "You want to send him to a bigger hospital? No one will question it since we can't get him safely positioned," he said.

Dr. Maroon said in my head again, *Lee, you know how to do this.*

I didn't like—and I still don't like—the lateral approach for spine surgery. It's out of fashion. It's hard. It hurts.

But I knew it would work.

I'd seen it done many times as a resident—whenever one of the three neurosurgeons had a severely obese patient whom others would struggle to get safely through surgery. Each time, the surgery would be done in the lateral position with no complications.

I didn't like it one bit, but I had to do something, and I was trained for it. "We're going lateral," I said.

He Lost It in Front of the Whole World

On June 7, 2004, with five million people watching, Dan Harris had a panic attack while on camera during a broadcast of *Good Morning America*. He was a rising star at ABC who had spent several years as a war correspondent, but this event threatened to ruin his career. In his bestselling book, *10% Happier*, Harris tells the story of how he suffered with crippling anxiety and his search for ways to regain control of his mind.

After Harris melted down on camera, he tried everything—therapy, drugs (legal and illegal), alcohol—but the panic kept wrecking him. Harris spent years trying to manage his problem on his own, seemingly running the plays familiar to everyone who has labored under the "Nothing can help me" approach. The cycle of anxiety, fear, turning to numbing agents to anesthetize himself from the pain, self-loathing, and then starting it all over again with the next panic attack pushed him to the brink of collapse.

When he suffered a second panic attack while delivering the news, he realized his inability to make his situation better through self-medication. When his therapist pinned his panic attacks on his recreational drug use, Harris did manage to end that. Even so, he realized he had spent the last several years living mindlessly, or as he put it, "sleepwalking through the entire cascade of moronic behavior."[2] That tendency was going to be the end of him unless something changed.

Then his mentor, news anchor Peter Jennings, asked him to cover stories about faith. Harris didn't believe in God, and he had no interest in spiritual matters. But in interviewing people like Deepak Chopra, Eckhart Tolle, the Dalai Lama, and numerous ministers all over the world, Harris realized that these people had in fact discovered something that seemed to help control anxiety and improve peace of mind: mindfulness meditation. Positive there must be a scientific explanation for how these meditators were able to calm their minds on demand, Harris dove into the neuroscience of how our brains process anxiety:

> Science challenges the common assumption that our levels of happiness, resilience, and kindness are set from birth. Many of us labor under the delusion that we're permanently stuck with all of the difficult parts of our personalities—that we are "hot-tempered," or "shy," or "sad"—and that these are fixed, immutable traits. We now know that many of the attributes we value most are, in fact, *skills*, which can be trained the same way you build your body in the gym.[3]

Harris kept digging, and he discovered that modern neuroimaging proves that prayer and meditation make helpful structural changes to the brain:

> Things truly got sci-fi when researchers started peering directly into the brains of meditators. A blockbuster MRI study from Harvard found that people who took the eight-week MBSR [Mindfulness-Based Stress Reduction] course had thicker gray matter in the areas of the brain associated with self-awareness and compassion, while the regions associated with stress actually shrank.[4]

Eventually, Harris began to pursue a meditation practice that was completely secular and stripped of any religious connotation. He had found a way to hack his brain and make it submit to his mind, and he conquered his panic attacks at last.

Harris is very honest that this sort of brain hack doesn't magically solve all of life's problems. It just allows him to thoughtfully respond instead of react.

To be clear, it's not a miracle cure. It won't make you taller or better-looking, nor will it magically solve all of your problems. You should disregard the fancy books and the famous gurus promising immediate enlightenment. In my experience, meditation makes you 10% happier. That's an absurdly unscientific estimate, of course. But still, not a bad return on investment.[5]

If Harris were to graph out his decision to change approaches, he might have called his new strategy the "Maybe *something* can help me" approach, and perhaps the chart would look like this:

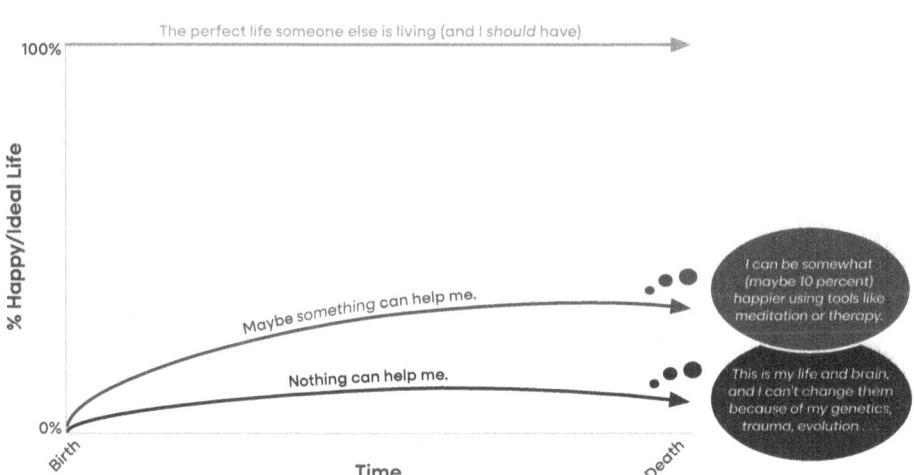

When *Something* Is Simple, Safe, and Effective

I hate the lateral approach for spine surgery.

It's inconvenient. It's uncomfortable. It's bloodier than I like as I am a meticulous and careful surgeon who likes to control everything, including every drop of blood that my patient loses.

But sometimes it's the right approach, as it was on that stormy night.

Although I chose to operate, notice that I was not obligated to. I could have bailed and sent the young man to a university hospital with the excuse that we were in a small town with limited resources. No one would have blamed or questioned me for that decision. However, I would have known that I'd failed to live up to my own training and capabilities, and that I'd caused the patient to wait hours for help that I could have delivered, just because I didn't want to change approaches and do something uncomfortable.

The surgery was difficult because it had been a few years since I'd used that approach and because of my internal aversion to it. But every moment during the procedure, I gained confidence that it was the right decision, and I felt a growing gratitude that we would be able to help this young man walk again.

An approach doesn't have to be perfect. You don't have to agree with all the reasons other people are using it, or even necessarily believe in the underlying principles of why it was developed. But isn't "Maybe *something* can help me" more hopeful than "Nothing can help me"?

Six months later, the young man walked into my office. He had regained bladder control, and his pain was gone. He was exercising and had started losing weight. He told me that the experience of almost dying had radically transformed his life, and he was determined to make better decisions about his health going forward.

I still believe that lateral position spine surgery is inelegant, inefficient, and cumbersome in modern times. But in this situation, it was the right call. It worked when nothing else would have. It was the *something* in "Maybe *something* can help me," and it saved a young man's life.

You've likely heard of breath work—the intentional focus on slowing and deepening your breathing—as a means of calming your mind and body. Why does it work? When you're anxious, you tend to take rapid, shallow breaths, which heighten your feelings of stress. Techniques like box breathing, in which you inhale for four seconds, hold that breath for four seconds, and then exhale for four to six seconds, activate your parasympathetic system, which moves your body into a calm and relaxed state.

Dan Harris found that becoming 10 percent happier through meditation was enough to overcome his panic attacks. Sometimes you can take small actions to improve your life in meaningful ways, like bumping your mood with exercise or an act of kindness, practicing breath work, or becoming more active to improve the release of dopamine in your brain when you feel stuck.

When we get to appendix A, you will learn some techniques to apply using the *something* approach. Many small, nagging issues can be addressed with a simple approach and do not require you to know or care much about the underlying science.

But when you're at the crossroads of a life that isn't working, only you can decide to try a new, even more intensive approach. Once you realize that something has to change, the next question is, Will you settle for *something*, or do you need more?

I don't want to forecast doom here, but some issues in life will move you off the trajectory you're trying to achieve by more than 10 percent. When Lisa and I lost our son Mitch, we were more than 10 percent sadder. Ten percent happier would not have been enough to make a difference for us, so the "Maybe *something* can help me" approach would not have been sufficient for us in that situation.

In the next chapter, we're going to become *absurdly scientific* in order to develop an approach that addresses some of the limits of the *something* approach, just as whoever first decided to place their patient in the prone position did so because the lateral approach had limitations and problems that the surgeon needed to overcome.

Remember that being willing to change approaches isn't a failure; it's the defining characteristic of good surgeons. If you're in a time of your life when it's become clear that you need to change your approach, let me remind you: *You know how to do this.*

The machines are beeping. The patient is waiting. Your old approach hasn't worked, and a decision must be made.

But you no longer believe that nothing can help you. You've learned that you have the tools to pick up the knife and use the power of self–brain surgery to change your mind and change your life. You're not the helpless patient anymore; you're a surgeon who's on the path to having all the training and skills you need.

Sure, no one would blame you if you decided not to operate with a new approach. You could offer many excuses: *It's too hard, I've been through too much, This is just how I am.* You could choose to defer to your diagnosis, your trauma, or the inertia of past failures. You could choose the comforting numbness of alcohol or whatever anesthetic agent or behavior you turn to when it's just too hard to think about your life.

No one would question you, but you would know the truth: You now have access to the training and the tools to choose another approach and take action.

So the question hangs in the air, swirling around with the beeps and hisses: "What are you going to do, Doc?"

7

Approach #3: Maybe Science Can Help Me

The highest aim of science is to help humanity to understand its own sense, its place, and its destiny in the universe.
KIRILL KOPEIKIN AND ALEXEI V. NESTERUK, EDS.
Consciousness and Matter

"It's like magic," Lisa said.

My wife and I were standing in the control room of the MRI Research Center at Auburn University, and what we saw on the computer monitor did look very much like magic.

We'd been back to work for only a few days after taking time off when our son Mitchell died. On this day we had a meeting to view the new functional capabilities of the 7-Tesla MRI machine that had been installed in the research center, which at that time was only the third MRI scanner that powerful in the United States. Our medical office was on the third floor of the building, so we were often invited to see the research progress the engineers and other scientists were making using their multimillion-dollar machine.

The meeting was a demonstration of a new experiment with some of the first human subjects in the 7-T scanner. A man lay inside, wearing a virtual reality headset that provided instructions of tasks to perform and what he was to think about while performing them.

Whenever the participant performed one of the assigned tasks—for example, "Move your left thumb; wiggle your right foot"—the screen showed us what areas of the brain were receiving increased blood flow, which was a proxy for understanding which parts of the brain had been activated. Next, the participant was given some instructions that involved only thinking: "Think of something sad. The worst thing you've ever felt or could imagine feeling. Now think of something happy. The best memory you can recall."

We watched spellbound whenever the colors on the screen changed as various parts of the brain became involved in the processes of thought, movement, and memory. Negative thoughts dramatically changed the blood flow to the amygdala, which is responsible for emotional processing, including the regulation of anxiety and depression. Positive thoughts caused similarly large changes in blood flow to the areas that produce rational thoughts such as the frontal lobes, along with areas that make helpful neurotransmitters like dopamine and serotonin. We were watching the human mind think, and we saw the neurochemical and blood flow changes in real time in response to changes in thought.

The experience of seeing with our own eyes evidence that you can *decide* to think about one thing and not another and that mental decision will structurally change your brain started a process of healing for Lisa and me, which I laid out in my book *Hope Is the First Dose*. It's relevant here because it taught me a lesson I need to share with you.

More than a century ago, psychologist William James figured out through observation that people could change their habits by changing their thinking. He wrote, "The philosophy of habit is thus, in the first instance, a chapter in physics rather than in physiology or psychology.... It is at bottom a physical principle."[1] He had recognized something about how the mind influences the brain, but he was a hundred years ahead of anyone being able to explain how. I observed that process with my own eyes in that MRI control room. Here's the life-changing takeaway for me:

You will either operate the system, or the system will operate you.

You will either operate the system, or the system will operate you.

Your mind, brain, body, and life are interconnected with one another and with the people and the universe around you in ways that scientists are only now beginning to understand. This isn't a physics book, but you need to know that the same phenomenon that gave me the A > SKD insight also teaches us that *how you decide to pay attention to something has an influence on the reality of how that thing behaves.*

Werner Heisenberg, a twentieth-century pioneer in the field of quantum physics, determined that we cannot know precisely both the velocity *and* the position of a particle because the act of measuring one changes the other. This so-called observer effect means that the choices you make in your life change your reality and that of those around you. You, my friend, matter. Whether you believe you're here because God made you in his image or you believe that you're just the random product of an uncaring universe, the truth remains that the universe, quite literally, would not be the same without you.

We're going to learn an approach to our lives that will allow us to operate our nervous systems from the perspective of a compassionate surgeon. We will use an honest application of the scientific method to make decisions about what works and doesn't work as we strive to reorder our minds, rewire our brains, and radically transform our lives.

But before we can apply such a method, we need to clarify some things about science.

Scientists Discover Things; They Don't Create Them

I'm not talking about inventions or products; scientists are, of course, responsible for creating smartphones, Post-it notes, and 7-T MRI scanners.[2] I'm talking about how Isaac Newton's observation that an apple falling from a tree always goes down and never up led him to *discover* and formulate the law of gravity, but his insights did not *create* gravity.

There's a clue in the etymology of the word *discover*. The prefix *dis-* means to remove, so the word literally means to *un*cover or remove from hiding something that was already there.[3] To discover something is to make the thing that was hidden visible for all to see.

Gravity, relativity, the ninety-two naturally occurring elements in the periodic table,[4] and neuroplasticity were all in effect long before Newton, Einstein, Mendeleev, or Konorski[5] got around to noticing and describing them.

Likewise, science didn't create your ability to change your brain's structure and function, and science did not create the incredible power you have to direct your mental activity and control much of that brain rewiring by changing how you think. Those powers are baked into the wonderful potential you've had all along. You, my friend, are fearfully and wonderfully made, custom-built with everything you need to operate your mind, brain, body, and life in a way that helps you.⁶ You're here to learn how to unlock, harness, and use that potential for your good and the good of others.

That's why I'm taking the time to make sure it's clear that science is not a creative force; it is a way of discovering, modeling, and explaining the world using a disciplined method that ideally works like this:

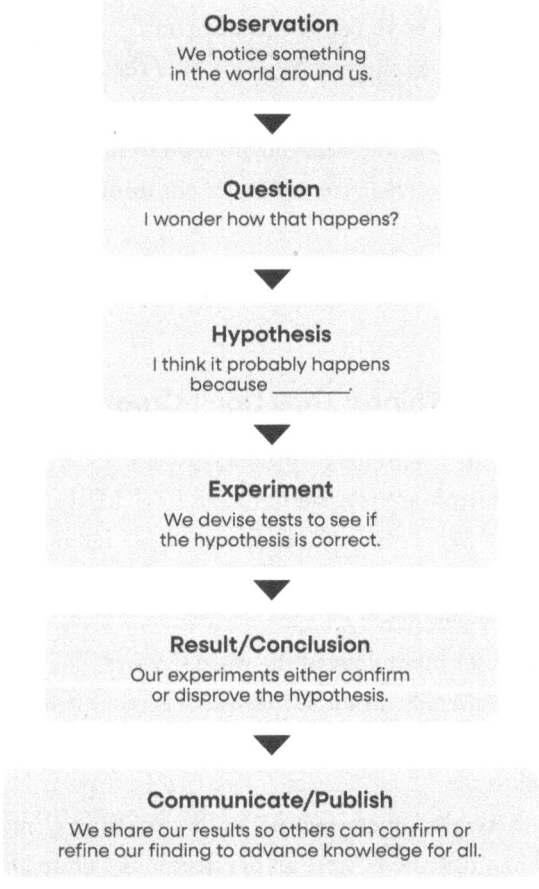

This is the famous scientific method you learned in school, and honest researchers follow it in their work. Note that we do not decide what we believe and then refuse to believe any data that do not support our belief. Rather, we continually refine our hypothesis based on our observations until we arrive at something that seems to be true.

APPROACH #3: MAYBE SCIENCE CAN HELP ME | 67

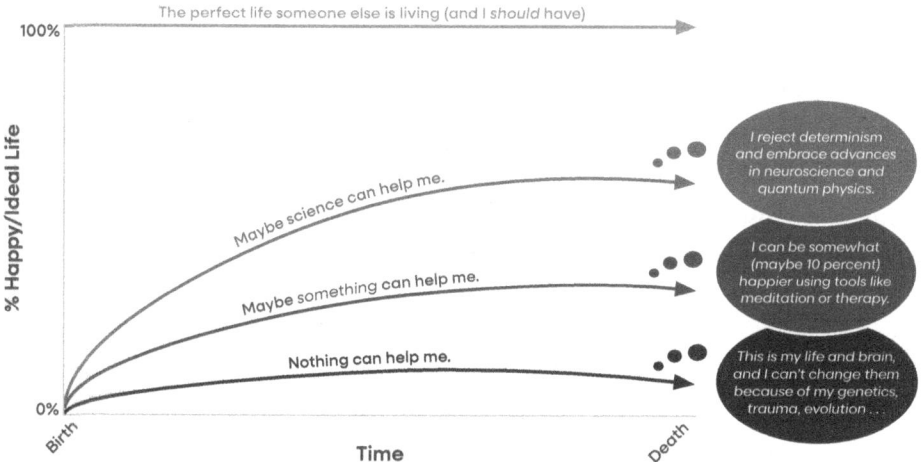

In the last chapter, I mentioned that Dan Harris learned that, despite his skepticism, practicing meditation could make him a little happier. Initially he didn't understand why; he just knew he'd found something that reduced his anxiety. But when he studied the underlying science of what was happening in his brain as he meditated, he learned why it worked and how he could maximize its benefits. He'd hacked the system, and the result was a scientifically backed approach he could use to manage his anxiety and panic attacks.

What's most interesting to me is the path people have taken throughout history to discover things that "just seem to work" in their lives, and what reliably happens when others become interested in trying to understand *why* those things are effective.

The common thread seems to be that someone accidentally stumbles onto a phenomenon that appears to have properties that cannot be easily explained. The results are obvious and reproducible, but the mechanism is mysterious. In most cases, long before a disciplined thinker comes along to investigate the phenomenon, rooting out its causes and explaining its effects, people are already using the method and attributing its power to mystery, magic, or miracles.

Magic Always Comes Before Science

People chewed on willow bark for millennia because someone noticed that it seemed to help them feel better when they were in pain. The local medicine men or folk healers would recommend it for a headache, fever, or back pain.

They would make salves from the bark that people could rub on their sore spots. Hippocrates wrote about the utility of willow bark in treating inflammation in the fourth century BC, but it wasn't until 1763 that English cleric Edward Stone published what amounted to a controlled clinical trial to prove that willow bark was, in fact, effective and safe in treating fevers from what was probably malaria. His paper was directly responsible for later work that led to the synthesis of aspirin and subsequently the whole class of nonsteroidal anti-inflammatory drugs (NSAIDs) that we still use today.[7]

This story of aspirin's development from someone noticing that tree bark made them feel better has all the elements of the typical magic-to-science sequence throughout history, and it's worth noting as we prepare to try out a new approach for our lives. See how the scientific method plays out in this example, and consider whether it reminds you of other examples you have seen:

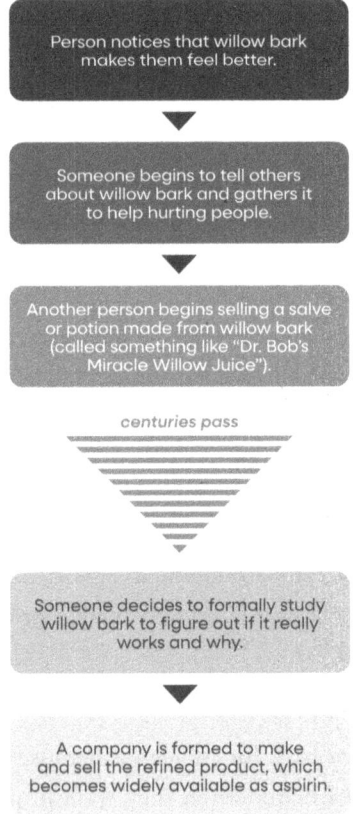

I'm laying this out to show you a pattern of how thoughts become things in the world. People stumble onto something, like the fact that chewing on tree bark seems to have healing properties. Lore and rumors spread that the bark has some magic about it. Since not everyone can go to the woods to gather bark, there's a market for the product, and inevitably someone steps in as the purveyor of the magic.

This person becomes widely known as the expert, the guru, and the source of the thing that can cure what ails you. Others hear about it and are curious. They want to know why and how it works. When they apply a scientific approach, they sort out facts from myths. Someone then refines the product into its active ingredients and proper formulation so it can be safely used. Finally, the product and the process for production are reproducible, and it's made available for everyone.

The developers of this product demystified the seemingly miraculous with science. They did not create the willow bark; they just figured out how it works and made it accessible to others.

We're not here to discuss aspirin, of course, or how science relates to magic or to business. We're here to learn how to develop an approach to life's traumas, dramas, tragedies, and massive things that will work and hold up under pressure.

I'm writing these words, coincidentally, on the anniversary of my son Mitchell's death. This isn't a book about grief, but losing a child is among the harder things humans can encounter in our lives, and it certainly remains the most massive emotional wound my family and I have experienced. After the initial and universal phases of shock, denial, and overwhelming sadness, it became obvious that Lisa and I were floundering. The faith to which we'd always turned seemed to crumble as we wondered where God was and how he could have allowed such a terrible thing to happen.

At baseline, Lisa and I are both happy, hopeful people. And we'd both been through our share of difficulties before we lost our son. But the perspective that had always worked for us before—"Hang in there, and it'll get better"—was not working this time. Losing a child is not a wound that can be remedied with the "10 percent happier" approach. We were confused, overwhelmed, and frustrated, and we realized we needed to adopt an approach to healing that would allow us to properly process the loss but also give us hope that moving forward in a healthy way was possible.

Friends and acquaintances wanted to support us in those early weeks after we lost Mitch, so they gave us books (including Harris's *10% Happier*), recommended support groups, and suggested therapists.

The books showed people's tendency to recommend what had worked best for them. They ranged from self-published guides for grieving parents ("This worked for us!") to self-proclaimed experts and gurus suggesting that healing could be found only through their program (with titles like "The Five Steps to Recovery After Loss") to scientific research (papers on complex grief and how the brain processes it) to books published by scientists ("Here's what brain imaging teaches us about grief").

These resources proved that psychological, philosophical, or spiritual cures go through the same discovery process as chemical ones; when a person figured out something that seemed to work, others started to use it too. Eventually, an organization formed to market it, someone else systematized and studied it, and finally someone made an online course or a copyrighted therapeutic paradigm from it.

All these resources offered some value, but perhaps it was too soon for us to be led through a program, join a group, or intellectually process research about how we could overcome our family's tragedy.

That's why the day in the MRI control room helped us make the breakthrough that put us on the path to finding hope again: To change our lives, we would first have to be deliberate about changing our minds. Though it hasn't been an instantaneous process, it has been an effective one. I believe the truths we learned will help you as well, no matter what you're facing.

From Fixed to Flexible

The hope I found in that MRI lab stemmed in part from what the test disproved. I'd trained as a scientist and neurosurgeon in the era when three foundational scientific principles were taught:

- The adult brain is structurally fixed and does not make new cells.

- The concept of mind is simply a perception generated by the activity of neurons in the brain.

- People's genetics and history, which are largely out of their control, determine brain function.

These three principles led to several conclusions that had dramatic effects on how people thought about their lives:

- *If I'm stuck with the brain I have, then my mental health and overall quality of life will inevitably degrade as I get older.*

- *If there is no real "me" (after all, my ideas of mind and self are really just artifacts of nerve cell activity in my brain), then nothing ultimately matters since it's all basically an illusion anyway.*

- *If my genes determine the structure of my brain, and some traumas, diseases, or experiences can harm my brain in irreparable ways, then I cannot reasonably expect to be happy or whole again if I experience any of these negative events.*

Because I'd been taught these things early on, they informed some of the ways I communicated with patients and their families in my neurosurgery practice: Some injuries can't be overcome, some tumors can't be cured, some mental health issues are overwhelming and hopeless. And I'd long labored under the gap between these teachings and my Christian faith, which proclaims that God can heal, that people can change, and that almost anything can be overcome—the very beliefs that helped me be an effective and compassionate physician who sought to offer patients hope despite the desperation of their circumstances.[8]

But as Lisa and I watched those research volunteers in the functional MRI scanner, I had an epiphany:

- We were not simply looking at pictures of what those people's brains were doing; we were seeing what happens to the brain in response to someone else suggesting that they think about one thing and not another.

- When the patients thought about something sad, chemical and structural changes happened in their brains immediately in multiple areas involved in stress, fear, anxiety, panic, and depression.

- When they instead thought about something happy, chemical and structural changes happened in their brains immediately in multiple areas related to resilience, regulation of behavior, well-being, and clarity of thinking.

- These brain changes produced shifts in heart rate, hormone production, blood pressure, respiratory rate, and a host of other physiological responses by the body.

- Since the brain activity that produces those physiological responses was initiated by intentional mental activity, there is a direct link between what someone thinks about and what happens in their body.

- In order for the body to change in response to the mind, real things had to be happening inside of cells in response to mental activity: genes had to be switched on or off, proteins and neurotransmitters had to be made and released, organs had to be stimulated, hormones had to be released or inhibited and blood vessels recruited to deliver them. *We were seeing thoughts become real things.*

This meant that we were seeing proof, in crystal clear resolution on the monitors, of mind-down control of the brain and body. The MRI machine did not give the research participants power to change their minds and their lives. The mechanisms and processes were inside them already; they simply needed to discover them and learn how to use them.

Lisa and I felt as if we were on holy ground that day. The implications of what we saw led us to a path of healing and hope after losing our son. That day inspired me to fully commit my professional life to understanding how the mind, the brain, and the body are connected. The lessons I learned led, step by trembling step, to you and me being here in "The Office." We are on the cusp of developing an approach to life that starts with realizing we are not just our brains, and ends with us deciding to use those inherent processes for our own good.

In the months and years following our epiphany in Auburn's MRI facility, Lisa and I followed a magic-to-science path of our own. We started paying attention to how we felt when we thought about different things. For example, I noticed that when I was feeling particularly sad about losing Mitch, if I could make myself think of something about his life that I was grateful for or that I always loved, I would feel better. It was a strange dichotomy of being impossibly sad and somehow a little happier *at the same time*, and it always made me appreciate that the mechanisms for using my mind to change my brain and body were already in place.

I could choose to see myself switch positions from the suffering, sad father to the one who gratefully remembered the joy Mitch had brought me. As I did, I could mentally view myself watching the control room screen as the MRI scanner revealed what was happening in my brain when *I decided what to think about and then paid attention to those things*. In my mind, I could watch the blood flow changes as my brain reacted to the top-down control of my mind. I could see my body's neurotransmitter environment becoming healthier and my body responding physiologically to produce some calm amid the chaos of my pain.

That patient-to-doctor switch did not erase the devastation of what happened, but it allowed me to remember an assertion often attributed to the psychologist Carl Jung: I am not what happened to me; I am what I choose to become.

Time after time, Lisa and I found that choosing to take control of what we thought about reliably improved our situation. We did not stop grieving or missing Mitch, nor did we magically start feeling happy instead of broken. Rather, our experience broadened, and we began to realize that we could still operate our lives *while we were grieving*.

In Edward Stone's landmark paper about how willow bark could be turned into medicine to help relieve the fever from malaria, he made a connection that we need to make here, my friend. Stone noticed that "many natural maladies carry their cures along with them, or that their remedies lie not far from their causes."[9] He figured out that an environment that provides a good habitat for, as an example, the mosquitos that carry malaria is often also a perfect environment for trees to grow that somehow, mysteriously, are a likely cure for the problem.

We saw from the MRI volunteers that the brain could either be pushed toward harmful activity or more helpful behavior by a *simple reordering of thought*, and we proved it in our own lives. And so can you, if you make this connection: *The solution is often very close to the problem.*

The troubles that hurt you, keep you stuck, frustrate you, or hinder you generally do so by making you believe that you are obligated to think about them in a particular way. And since thoughts become things (see page 165), your life is not defined by your circumstances but rather by *how you think about them.*

When you look to other people for the solution, you generally end up on a path leading to a potentially endless "take this, do that, attend this, read that, stop doing this" cycle of advice from friends, self-proclaimed experts, gurus, therapists, pastors, and doctors. All of their recommendations can offer some help in the right context, but if you're looking for magic, you must first recognize that you've been aiming at the wrong target.

I want to offer you the approach that finally moved the needle for us. It's called "Maybe science can help me," and it's very simply built from the following realizations:

- We've seen with our own eyes that people can change their brains and their bodies (and thus their lives) by changing their thoughts.

- This means we cannot be reduced to the activity of neurons in our brains since those neurons change in response to our thoughts.

- The future or quality of our lives, therefore, cannot be determined by the activity of our brain cells.

- If we replace a reductionist/determinist belief system with the belief that our thoughts can either harm or help our brains and bodies, then we can adopt a scientific approach to figure out what helps us become healthier, feel better, and be happier.

A scientific approach rejects the idea that we are stuck and unable to change because the solution is close to the problem. In other words, if our thoughts are the problem, then our thoughts can also be the answer. We can adopt the scientific method to solve our own issues, formulating hypotheses and testing them until we figure out what produces the results we're after.

Because you're likely to find the answer close to the problem and the scientific method enables you to test possible solutions, you can become the expert on remedies for the issues troubling you most. For example, if you struggle with crippling anxiety or panic attacks, you likely become aware of the rising tension internally before your anxiety spirals out of control. The 5-4-3-2-1 method (read more on page 280) directs your attention elsewhere and lowers panicked thinking in many people. Will it work for you? Give it an honest shot and evaluate its effectiveness by using the scientific method outlined on page 66.

Note that in order to make this approach work, we must reject the idea that our brains are unchangeable. Genetics, circumstances, and traumas may change our brains negatively, but if we are willing to practice self–brain surgery on our own behalf, our thinking can lead to positive changes to our brains.

This allows us to take the advice of therapists, books, gurus, and ministers; test it for ourselves; and then refine our approach based on whether the counsel was helpful *without blaming ourselves if we don't make progress since we know that the mechanisms for progress are in place.* We just remain willing to try new approaches until we find the solution.

We remember that we are good scientists who apply the scientific method. If, for example, we discover that hours of nighttime social media scrolling does not relieve our anxiety and move us forward but instead causes other problems, then we reject that approach and pivot to something more helpful. We are, as good and compassionate self–brain surgeons, unwilling to commit self-malpractice in service of an approach that isn't working. Rather, we care for our patient (ourselves) by being willing to learn a new approach until we find the progress we're seeking.

Small problems can sometimes be addressed by small approaches. Something that is a nuisance to our lives may be appropriately managed with a technique gleaned from hacking a system for minor improvements. But I'd like to propose that if reordering our minds can rewire our brains, then learning to perform that procedure in every situation of our lives can produce much more than a minor therapeutic advance. We're after radical transformation, major positive change for the big factors that keep us sad, stressed, sick, or stuck in our lives.

As you step into the role of self–brain surgeon and begin to see the amazing results that practicing from a "Maybe science can help me" paradigm can achieve, you'll realize that it isn't magic and that everything you ever needed to become healthier, feel better, and be happier was always there, waiting for you to learn to operate it in a healthy way. But when I show you more about how your mind works, it will probably still feel like a miracle.

That's what the next approach is for.

8

Approach #4: Maybe God Can Help Me

The tools of our consciousness—including our beliefs, prayers, thoughts, intentions, and faith—often correlate much more strongly with our health, longevity, and happiness than our genes do.

DAWSON CHURCH
Genie in Your Genes

As we've seen, there are multiple approaches available to address a given problem. Without even realizing it, many people default to the first approach we covered, and it's not surprising that it offers little to no benefit: The "Nothing can help me" approach can lead you to despair, apathy, or the choice to use a numbing behavior (alcohol, mindless scrolling, overeating, etc.) to manage the cognitive dissonance associated with recognizing that you seem to be stuck while other people are finding their way through the same issues.

Given the obvious limitations of the first approach, the wise person is open to learning alternative approaches. When someone realizes that their approach leaves them needing something more, it is *reasonable and rational*, even *right*, for them to seek another way of operating. This evolution of thought and practice is not a character flaw or an acknowledgment of failure; it is a mark of maturation and a desire to be the best surgeon possible. The overarching goal of this book is to help you see the times and the ways in which moving from one approach to another makes sense, and to help you consider making a change when you know it's needed. And so we looked at two other approaches that can be helpful in certain circumstances.

The "Maybe *something* can help me" approach can relieve the stress of everyday irritations and negative emotions, but if you are hit with something extremely challenging, you may find it ineffective. Hacking the system for modest gains is a great way to work through some issues, but it can leave you needing more.

The "Maybe science can help me" approach relies on a diligent, methodical way of discovering how things work, which can offer insights into how to operate your life constructively. Recall that the scientific approach involves observing something, wondering why it happens or how it works, and then devising experiments or tests to figure it out. We do not decide what we believe before we run the experiments and then refuse to modify that belief regardless of the results; that would be inherently *unscientific*. So using the approach properly requires us to be willing to modify our hypotheses based on our research.

Keep in mind that the word *science* has many connotations, and the one we're using here specifically refers to the diligent, methodical approach to discovering the true nature of how things work for the purpose of operating our lives in the best way possible. In the case of self–brain surgery, we have come alive to the knowledge that we are all operating the most complex computer network in the universe, the human mind-brain interface, and that most of our problems stem from not knowing how to operate that interface effectively.

If, at this point, you are convinced that self–brain surgery has transformative power and you are satisfied with the few new approaches you've already learned, you may choose to skip the rest of this chapter. Most of the remaining chapters are profoundly tactical and will arm you with specific steps you can take when facing a particular issue.

However, note that these approaches will sometimes fall short. The limitations of science and simple hacks will become glaringly apparent if you lose a child, face a divorce you did not want, receive a terminal diagnosis, discover a spouse's affair, or don't get the job you so desperately need. If you believe that science will eventually explain everything, you may be frustrated because it can never answer the big questions of meaning and purpose. Science is insufficient to answer such questions since they are untestable by the methodologies of science. That's why I believe that, even if you move ahead to the next chapter now, you may decide to come back to this chapter should you ever find yourself on the wrong side of our equation, A > SKD, as Lisa and I did when our son died.

These massive things produce huge gaps between what you thought was true of life and what is true now. Even in those moments, practicing self–brain surgery to manage the inevitable avalanche of anxious, grieved, desperate emotions and thoughts will prove incredibly helpful. But that practice will not comfort you or satisfy your questions about why these things happen or what the future will look like for you. And as it turns out, "why?" and "what now?" will be what you most desperately want to know, even when you are not in the middle of some trauma, drama, tragedy, or massive thing.

Since we are gathered here in "The Office" from our practices all over the world, this is a good time to acknowledge again that we all have different backgrounds and belief systems. And so, as we discuss the various approaches available to us as self–brain surgeons, it is good to note that even here lies some common ground for the doubter, the atheist, the agnostic, and the devout believer or practitioner of any faith.

As I mentioned earlier, quantum physics clearly shows that the mind of the observer of an experiment has an effect on the outcome of the experiment. The relevant self–brain surgery lesson we learn from this is that *how you pay attention to things and how you think about them has creative power to change what happens to them.*

I'm not talking about the law of attraction or manifesting everything you want, but there is a secret to learning how your mind can turn on filters in your brain to make you pay attention to things more carefully, which then leads to you being more likely to find what you're looking for in life. You'll learn about this incredible filtering mechanism when we get to "The Operating Room," but for now, the mic-dropping, stunning conclusion is that science shows that your life has a purpose regardless of whether or not you believe in God or spiritual matters. Because, independently of any belief in a God who created you, *your life and your interaction with the people and the universe around you matters. You matter, my friend. Your choices and decisions have real-world consequences.*

To reach this conclusion, we must reject the reductionism and determinism of classical physics, most mainstream psychology, and the twentieth-century neuroscience I learned in medical school. In the determinist worldview, every decision we make is determined by undirected biological processes set in motion by the random physics of an accidental universe. That outdated view is the reason modern media and culture often present science and faith as enemies.

However, neuroscientists have known conclusively since the late 1990s that the adult brain is constantly undergoing neurogenesis (the creation of new neurons) and neuroplasticity (the formation of new connections between neurons). Since the development of functional brain imaging in the early 2000s, we've known that thoughts can direct structural changes in the brain as well as or more effectively than medicines or surgery—and can do so much more quickly.

The stakes are high, because how you operate your mind, your brain, and your life isn't just about you. Your decision to master self–brain surgery and get your thinking under control will change how you function in every area of your life, including your relationships. It will change how you relate to your spouse, how you parent, how you interact with your friends, and how you view others.

From this ground, tilled by our desperate search for purpose and answers in life's hardest moments, there grows a final, needed approach. Before we dive into that approach, let me make a few things clear so that we both know exactly what we are discussing:

1. This book is designed to train you in self–brain surgery and to give you the theoretical and tactical tools you need to operate your mind and your brain. To that end, we are going to discuss the possibility that God can help you operate them in a way that is fundamentally different and more powerful than you can achieve alone. This is not an altar call; it is an acknowledgment that pursuing truth through a scientific approach leads to questions that cannot be answered by that method, and it is an invitation to a path we can take from there when needed.

2. Our study of various approaches has been built in a rational, reasonable, and scientific way. I propose that we can use this same path to get to the next approach. Even though discussions of God or spiritual matters seem unscientific to many people, I will show you that this is not the case.

3. We will not debate doctrinal issues here. This chapter will show you that in our search for a process *that works when we're under pressure*, the "Maybe God can help me" approach adds value to the purely scientific one we learned earlier by answering the "why?" and "what now?" questions science alone cannot answer.

4. I am a Christian and believe that God created the universe from nothing, that we were created in God's image, and that Jesus—God in human

form—died for our sins and was resurrected, which gives us the hope of salvation. This is the "good news" as taught in the New Testament of the Bible. You may not share my belief in Christianity—or in any one path to God—but if you are interested in understanding why I find it convincing, please refer to the books in appendix E.

5. When I speak of God, I am referring to a living being who created the universe but who is both independent of and actively at work in it.[1] Though I want to explain my view of God, the rest of this chapter will stay in the lane of how our nervous systems seem designed to communicate with God and benefit from that interaction in numerous ways.

If we're looking for an approach that works, then we should be able to use science to investigate the approach and evaluate its efficacy. As discussed earlier, you do not have to believe everything someone else believes to operate from their approach and see if it works for you. In this chapter, I merely want to show you an approach that billions of people use in their lives, and soon I'll introduce some science to hopefully convince you that it is a reasonable, rational consideration.

The Origins of Modern Science

We're here to find the best operating system for our lives—the approach that best helps us use our minds and brains to overcome the things that hurt, frustrate, or keep us stuck and that we need to manage better.

And so, friend, if you agree with me that taking a scientific approach here—following the evidence to determine what works best in our quest to become healthier, feel better, and be happier—is an intellectually honest endeavor, then we need to clear up one point. Modern academia and popular opinion tell us that there is no need to invoke God in our search for answers because science will eventually answer all our questions. They believe that you have to check your brain at the door if you want to believe in God *and* practice science. It might surprise you, then, to learn that organized science began as a way to explore and explain God's creative work for the purpose of helping people see and be in awe of him.

Scientists like Nicolaus Copernicus, Johannes Kepler, and Gregor Mendel were fervent believers who brought science out of the realm of Aristotelian logic that argues one can use reason and abstraction to deduce how nature was formed.

Instead, they used principled investigation to actually learn what God had done and to try to inspire others by explaining how God did those things. The philosopher Holmes Rolston III puts it like this: "It was monotheism that launched the coming of physical science, for it premised an intelligible world, sacred but disenchanted, a world with a blueprint, which was therefore open to the searches of the scientists. The great pioneers in astronomy—Copernicus, Galileo, Kepler, and Newton—devoutly believed themselves called to find evidences of God in the physical world."[2]

Learning that smart people in past centuries used science to explore spiritual matters might allow you to consider an approach you would not previously have tried. We don't use science to investigate things only if we already believe them; we use science to learn what's true.

You might also not know that James Clerk Maxwell, the father of electromagnetism (which taught us that electricity, light, and magnetism are different forms of the same phenomenon) and a major influence on Einstein as he developed theories in relativity and quantum physics, was a Christian. Maxwell founded the Cavendish Laboratory at the University of Cambridge and had the words of Psalm 111:2 inscribed in Latin above the doorway of the lab's entrance: *Magna opera Domini: exquisita in omnes voluntates ejus*. When the laboratory was rebuilt in 1973, the new doorway, as a nod to Maxwell, was inscribed with the same Scripture, this time in English: "The works of the LORD are great, sought out of all them that have pleasure therein."[3]

I find it somewhat ironic that the Cavendish Laboratory is where James Watson and Francis Crick worked out the structure of DNA in the 1950s. They walked through that doorway every day under the words of Scripture while maintaining a naturalist worldview. They believed that their discoveries would eventually make God unnecessary to explain anything.

But science, honestly pursued, continues to frustrate those who think it will eventually lead to a simple explanation for how we got here and how everything works. For example, discovering DNA led to the science of molecular biology, which has produced the surprising result that simple Darwinian evolution has a very hard time explaining the arrival of new information from gradual changes in organisms, not to mention the enormous chemistry problem of how those molecules assemble themselves in an organized way.

As we talked about when examining the scientific method, the solution often lies close to the problem.

What If God Can Help You?

Once you accept the idea that you can change your brain, body, and life by changing how you think, you must consider two critical truths:

1. How you think affects how other people think.
2. How you think affects your entire life and even the generations after you.

Since you are a wise and compassionate self–brain surgeon, these truths lead you to the shocking realization that, because thoughts structurally change your brain, every thought you take action on also changes *you* in a material way. And those changes inevitably impact the people around you, which influences the kinds of thoughts they think and act on. This is what I call the two-patient rule (see page 224): Your thoughts do not happen in a vacuum, and self–brain surgery is never just about you.

> Because thoughts structurally change your brain, every thought you take action on also changes *you* in a material way.

This should be equally encouraging to you regardless of your beliefs, but if you are a doubter or atheist, or you've simply never put much thought into these matters, here's your callout: If you accept Heisenberg's "attention changes reality" discovery (see page 65) and that your choice of thoughts matters in the universe and other people's lives, isn't it scientifically reasonable to ask how it came to be this way?

Although understanding that our ability to affect the world around us with our thoughts can rightly give us a sense that our lives do matter, it does not answer the big "why?" and "what now?" questions we mentioned earlier.

At this point, I want to call out the faithful as well: If you believe in a God who created you on purpose and for a purpose, then learning to operate your nervous system as it is designed to operate is your responsibility. Approaches have consequences, remember? The Bible gives us a good definition of sin when it says, "If anyone, then, knows the good they ought to do and doesn't do it, it is sin for them."[4] Once you realize that you are not obligated to suffer at the behest of every thought and feeling that pops into your head, and that you have the power to manage your mind and change your life, you may start to see self–brain surgery as a form of obedience to God's design for your flourishing—the *abundant life* Jesus promised. When you reach this level of "The Practice" (as we will discuss in part 5), the transformation of your thinking will begin to affect your whole life in a radical way.[5]

So now let's return to our graph, adding a new approach called "Maybe God can help me," which would look something like this:

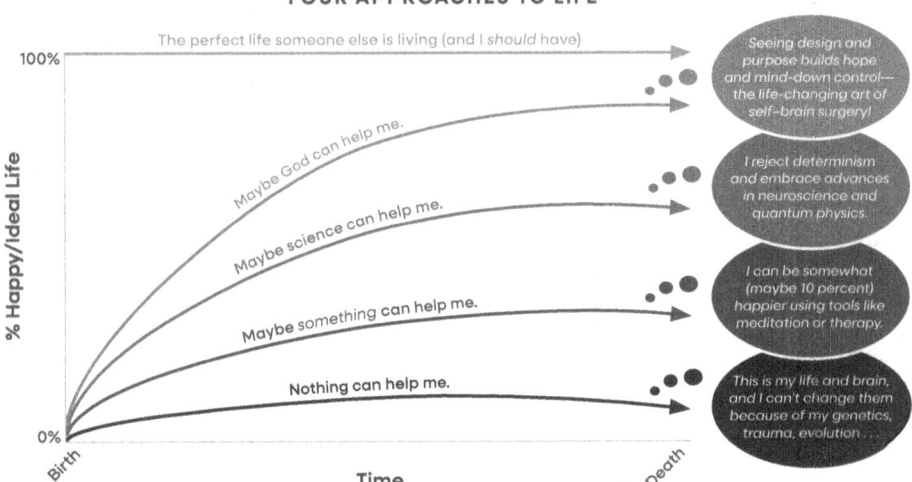

Remember that the graph represents the internal sense we all have that someone out there is living a life that's "better" than ours. We assume that more is possible and that as time goes on, we should be getting better at getting better, but we bump into constraints when our approach doesn't allow us to make progress.

If something appears optimized to perform in a certain way, then isn't it reasonable to consider whether it was designed for that purpose? We mentioned earlier that, when we are pondering why we're here or what to do when something hurts, one thing we seek is a sense of meaning and purpose. It might surprise you, then, to notice the ways in which choosing to focus our thoughts on God when we face problems has many measurable, positive benefits:

- Numerous studies using functional imaging have shown that various forms of meditation produce increased size and function of brain areas involved in reducing anxiety, increasing resilience, and improving the ability to reason and make decisions.[6]

- Prayer and meditation together and independently have been proven to produce these same changes even more powerfully, along with significant improvements in brain wave activity.[7]

- Prayer and meditation have been proven to reduce the self-referential activity of the brain's default mode network, which is the network that activates when we are at rest and often floods our minds with regret about the past or worry about the future.[8]

- These activities have also been proven to reduce blood pressure, stress, and levels of pain, as well as lower cortisol levels and cardiovascular risk.[9]

- Spiritual prayer and meditation have been compared to secular forms and found to be superior at decreasing anxiety, improving mood, and improving tolerance to pain.[10]

Of course, people have known for centuries that managing their thoughts and engaging in prayer and meditation are helpful, though they did not always know why. Still, ancient sacred and secular writings from all over the world mention these as ways to reduce anxiety and address other problems.

The "Why" Factor

Until a few decades ago, many scientists attributed the positive physiological and psychological benefits of prayer and meditation to the brains of those people who engaged in such behaviors. These people were assumed to have certain structures in their brains or particular genetic characteristics that predisposed them to want to pray *because* of the type of brain they had. But in the early 2000s, the development of functional brain imaging technologies laid an axe to the root of that tree by showing that the structural changes in the brains of people who pray and meditate happened *after* they engaged in these activities. In other words, it's not their brains that made them want to pray and meditate.

This is a good example of what science is supposed to do: allow for the reformulation of a hypothesis when the data show it to be false. The old idea—that there's no God, but some people have a "God neuron" in their brains that has evolved to make them operate better when they imagine a God out there who can help them—is challenged by a new technology (functional brain imaging). Thus the honest researcher must reconsider and revise the hypothesis: "Wait, even when nonbelievers pray and meditate, their brains structurally change in positive ways that were not there before. Perhaps this means there is a benefit to these practices that is not predisposed by but rather caused by them."

I acknowledge that this discovery still does not prove the existence of God. Some scientists even propose that these changes are somehow illusory and that they have evolved that way simply as some sort of neuronal survival advantage. *If that is the case, however, it still behooves us to use our thinking to change our brains to become healthier, feel better, and be happier, even if we're just learning to practice self–brain surgery to gain a benefit and there's nothing spiritual about it at all, right?*

Many people, including the "10 percent happier" types led by Dan Harris, have settled here: "The science says these practices will help me, so I will use them to feel and perform better."

We're good scientists, though, and we have a responsibility to be the best physicians we can be in order to take care of our patients (ourselves). And so we are not going to settle for this "Maybe *something* can help me" level of operating our lives. We're not going to be satisfied with simply using science to squeeze more performance out of ourselves. No, when our investigation's results imply that there is more to the story, we are the type of scientists who want to pull on that thread.

That's where my grandson Ryker comes in. Ryker is a curious, brilliant little boy. He's four years old as I write this, but his vocabulary and conversational skills rival those of children much older (and some adults I know, frankly). One thing I love about Ryker is that he's never satisfied with being told something. He always wants to know *why*.

Here's a typical interaction over FaceTime with Lisa and me (whom he calls Missy and Pop):

Ryker: Missy and Pop, can you come to my house today?

Me: No, Buddy, we can't come today.

Ryker: Why?

Me: Because you're in Texas, and we are in Nebraska.

Ryker: Why?

Lisa: Because that's where we live.

Ryker: Why?

Me: Because my job is in Nebraska.

Ryker: But why?

Before long, we're discussing economics, the realities of the supply and demand of the neurosurgical job market, the post–Affordable Care Act shift in employment of physicians from private practice to hospital-based work, and how if we'd bought Bitcoin in 2009 we'd be independently wealthy and could all live together on a private stretch of beach on South Padre Island.

And, inevitably, that leads to me saying, "You're right, Ryker, we should have followed that investment advice from your Uncle Nate, but it seemed like a scam to me."

Then Ryker shakes his head and says, "But why?"

There are immense benefits to this type of curiosity, especially if we're amenable to changing our approach as our questions lead us deeper. One of those benefits is that it opens up a willingness to accept possibilities that we may have previously dismissed.

For example, if the MRI research keeps showing us that spiritual practices are good for our brains, our bodies, and our overall lives, then maybe we should channel Ryker and say, "Why?"

That might open us up to other questions: If prayer seems to improve the parts of our brains that make us less anxious and better at decision-making, is it possible that it is not just a neurological phenomenon but a mechanism of communicating with God? If so, then is it really a mind-up connection that allows for the possibility of guidance, healing, comfort, and strength for our lives?

If we become comfortable with such questions, then we can begin to follow a trail that leads back to the wisdom of those who engaged in spiritual practices long before us. Perhaps we thought it was just coincidental that people figured out ways to improve their lives when they didn't know anything about neuroscience. For example, the apostle Paul points out that anxiety dissolves when we choose gratitude (see Philippians 4:6-7). Now, as science reveals that our nervous systems are designed to flourish with intentional thought surgery, maybe it's reasonable to conclude that ancient prescriptions like the apostle Paul's are effective because they were prescribed by the Great Physician.[11]

Since we've seen how spiritual practices make positive structural changes in the brain, consider this: The Bible presents Jesus as a man who never did anything wrong. He did, however, often teach that it is possible to err with our thinking.[12] But if Jesus never erred or sinned with his thinking, that means that he *never hurt his brain with harmful thinking.*

Following this stream of thought, then, Jesus' brain would have always and only been structurally improved by his thoughts. He would have had the ideal human brain, unspoiled by harmful synapses, aberrant neurochemistry, or unhelpful emotion/thought loops. What does this mean for us? The Bible makes a few curious statements about believers and their minds. Romans 12:2 encourages people to "be transformed by the renewing of your mind," and 1 Corinthians 2:16 says that believers have been given the "mind of Christ."

What if praying that God would progressively show us how to align our thinking with the types of thoughts Jesus had would structurally make our brains more like his over time? What if this type of progressive mind-brain improvement would allow us to flourish—to live in the "A" (abundance) of our A > SKD equation *while* we're living in the world full of steal, kill, and destroy?

To test the idea that "Maybe God can help me," try the experiment in the paragraphs below. Be sure to record your observations as you determine how this approach may be helping you.

Regardless of your belief system, since we know that spiritual practices make our brains better and we have committed to follow a scientific approach as we change our minds and our lives, what if you decided to do an experiment? Perform the self–brain surgery practice of devoting a few minutes a day to calming your mind and simply asking God (If you're not comfortable with that, just do it as a science experiment) to optimize your brain. Then, over the next few weeks, pay attention to changes in your automatic thoughts, your feelings of resilience, your emotional control, and other areas in which you normally struggle.

If you find that it's working, it might be an approach worth continuing. If it produces helpful results over time, then perhaps a reasonable, rational, scientifically valid conclusion is, "Maybe this works because it's true."

The "Maybe God can help me" approach does work for many people, and the imaging results are consistent with Scripture and with billions of people's lived experience. So I'll leave you with this before we move on: If you, like some of Dr. Fukushima's colleagues, can see the value of this approach but are not willing to try it, then my grandson Ryker has a question for you.

"Why?"

9

Your Role in Rewiring Your Brain

If you haven't the strength to impose your own terms upon life, you must accept the terms it offers you.

T. S. ELIOT
The Confidential Clerk

"He wants to know how you would do it."

I couldn't make sense of what the nurse was saying on the phone. "Please repeat that," I said. "I don't understand what you're asking me."

"Dr. Anderson is trying to do a case, and he keeps asking us what *you* would do in this situation. He's stopping the operation every minute or two and asking the staff questions about how you perform this type of surgery."

Dr. Anderson (not his real name) was a young neurosurgeon I'd hired temporarily to cover my practice so Lisa and I could take a trip to Texas to visit family. These locum tenens physicians are doctors who, for many reasons, are willing to take short assignments in hospitals to provide coverage when local doctors need to travel or when hospitals have staffing shortages.

I'd used locums doctors several times, and generally they fell into two categories: older surgeons who didn't want to work full time but weren't quite ready to retire, and others who simply weren't busy enough in their own practices and needed to make more money. I'd found the quality of the locums surgeons to generally be excellent, and they enabled me to be sure my patients were cared for when I needed to be away.

Dr. Anderson was an exception. When he first applied, his credentials looked impressive. He'd gone to a top medical school, done his residency in one of the premier programs in the country, and even completed an extra yearlong fellowship in complex spine surgery under the direction of the surgeon who wrote one of the textbooks I have on my shelf. He was, on paper, a wonderful candidate.

The only odd thing about Dr. Anderson's resume was that he wasn't practicing anywhere. He finished his training and then immediately began to do locums assignments all across America. When I interviewed him, I asked him why.

"Well, I'm young and single, and I just want to see a lot of hospitals and cities before I decide where to put my roots down. I want to get experience without being committed to one place for a while."

That answer made sense to me and his references were solid, so I decided to give him a try while we went to Texas.

Two days later, while visiting with family, my phone rang. That's when my nurse frantically told me that Dr. Anderson was struggling.

"He seems unsure what to do, Doc. The patient has been asleep for a while, and Dr. Anderson has barely gotten started. Is there any way you can help him?"

I went to another room, and the nurse called me via FaceTime. She held the phone up, and I could see Dr. Anderson looking down at the patient.

I asked, "What's going on, David?"

He looked up and said, "Oh, I just wanted some advice. This patient has a large disc herniation with spinal cord compression, and I'm doing an anterior fusion. But the approach has been really difficult, and she's lost a fair amount of blood. I can't seem to get the spine exposed without running into more bleeding. Something is off with her anatomy."

"Okay," I said, "take the retractors out and show me how you got in there."

David removed the retractors, and the nurse moved the phone around so I could see the approach the young doctor had taken. I asked him then to slowly show me each layer he had gone through to get to the spine, and the problem became obvious.

"Looks like you just started a few centimeters too far laterally, David," I said. "You're going through the sternocleidomastoid muscle, and it will be a lot cleaner if you come in medial to it instead. Extend your incision a little more toward the midline, and you should be able to get to the spine with less bleeding."

David's approach had been off by less than an inch, and it had placed the trajectory of his surgery directly through the middle of the large muscle that runs up and down the neck. A cleaner and safer route to the spine is to work along the inside border of the muscle, in a natural cleft between the muscle and the trachea, which also allows the surgeon to sneak past the carotid artery and jugular vein without making them bleed.

Over the next half hour, I watched David make the incision a little longer, replace his retractors in the proper spot, and expose the spine nicely. There was no more bleeding, and he was able to find the disc herniation and decompress the spinal cord safely.

I noticed a few important things along the way:

- The problem was never with this young doctor's technical skills or his understanding of the pathology he was there to treat.
- The issue was only that his approach was off, and he'd failed to recognize it.
- Because he had taken the wrong angle, he was struggling mightily to expose the thing that was hurting his patient, leading to other problems.
- He hadn't called for help, mostly because he seemed too busy blaming his struggle on the patient's anatomy to question his role in the situation.
- Once he got help, he backed up a few steps and corrected the approach. Then the case proceeded in a smooth and safe manner, and the patient ultimately made a good recovery.

Later, I had long conversations with David's former professors and his other references. It became clear that none of them had ever seen him operate independently. He had been in a training environment, surrounded by other surgeons, and he always had someone around suggesting ideas and helping him along.

His former chief, the one whose name is on the cover of my textbook, was shocked when he realized this. He told me, "We really did David a disservice. It never dawned on me that every case he ever did was with another surgeon, so we did not realize he wasn't developed enough to practice independently."

David and I had an honest talk. He said, "Surgery always seemed so easy when I was in fellowship. Now every case seems really difficult and dangerous." I helped him recognize that he wasn't ready to be in practice.

I worked with his former professors, and they created an opportunity for him to do another year of hybrid training, in which he was progressively less supervised and was expected to become more independent.

Notice that David's problem was not his intelligence, his technical skills, or his concern for his patients. His entire problem was a lack of insight into how to recognize when an approach was off and when an operation needed to change. He had to stop blaming the patient and to develop the willingness to honestly assess his own performance and change his approach if necessary. Only then would he become a safe and independent surgeon.

I heard from David not long ago, and he thanked me for investing in him and taking the time to help him get better and move forward in his career. He said that he had flourished in his new training environment, and today he is in a successful academic practice and doing very well.

Launching from Student to Practicing Surgeon

Training a surgeon to begin practicing and do more good than harm requires so much more than teaching them a bunch of techniques. Signing off on graduating trainees is one of the biggest responsibilities of an attending physician's career because it means that their former students will now be practicing on real patients when there will be no one there to watch over them.

Our time remaining in "The Office" is short. It's almost time for us to go to "The Operating Room," where you'll learn procedures to apply to and operate on essentially any issue you may face. That part of the book will be a reference you can return to anytime you encounter something that requires a specific type of self–brain surgery. It's also a place to turn for help as you consider various approaches.

But should you ever find yourself struggling to get results, if everything seems hard and you feel stuck, then perhaps remember David and the lesson he learned: When the anatomy seems off, when things are bleeding more than they normally do, and when nothing seems right in an operation that usually works, *the problem is often with your approach.*

Why does this matter? Because there's a difference between being a person who knows lots of techniques and procedures, and being a trustworthy, wise, and compassionate surgeon. And in the world of self–brain surgery, you're operating with yourself as the patient, and everyone in your life is being helped or harmed by the outcome of your practice.

I can teach you the techniques, and you're smart enough to master them. But as we saw in David's story, having a vast array of technical knowledge won't help if your approach is off (even by a little) and you refuse to seek counsel when you need it. You must develop a discipline of checking for approach errors and a willingness to course correct when you're off.

Knowing what to do *when* you think about certain things is what you'll learn in "The Operating Room." But knowing *that* you're thinking in an unhelpful way is more philosophical than scientific, and it requires a disciplined and systematic process that is hard to teach. The reason it is so difficult is because it's as much about character as it is about concepts.

The move from floundering to flourishing in your life is the most dramatic and liberating journey in the human experience. It breaks chains, overcomes trauma, ends generational troubles, and sets people free from all the different ways in which life can make them feel broken.

That's why this matters so much. And it starts with the insight that sometimes your entire struggle can be resolved by changing your approach and asking for help.

And *that* starts with you, right now.

You have a role to play in this that no one else can play for you.

Hold out your hand and say, "Scalpel."

It's time to operate on your own life, Doctor.

Helping Hands

The first time you cut a person with a scalpel is terrifying.

I remember my first time like it was yesterday. I was a lowly intern in Pittsburgh, scrubbed into an appendectomy on a teenager with belly pain and a fever. The attending physician was a grumpy older surgeon who happened to be chairman of the department. (After all these years, I can't even remember his real name; we all just called him The Chairman. I mostly strove to avoid him and tried not to make eye contact with him.)

Through some terrible turn of events, the chief resident and both of the senior residents on call that night were busy with trauma surgeries, so The Chairman found himself having to come in to scrub a minor case with the person least qualified in the hospital to operate—me.

Not only was I an intern and just a few weeks out of medical school, but I also wasn't even one of *his* interns. As a neurosurgery resident, I was required to spend one year of internship with the general surgeons, but from day one I was treated differently from the "real" general surgery residents. A handful of us were future surgical specialists there to pay our dues as interns—nascent oral surgeons, orthopedists, otolaryngologists, and me. Everyone knew we weren't there to learn how to operate on livers and colons, so from the start we were assigned the least desirable and most arduous rotations and tasks.

My intern year consisted of four months on the trauma service—valuable experience that paid huge dividends for me later in Iraq—and several months on other rotations that needed warm bodies to hold retractors, drain abscesses, check labs, and write orders. I was there to learn how to take care of sick people, gain some experience in the operating room, and generally learn to work up to 120 hours a week and not complain about it.

I had seen the patient in the emergency department, felt her tender abdomen, noticed her abnormally high white blood cell count and fever, and made the diagnosis of appendicitis. Then I called the senior resident to tell her that this young lady needed surgery, and that's when my night went off the rails.

"There was a big crash in the Fort Pitt Tunnel; multiple trauma patients coming in, Lee," she said. "All of us are going to be tied up for a while. You'll have to call The Chairman and do it yourself."

After suffering through two minutes of The Chairman yelling at me on the phone for basically existing, he agreed to come in and do the case. Half an hour later, the patient was prepped and draped, and I was mentally prepared to hold a suction tube and be ignored for the next hour.

That's when it happened.

The Chairman looked down at the patient's abdomen, seemingly pondering something while the scrub tech and I waited for him to start the surgery.

After what seemed like hours but was probably only a few seconds, he looked up at me and said with a snarl, "What's your name again?"

I said, "Dr. Lee Warren, the neurosurgery intern."

He shook his head. "You guys are like psychiatrists with knives. Never understood anyone wanting to do that for a living."

"I'm sorry," I said, although I'm still not sure whether I was apologizing to him for being a future neurosurgeon or just being there at all.

There was another long pause until The Chairman said, "Well, Warren, are you going to do this case or not? This girl's not going to operate on herself."

I looked at him, the scrub tech looked at me, and I tried not to pass out at the idea that I was about to perform my very first operation in the middle of the night on a very sick young girl in front of the head of the whole department. That realization hit me like a sucker punch in the solar plexus.

"Scalpel," I said. And thus began my career as an operating surgeon.

For the next hour or so, literally every move I made was met with scolding and questioning from The Chairman.

Him: What incision are you going to make?

Me: Rockey-Davis.

Him: Why not McBurney?

Me: She's young; it should leave a prettier scar.

Him: What layers will you need to open?

Me: Well, the muscles are external oblique and internal oblique, then we should see the transversalis fascia, and finally the peritoneum.

The Chairman continued to question everything I did, tell me I was holding every instrument wrong, and remind me often that it was late and if I were smarter or more talented, he'd be home and in bed already. But he never stopped me or took over. I opened the peritoneum, mobilized the colon, found the appendix, and then identified the appendiceal artery and vein, the only blood vessels I had to worry about in that operation.

I placed a clamp across the vessels and then clumsily tried to pass a suture around them so I could tie them off. The Chairman watched me struggle for a few seconds and said, "What am I doing here if you're not going to ask me to assist you?"

I hadn't thought about asking *the professor* to help *me*. The operation requires more than one set of hands to complete, but I was so shocked to be operating at all that it never occurred to me to think he was there to teach and support me. I said, "Do you mind holding this clamp, sir?"

He took the clamp, which freed up both my hands to pass the tie around the vessels, but the angle was awkward due to the size of the swollen appendix. The Chairman said, "Go ahead and cut the artery and vein, and then you can get the appendix out of your way before you tie off the vessels."

I took the Metzenbaum scissors from the scrub tech, cut the two blood vessels, and then lifted the appendix out of the patient's abdomen, the first human organ I'd ever removed. My heart leapt up into my throat as I realized I'd just performed an operation as the operating surgeon, a huge step in my professional development. I was basking in this internal glow of my own accomplishment when The Chairman gently cleared his throat and brought me back into the moment.

There was still work to be done, and now I had to show the boss that I could tie a knot.

I used a right-angle forceps to pass a silk suture behind the clamp and then make a knot with a two-handed technique I'd learned in hundreds of practice sessions in call rooms and labs during medical school. As I slid the knot down toward the clamp to secure the vessels, The Chairman opened the clamp and let them go. Blood sprayed everywhere, and I panicked.

What had been an organized, clean case was now a hole in a teenager's abdomen that was rapidly filling with blood, and The Chairman started yelling. "What are you going to do, Doctor? Your patient's bleeding!"

I grabbed a sucker and began to try to clear the blood from the wound, but it was filling up too fast. "What are you going to do, Warren?" The Chairman screamed.

That's when I saw it. I can't explain it exactly, but it was like that scene in *The Matrix* movies, when time slows down for Neo and he can see things so clearly that even the bullets flying at him appear to be just bits of information he can easily process and swat away. Somehow, I heard in my head, *This is a game for him, and he's testing me.*

I recalled what The Chairman had said earlier when he'd told me that he was there to help me (the solution often lies close to the problem, remember?).

"Grab a sucker," I told him, "and help me clear this blood."

He picked up a second sucker, and with both of us working, we were able to quickly gain control of the field so I could see where the vessels were. I used my other hand to pick up the ends of the vessels with a DeBakey forceps, and then I told The Chairman, "Clamp these off again, please."

He did so, and I irrigated the wound with sterile saline to wash all the blood away. I passed the suture around the clamp and began to slide the knot around the vessels. But this time I stopped for a second and looked The Chairman in the eyes. "Don't open that clamp again, or I'll get an assistant with steadier hands."

The scrub tech made a little sucking sound under her mask, and I wondered for a second if I'd just ended my own career. But The Chairman chuckled and said, "Nice. A surgeon has to give good instructions to the assistant. Go ahead and tie the knot so I can go home."

I tied off the vessels, and The Chairman actually made small talk with me as we closed the wound. He scrubbed out as I was placing a dressing on the patient's abdomen, and on his way out of the room he said over his shoulder, "Good job, Warren. We might make a surgeon out of you after all."

Natural Resources

I've thought about that night many times over the years, particularly how scared I was when the clamp came off. And then about how it was clear that I could not have safely finished that operation without asking The Chairman for help. I realized that he was forcing me to fully step into the role of operating surgeon, which required me to make a mindset shift in the middle of a very stressful situation. And I now know that although I freaked out for a moment, the situation was never out of his control. He would not have let anything bad happen to that patient if I'd failed to step up, and he knew without a doubt that he could take over and set things right if needed.

But he was a good professor, and he knew that there would be times in my future career when the unexpected would happen, and I would not have him there to save me or my patient. I learned later that The Chairman was famous for using "the clamp trick" when he was teaching young interns how to operate. It was his way of testing their ability to handle stress and use the resources available (including other surgeons).

As part of my medical training, I had read about the appendectomy procedure until I had memorized all the steps, and I had scrubbed in as an assistant and watched others perform it dozens of times in medical school and earlier in my intern year. I'd thought about the operation plenty. But until that night, I'd never performed it. I'd been contemplating but not operating.

That night when the clamp came off, there was no more time to think. I had to *do*.

Chris Voss, the former FBI hostage negotiator who wrote the book *Never Split the Difference*, said, "When the pressure is on, you don't rise to the occasion; you fall to your highest level of preparation."[1] And in the case of self–brain surgery, my friend, we *prepare* for the pressure by recognizing that the things we think about, and the ways in which we think about them, turn into the things we do when life gets hard.

A few of my fellow interns quit that year. It was too hard, the hours were too long, and they didn't enjoy the lifestyle of surgeons who have to work all night. One intern was fired because he simply could not perform under pressure. He could do everything perfectly in the lab; he could tie all the knots and answer all the test questions about the anatomy and physiology of every problem he might encounter. But he failed the clamp test because he hadn't mentally prepared for what to do when things did not go according to plan. He also hadn't learned when to ask for help.

I told you that story as we're ending our time here in "The Office" because I need to convince you that you have a role to play in your own mental health, decision-making, and performance improvement that no one else can play. That's a critical lesson before you begin learning the tactical techniques of self–brain surgery.

In order for your life to start to mirror that slow-motion scene from *The Matrix*, as mine did once I saw the game The Chairman was playing in the OR, you must see this clearly: *The ultimate impact of almost everything that happens in your life is determined by how you think about it.* Once you realize this, you will begin to view your automatic thoughts and feelings, which you previously thought were as real as the bullets flying at Neo, as simply bits of data that you are empowered to investigate, examine, and choose a proper response to. No longer will you assume that you're obligated to react to or be wounded by them in an endless repetition of the same scenes playing over and over.

Obviously, I'm not saying that if you get hit by a bus or crash in a plane, how you think about it will change the damage it caused. Sometimes horrible things happen, people die, and life is hard. But the vast majority of our circumstances lack the inherent power to make us flounder or rob us of flourishing unless we give them mental consent to do so. This is because, as Gabor Maté said, "Trauma is not what happens to you; it's what happens inside you as a result of what happened to you."[2]

This may seem hard to believe because the prevailing message today is that we are inherently fragile; it seems like every other person on Instagram claims to be a trauma expert and tells you that your body keeps a record of everything that's ever happened, that certain adverse childhood experiences can wreck you even if you don't remember them, or that the wrong genetics or upbringing can determine the whole course of your life. But the objective truth is that humans are not inherently fragile or easily broken. Evidence of this is everywhere; not everyone who went through the Holocaust or who lost a loved one on 9/11 or to COVID-19 developed PTSD. Not every one of my patients with fatal brain cancer loses hope or suffers a loss of quality of life, even though they are dying of their illnesses.

I do want to note that, on a personal level, I understand how difficult it can be to move forward after experiencing trauma. I went to war and came home with my mental health and my first marriage blown up, developed PTSD, and spent years putting myself back together. Then I lost my son in a horrific way and found myself blown up again. But when I saw other people change their minds in that MRI scanner in Auburn, I realized that I could too. I saw my heartbroken wife, Lisa, make the same mental switch, and we, with our tired hands and weak knees, found a straight path for our lives again that led us back to hope.[3]

Anne Lamott writes, "There is almost nothing outside you that will help in any kind of lasting way, unless you are waiting for a donor organ,"[4] and it's a fact. Modern neuroscience has proven it conclusively: You have the tools inside you to perform self–brain surgery and take mind-down command of the processes your brain performs that determine how most of your life plays out, even down to the switching on and off of a huge percentage of your genes through the miracle of epigenetic control.

You are not inherently fragile, and it's not a simple luck-of-the-draw situation in which some people are robust and others crumble when things get hard.

No, the truth is that humans are, as Nassim Taleb has written about brilliantly, *antifragile*.[5] That is, we have the systems in place not only to *survive* hard things but to get stronger *because we go through hard things*. Society has made the wrong diagnosis and prescribed the wrong treatment: "Life is scary and painful, and it can break you, so avoid anything that might hurt." While it is true that some things in life hurt, real living requires learning a process of navigating those circumstances so that each event makes us stronger and more prepared for what comes next.

In that respect, we're not all that different from trees. Dendrologists (a fancy term for tree scientists) know that, to withstand high winds and erosion, healthy trees develop reaction or stress wood within their trunks and branches so that they will not crack or break during extreme weather events. Yet reaction wood develops only as the tree is buffeted over time by wind gusts. In other words, trees require the stress of wind to develop both the strength and flexibility they need to withstand other adverse conditions.[6]

The same is true for you, my friend. You are designed to become more resilient and robust when you face difficulty.[7] Everything you need to develop your root system and be ready for the winds life will bring is already wired into the way your mind and brain interact with your body. You can use self–brain surgery to create a mind and a brain that are resilient and antifragile, ready with a healthy response to anything that may come along instead of reacting in the less helpful ways you've thought were unavoidable in the past. Resilience means that you can go through stress and remain intact; being antifragile means that you can face stress and get stronger because of it.[8]

The problem is, as we've discovered, those rewiring processes are playing out whether you choose to control them or not, and the default state is to keep doing what you've always been doing. You were born into a certain family with a baseline genetic starting point, with a culture and a worldview that were imprinted onto you before you developed language or were even aware you were being shaped in this way. Where you started is not your fault; nor are many of the things that have happened to you along the way.

And yet here you are in the middle of operating on your own life, and you now know that you are not stuck with the brain you have, and you can change the future course of your life by changing how you think.

Consider any traumatic event, diagnosis, or label you may have taken on as part of your identity (or even as your complete identity). How might thinking of it as a starting point that gives you insight into your default ways of thinking enable you to move beyond it toward the life you want?

Realizing that where you started wasn't your fault but that you have agency as to what happens now changes the whole game. Just like the various approaches we've talked about, this insight has consequences:

- Whereas previously you could blame genetics for certain things, now you know that genetics determine where you start but do not have the power to determine where you end up (except for eye color and other immutable characteristics). As T. D. Jakes notes, "We are born looking like our parents, but we die looking like our decisions."[9]

- At one time you may have believed that your personality type, neurodivergent brain, or diagnosis determined your way of thinking and became your *identity*. Now you know that it is simply a baseline that gives you *insight* into how you are predisposed to think, and that you can use self-brain surgery to start there and operate in healthier ways.

- You may have thought that a particular trauma, tragedy, massive thing, or even just the steady drip of life's disappointments could change you in irreparable ways. Now you know that your previous response is changeable if it fails to serve you in your goal of becoming healthier, feeling better, and being happier.

- You thought you were destined to be on the wrong side of the steal, kill, and destroy versus abundance equation, but now you see clearly that your Creator has given you everything you need for life,[10] and you're already equipped to use those things for your good and not for continued self-malpractice.

It is a simple fact of life that sometimes the clamp comes off, the artery sprays blood, and all you can see is the flood of life's realities that rushes in and obscures the way forward. That's when your role comes into clarity:

Are you going to shrink back in fear, allowing the default processes of how you have previously handled adversity to play out again, even if those processes have not served you well before? Or are you going to fall back on your preparation (which the rest of this book will give you) and chart a new path forward for your own life as a surgeon who is ready to operate?

As part of your preparation, in the next chapters I am going to reveal the ten most important principles I've discovered in my search to understand how neuroscience and faith can smash together to enable us to navigate our lives in an empowered and responsible way. Drawn from neuroscience, philosophy, theology, and psychology, "The Ten Commandments of Self–Brain Surgery" will serve as guardrails, guiding you through the noise and confusion of the different situations that can leave you sad, sick, stressed, stuck, or even just tired of continually settling for less than you believe your life should be.

Once you learn the ten commandments, it will be time to stop contemplating and start operating.

The Chairman has asked the question, "What are you going to do, Doctor?" How you respond will change your entire life.

PART 3

The Ten Commandments of Self-Brain Surgery

The kind of attention we pay actually alters the world: we are, literally, partners in creation.

IAIN MCGILCHRIST
The Master and His Emissary

10

Why We Need Guiding Principles

When we look inside, we wake up.

ANNE LAMOTT
Almost Everything

Leonid Rogozov saved his own life, but he had to change his mind first.

In mortal danger from appendicitis while serving at a remote Antarctic research station, Rogozov had to choose to change perspectives. Once he realized that he was not only a patient—scared, helpless, suffering, dying—but also a surgeon—empowered, trained, intelligent, capable—he felt hope for the first time.

Hope has been defined as the belief that "you can get there from here."[1] Before he ever picked up the scalpel, Rogozov had to see in his mind that there was a path forward, that the outcome was not predetermined, that the situation he was in was manageable, even though objectively it seemed impossible.

He had to believe before he could proceed.

And the same is true for you, my friend.

Consider the places where you feel sad, sick, stressed, stuck, or as if you're settling for something less than you know you're supposed to. In that respect you are, like Leonid Rogozov, a patient. But if you have now assessed your situation and decided it's time to operate, you are also a surgeon.

Hopefully, by now I have convinced you that you are not just your brain and that your mind has tremendous influence over the structure and function of your brain. That's very good news, because it means that you are not stuck with the brain you were born with, or the brain shaped by the traumas and tragedies of your life. Your brain is constantly changing, and it does so largely under the influence of your mental direction if you choose to switch positions and operate rather than allowing the automated, default processes to proceed to your own detriment.

Now that you know the influence your mind can have over your brain, a stunning thought occurs: *If the way my brain works is not helping me, I need to change from patient to doctor and do something about it.*

The fact that you can change your mind means that what you used to consider your identity—things like your personality type and any diagnoses or traumas—does not have to define you. Identity, when based on your behavior or challenges rather than your inherent dignity, creates excuses, but insight generates responsibility. You are not just a patient hoping against hope to find a way to become healthier, feel better, and be happier. No, you're also a surgeon tasked with the solemn duty of applying what you've learned to the care and improvement of your own life and the lives of those around you. Your thoughts, when made deliberately and oriented constructively, actually change the physiology of your brain, which potentially leads to a cascade of other positive changes in your body, spirit, and relationships.

That's why I keep stressing that self–brain surgery is not a metaphor or some kind of self-help program. It is also not therapy. While a therapist can help you see where you're stuck, point out the patterns of thought and behavior you need to change, and provide accountability, they cannot make those changes for you or force you to believe that you are capable of making them for yourself. Self–brain surgery is a lifestyle that stems from the belief that you have control over how your brain works and how you respond to whatever life brings you.

> **Identity, when based on your behavior or challenges rather than your inherent dignity, creates excuses, but insight generates responsibility.**

This section, then, describes ten principles underlying self–brain surgery. These propositions emerged over the past two decades as I distilled what I'd learned from neuroscience and applied those lessons to my own life in the context of my faith. Just as we have our own code of ethics, standards of care, and best practices in medicine—evidence-based guidelines for the best ways to manage our patients' troubles—we require similar direction in self–brain surgery. These ten commandments are not intended to prove the science to you; their purpose is to give you a framework for using neuroscience to your advantage in practicing self–brain surgery as a lifestyle.

To keep our focus on the practical, I won't be going deep into *how* I formulated these ideas, but in the endnotes and appendix E, you'll find an exhaustive list of papers and books that shaped my thinking. I invite you to dig into them if you want to do the research yourself.

Remember that, in part 2, we learned the value of changing approaches when something is not working. You do not have to agree with every aspect of how an approach was developed to be able to use it to get better results, so these principles will be helpful to you regardless of whether or not you agree with my Christian worldview or my interpretation of neuroscience. Even if you believe that "it's all just neurons," you might at least appreciate that there are functional advantages in *thinking about your brain as if you can control it with your mind*, since neuroscience and imaging studies so clearly show that the mind-down approach makes positive structural changes in the brain. People have more satisfying lives when they believe they have agency to change, which means that the science is on your side when practicing self–brain surgery as if your choices matter.

With that foundation, I present to you the ten commandments of self–brain surgery:

1. I must relentlessly refuse to participate in my own demise.
2. I must believe that feelings are not facts; they are chemical events in my brain.
3. I must believe that most of my automatic thoughts are untrue.
4. I must believe that my mind is in charge of my brain.
5. I must believe that self–brain surgery is not a metaphor; it is the mechanism of transforming my life.
6. I must love tomorrow more than I hate how I feel right now.
7. I must stop making an operation out of everything.
8. I must not perpetuate—or start—harmful generational thought or behavioral issues in my life or family.
9. I must believe that I'm getting better at what I'm doing.
10. I must understand that thoughts become things.

I devote one chapter to each of these commandments in part 3, which is the reason this section is laid out differently from the other parts of the book. After introducing that chapter's principle, I summarize the neuroscience that undergirds it, along with ancient wisdom from Scripture that reflects it. This is also the part of the book where things get personal. Each chapter ends with several questions, and I encourage you to take time to answer them. They will help you put your mind in control so you're ready to become your own surgeon.

The Ten Commandments found in the Bible can be organized into two sections. The first four govern how people are to relate to God, and the next six regulate how people are to relate to others. Similarly, the ten commandments of self-brain surgery guide us in two main ways. Imagine a staircase leading up to a platform. Commandments 1–4 give us the steps to understand how our minds are designed to work so that we can avoid harming ourselves and others. Commandment 5 is the plateau, the high point from which we can view our lives with the proper perspective. And commandments 6–10 guide us as we then live in the power of such transformation.

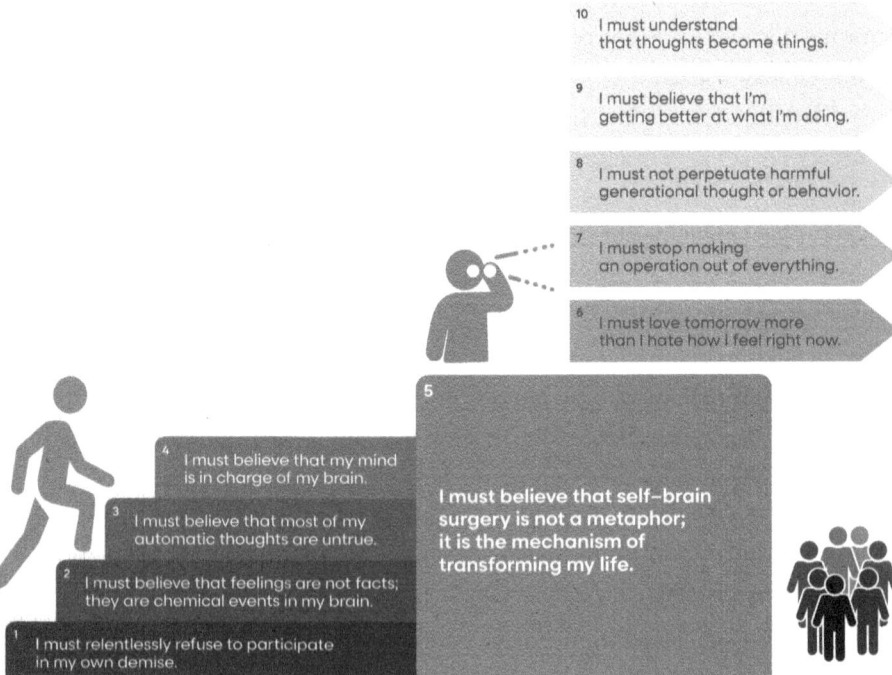

These are the ten foundational principles that will guide your self–brain surgery practice. Each one presents a shift in thinking that will literally reshape your brain and, ultimately, your life.

Are you ready to take the first step on the path of hope, which will lead you from here to there?

11

The First Commandment
I Must Relentlessly Refuse to Participate in My Own Demise

*On some days I'm embarrassed, even ashamed,
by my failure to try to fight back.*
SALMAN RUSHDIE
Knife

During the first year of their professional education, students in medical schools all over the world take an oath. The history of this tradition traces back to the ancient Greeks and is most famously attributed to the physician Hippocrates. Originally the apprentices and nurses who would train and work in a doctor's surgery (itinerate medical clinics set up to provide care in different cities) would swear this oath to a physician. Over time, the idea spread to the academy, and the oath began to be taken by students as they became physicians.[1]

Although the wording has evolved throughout the centuries, most versions contain the idea that a doctor is supposed to consider the potential benefits of their proposed treatments and weigh them against the possible ways those treatments could make things worse for the patient. The most often quoted line in this regard is *primum non nocere*, "first, do no harm," but that phrase is not found in any surviving writings that can be tied to Hippocrates himself. Instead, it probably came from a British doctor named Thomas Sydenham.[2]

In surgical specialties, it is impossible to follow this guidance exactly, since literally every time we make an incision in a patient's body we are harming them in some way—cutting skin, traumatizing muscles, removing body parts—but the surgical wound is necessary to accomplish the greater good of addressing a bigger threat to the patient's life (or quality of life).

Likewise, in the practice of self–brain surgery we must face some painful realities as we contemplate dedicating ourselves to the reordering of our minds, the rewiring of our brains, and the resultant radical transformation of our lives. And one of those realities is that life is hard enough without us making it harder for ourselves.

> **Life is hard enough without us making it harder for ourselves.**

Malpractice is when a provider harms a patient because of negligence or improper treatment. If you hit your head and have a brain bleed but I am not there and don't know it happened, it's not my fault. But if you're in the hospital and someone calls to tell me you need my help, then I'm obligated to come to the rescue since I have the training and ability to intervene and try to save you. If I know about the problem and do not take action, or if I do the wrong thing, that's malpractice. Likewise, once you know the principles of how your mind and your brain can work together to help you, then choosing not to apply them is self-malpractice. The Bible says that when we know what we should do and don't do it, it's sin.[3] It's time to stop sinning against ourselves.

The first commandment is a call to action: Seek to engage only in those mental, physical, and spiritual habits that bring life and health. Learn mental habits that will allow you to flourish rather than struggle with thoughts, feelings, limiting stories, and beliefs that have held you back for too long.

Primum non nocere, or "first do no harm," even to yourself.

Relentlessly refuse to participate in your own demise.

Relevant Neuroscience

Actively choose not to engage in self-sabotaging behaviors. Your brain's reward system can reinforce harmful habits over time, but neuroplasticity allows you to break these cycles. By consciously avoiding negative behaviors, you will create new, healthier neural pathways that support resilience and positive change.

Guiding Scripture

> *Brothers and sisters, in light of all I have shared with you about God's mercies, I urge you to offer your bodies as a living and holy sacrifice to God, a sacred offering that brings Him pleasure; this is your reasonable, essential worship.*
>
> **ROMANS 12:1, THE VOICE**

Taking care with your thoughts is a form of offering your body (including your brain and mind) to God as an act of worship. When you feel like it's too much work and are tempted to give in to the same old ways and commit malpractice against yourself, it helps to remember that when you take good care of yourself, it's not work—it's worship.

Questions for Reflection

1. In what area(s) of your life do you struggle with self-malpractice?

2. How could relentlessly refusing to participate in your own demise help you?

12

The Second Commandment

I Must Believe That Feelings Are Not Facts;
They Are Chemical Events in My Brain

> We all understand intellectually that the brain can regulate functions throughout the rest of the body, but it is still surprising to be reminded of how far-reaching those effects can be.
>
> **ROBERT M. SAPOLSKY**
> *Why Zebras Don't Get Ulcers*

Imagine that the next time you open your mailbox, you pull out a letter marked INTERNAL REVENUE SERVICE.

Immediately, your skin begins to tingle, and you feel the hairs on the back of your neck stand up. You feel goose bumps on your arms, and your heart begins to race. You feel a little dizzy and short of breath, and your stomach clenches.

Is that anxiety because you were unusually creative on your tax return last year and the letter might be a notice that you're being audited? *Oh no! They caught me!*

Or is it excitement because you're desperately behind on your bills and you've been praying that your tax refund would come today? *Maybe this is it!*

Notice that neither of these two outcomes is true yet. In fact, they could both be false. The letter might be a notice that your return is still being processed so you won't be receiving your refund for several more months. It could be a request to verify your identity. You might even notice, if you look more closely, that the letter is addressed to your neighbor and was put in your mailbox by mistake.

But regardless of the truth, your body is sending the *exact same set of physiological signals*, and your conscious brain is interpreting them as either anxiety or excitement.

Emotions are the unconscious indicators our bodies and brains generate to alert us to potential threats, opportunities (real external stimuli), or to *perceived* or even *imagined* situations. Feelings are our conscious processing of those signals and the thoughts we have in response, and we *decide what they mean* based on our past experiences and our present state (e.g., mood; location; being sick, hungry, or tired).

Emotions are objective in that our bodies *are* sending us signals that *do* have real physiological effects: Our heart rate, blood pressure, respiratory rate, gut function, skin sensation, and more really are changing. These biological events serve as barometers and not as GPS navigation systems. They alert us that something is or might be happening, but they do not tell us what it is.

The "What is happening outside of my body?" question is left to feelings. We decide what is occurring and attach meaning to it. There are two problems with this:

1. If we believe that everything we feel is true, we may conclude that we are obligated to react to every emotional signal. This leads us to assume that external events can control our internal state, a belief that numerous studies have shown to be associated with depression, anxiety, and hopelessness. This is particularly troublesome in light of the fact that the more we do something, the better we get at it (our ninth commandment, which we will explore soon).

2. If we are unaware that some emotional signals happen even when the threat is purely imagined, we may create and react to feelings *when nothing bad at all is happening.*

Shawn learned this the hard way. He was at his desk, trying to wrap up a phone call with a huge potential client he hoped to land for his law firm, when he heard the *ping* of an email notification on his computer. Shawn was a rising star in one of Denver's largest law practices, rumored to soon have his name on the wall as the youngest to ever make partner. The path there involved lots of billable hours drumming up prestigious new business, and landing this whale of a client would go a long way toward both of those objectives. Jonah Resources was an up-and-coming player in the oil and gas industry that had recently fired their legal team after losing a lawsuit from the EPA. That loss cost them the mineral rights on a property that they thought might be worth hundreds of millions of dollars. Shawn could see his dream playing out: *I sign Jonah, they get the land deal on appeal, then I get a bunch of stock options and make partner. They go public, and I cash in. Just need to reel this guy in and I'm set.*

Always multitasking in his quest to make partner, he glanced at his computer and saw the message subject line from Ian, one of his firm's senior partners: "Nice job, Genius!" Shawn clenched his teeth so hard that he bit his cheek. He winced but tried to steady his voice so his hopefully soon-to-be-client Jason couldn't hear his anger as he thought, *Ian is such a jerk! How dare he mock me like that after how hard I've been working!*

Jason was droning on about the things Jonah was looking for in a firm, but Shawn was already mentally composing his reply to Ian's message as he tasted the blood from his cheek and the acid rising in his throat, mixing to make him a little nauseated. He cut Jason off midsentence just as he was saying that a round of golf this weekend just might convince him to sign with Shawn's firm. Suddenly none of that mattered to Shawn—he had to respond to Ian's insult.

"Jason, I'm going to have to call you back. Something just came up."

"But what about this weekend?" Jason said. "We on for eighteen holes on Saturday?"

"I'll get back to you," Shawn said, clicking off the phone just as Jason said, "Maybe 9 a.m.?"

Shawn blinked hard and tried to think of the perfect comeback to Ian's message. He hadn't come this far to be belittled by some arrogant old lawyer who thinks it's okay to call people names. *I don't deserve to be treated that way, not from anybody.*

Shawn hovered over the email, his pulse pounding in his ears. He was ready for the gut-punch he knew was coming. He was sure Ian was dressing him down for *something*, although he couldn't think of anything he'd done wrong. *Doesn't matter what it is. I'll probably get fired for telling him off, but I don't want to work for somebody who makes me feel so bad anyway.* With a deep breath, he clicked. His eyes darted over the words, but something didn't compute. He blinked. Read it again. The sentences weren't lining up with the anger and humiliation he had braced for.

Subject: Nice job, Genius!

From: Ian Anderson, Senior Partner

Shawn, I just heard from Zane Thomas over at Jonah that they love the work you've done in pitching them. He said that his associate Jason is going to sign with you, as long as you don't beat him too badly at golf this weekend! Just wanted to say congrats and we're proud of the brilliant work you're doing. You're a genius! Best, Ian

Shawn read the message again, feeling even sicker to his stomach as he realized the Olympic-record-length conclusion he'd jumped to.

That's when it hit him: *I have to call Jason back!*

Can you see why feelings are horribly unreliable in terms of guiding your decisions and leading you to success? *Feelings are not facts.*

Feelings arise as our conscious thoughts attach meaning to emotions we perceive subconsciously. The problem is, there is a limited palette of neurochemical signals in our brains that generate the entire range of physiological responses we perceive as emotions. As a result, the truth about what a particular emotion is alerting us to or reminding us of is determined by the context of the current moment and our retrieved memories of prior situations in which we felt something similar.

> **Feelings are not facts: They arise as our conscious thoughts attach meaning to emotions we perceive subconsciously.**

As Shawn redialed Jason's number, a different voice echoed in his mind—one he hadn't heard in years but had never truly escaped. *Way to go, dummy. Nice work, brainiac. Good job, you moron.* His father's words from his childhood, sharp as ever, surfaced like a reflex. And suddenly, he understood. Ian hadn't insulted him—his past had. His old wounds had hijacked his present moment, making him react to a battle that wasn't even happening.

His call went to voicemail. He left a message for Jason: "Hello, it's Shawn. So sorry I had to go so quickly earlier. I'm in for golf if you still want to play!"

Shawn hung up the phone and cradled his face in his hands. *Please don't tell me I just blew up this deal.*

If we are honest in our pursuit of truth and do not violate our first commandment (no self-malpractice), we must acknowledge that reflexively following our emotions does not produce lasting happiness or real improvement. This may be an unpopular position in our current cultural environment, but my job as a physician is always to give you the diagnosis honestly.

Let me be clear: I am *not* saying that it is bad to feel things deeply, and I am *not* saying that you should ignore emotions. On the contrary, healthy and flourishing people must be able to experience and process emotions, express them as feelings in a healthy way, and contextualize them appropriately.

One of the first procedures you will learn in "The Operating Room," the Whole-System Scan, will equip you to discern what you are feeling and decide how to process and respond to it rather than simply react to it because you assume you are powerless to choose your response.

The fully felt and lived human experience comes stocked with feelings and emotions. God gave them to you so you can have abundant life in spite of everything that seeks to steal, kill, and destroy. When it's time to be sad, to grieve, and to mourn a great loss, then experiencing and expressing those emotions in healthy ways *is* the appropriate and necessary response. When it's time to rejoice, be happy, or be giddy over some triumph, you should fully embrace those feelings.

But when you're holding the envelope from the IRS, it's best to open it and learn what's really inside before you react to it. It might be bad news that requires a response. If so, you want your frontal lobes engaged to help you make good decisions about what to do next, not your amygdala telling you to freak out and run away. That's what taking a moment to learn the truth does for you: It keeps *you* in control even when the news is bad.

Sometimes the news is good. You want to feel that too. But it's best to feel it when it's true, so open the letter already and find out.

Feelings aren't facts, my friend. They are chemical events in your brain.

A Word About Triggers

This would be a good time to mention that feelings are especially prone to make us believe that we have no control over how we react to something. We find ourselves, like Shawn, having such an intense reaction to something someone says or does, or sometimes to something we just worry about or imagine, that our reaction seems programmed and unchangeable. (Even if you have PTSD, you have some control over your reaction.)

We say things like, "I couldn't help it; that triggered me," "It's not my fault; that's how we react in our family when people insult us," or "You made me yell because you just wouldn't shut up."

Think about the word *trigger* for a moment, and what I'm about to tell you will seem obvious: *A gun does not fire until the trigger is pulled, and the person holding the gun decides when to pull the trigger.* It's not the environment around the gun, the behavior of the people standing near the person holding the gun, or the type of targets set up downrange from the gun that makes the gun fire. It is solely the decision of the shooter to pull the trigger.

Using a term like *triggered* implies a belief that your brain controls your behavior and that certain types of reactions are forced upon you because of how your brain works. Here is the life-changing truth: Nothing outside of you can ever force you to pull the trigger on your own decisions. If you choose to believe that, you will become empowered to *respond* to things from the position of a self–brain surgeon. You will no longer believe that anything or anyone else can set you off; instead, you'll know that you can choose a healthy response.

This is one of the most awakening moments in life. When you finally see the truth that you've been liberated from the lie of "That's just how I am," you will be able to step forward in your life infused with the God-given and hope-giving agency that comes from being in control of your emotional state, your inner dialogue, and your future decisions. And, as Jesus said, when you taste this kind of deliverance, "You will know the truth, and the truth will set you free."[1]

Relevant Neuroscience

Emotions are the result of neurochemical reactions in the brain, specifically involving neurotransmitters like dopamine, serotonin, and cortisol. Recognizing that feelings are temporary and chemically driven allows you to engage your prefrontal cortex to reinterpret and regulate your emotions rather than being ruled by them. Remember: Only you can pull the trigger.

Guiding Scripture

Search me, O God, and know my heart; test me and know my anxious thoughts.
PSALM 139:23, NLT

This verse reminds you that feelings aren't facts. You can, as the psalmist says, recognize when you're *feeling* anxious and ask God to help you discern what the facts are before you react.

Questions for Reflection

1. In what ways have you let feelings lead you before realizing they weren't telling you the truth?

2. How has this caused you more harm than good in the past?

3. Now that you know that your body has a limited number of chemical messengers that create your full range of emotions, how can you be more diligent about how you interpret those emotions in the future?

13

The Third Commandment
I Must Believe That Most of My Automatic Thoughts Are Untrue

*The mind defaults to wandering between miserable
past memories and fearful future possibilities.*
DAWSON CHURCH
Bliss Brain

You spend most of your time thinking, but not all of your thoughts are helpful to you.

Estimates of how many thoughts you think per day vary widely, but functional imaging research puts the number at over six thousand.[1] What you do with those messages determines the course and quality of your life, so it's critical to understand what's really happening when you hear them.

Research suggests that a vast majority of our thoughts are automatic, and that most of them are untrue.[2] They are negative by about five to one, so you are much more likely to hear something like *I'm such a loser* from your brain than you are to be awash in mental messages about how beautiful and brilliant you are. With all the chatter in your head, how do you determine which thoughts are "real"—productive, true, and worth paying attention to because they are generated by your mind? And what are we to do with the never-ending stream of mostly untrue, generally negative, and largely in-our-own-voice brain-generated thoughts we hear in our heads?

We will learn a few specific procedures for handling automatic thoughts in "The Operating Room" soon. But before those operations can be useful, you must first realize that at least three different types of scripts are running through your head. The word *script* makes sense, because that's what the stream of thoughts in your head often feels like: a script you didn't write and can't control—especially before you knew that you can change how your brain behaves by directing your mind. Until you learn to recognize these various types of inner chatter for what they are, you will perceive them all as "thoughts," but I am going to teach you that they are not all the same. I think it is helpful to label them differently so you can begin to recognize exactly what is happening and then implement an appropriate treatment plan for managing them.

Script #1. The bulk of the thousands of automatic "thoughts" *you think* that you think every day fall in this category. Notice the phrase "*you think* that you think" in the last sentence. That wording is intentional because script #1 does not come from your mind but rather your brain. If you accept the idea that the mind and brain are not the same, then it makes sense that some of the thoughts you hear are generated by the brain and others are generated by the mind. In that context, let's refer to those script #1, brain-generated "thoughts" as brain-side inputs. These are basically queries, in which your brain is seeking permission from your mind to automate a response to a particular situation (real or perceived). They sound like you, and they're wrapped in familiar feelings and contextualized in terms of how you felt, thought, and behaved the last time something similar was happening. When these inputs are false, they can contribute to all kinds of trouble, as in the repetitive ruminations of people with obsessive-compulsive disorder. Psychiatrist Jeffrey Schwartz calls these "deceptive brain messages."[3]

So when you're tired and hungry and then get into a huge fight with your favorite person, your brain may send up an automatic input to your mind that says (in your own voice), *They are going to leave me, and I'm going to end up alone.* You may react to that input with anxiety and panic before you even stop to process the fact that you've made it through rough spots in your relationship before. Once you give consent to your brain to run the anxiety-panic program, it will produce the physiological changes associated with stress. Your body suffers, and you have made a new synapse that makes it more likely that you'll have that same response the next time you have a fight. (You'll understand why when we get to the ninth commandment.)

Remember that the brain's main job is to automate as many processes as possible to keep you alive. This frees up mental resources so you can perform higher-level tasks without having to think about basic functions like breathing and walking. Your mind is in control of what your brain does, but if you don't live that way, over time, your brain will ask for consent in a progressively less conscious way. It now assumes you will say yes to whatever input it presents to you.

Brain-side inputs can be conceptualized as computer programs your brain runs that send messages to your mind. They are reflexive, preprogrammed events that occur automatically, formed by your experiences, habits, culture, upbringing, and emotional state. They arise from synaptic connections between neurons you have developed, consciously or unconsciously, over the course of your life. Because they sound like real thoughts, they may lead you to respond reflexively with anxiety or doubt, or to jump to conclusions.

Understanding these brain-side inputs is the first step in learning to recognize and control them. Script #1 can be understood and managed using approaches 2 through 4 discussed in "The Office." Even if you believe that everything you think arises simply from neuronal activity, you can accept the evidence from functional MRI research and quantum physics showing that you can influence the brain's system with self–brain surgery. If you remember that the observer affects the outcome, then you can learn to operate your nervous system from an empowered perspective and tell your brain who's boss.

The next two types of scripts are harder to accept if you are practicing from a brain-out worldview. But if you believe that your mind has controlling power over your brain, then these two scripts will dramatically change how you think about all the things you hear in your head.

Script #2. These are what we will call "real thoughts." Rather than being presented to the mind by the brain, these arise in the mind out of your consciousness and then interact with your brain in a mind-down way. If you practice becoming mindful of what you hear in your head, over time you will begin to discern that some of your thoughts feel more intentional and conscious, less automatic. These mind-generated real thoughts are not brain programs but come from you—your consciousness and your "self." You have some ability to exert control over the process of thinking them.

Script #2 thoughts lack the alarming tone of many script #1 messages. They sound less like, *I'm terrible at my job, and they will eventually figure it out and fire me*, and more like, *Hey, did I really do my best today? Maybe tomorrow I can be on time and try harder, and I can make myself more valuable to the company.* Script #2 messages show us opportunities and issues that need to be addressed but are not incessantly negative or condemning.

Script #2 thoughts are also where we engage with God. If our minds are indeed separate from our brains—as functional imaging, quantum physics, and Scripture validate—then we can begin to understand what happens on a physical level that turns a mental event into a brain activity. Have you ever wondered, *What exactly happens when I think a thought?* Something happens in your mind that activates something in your brain, and that brain event produces electrical signals that cause activity in multiple brain regions and networks. This ultimately results in such things as gene expression, neurotransmitter and hormonal release, physiological responses, and real-world impact on other people (as we'll see when we get to the tenth commandment).

This thoughts-become-things sequence represents, at the particle level, the conversion of a mental event into a series of physical events. It has been the subject of a vast amount of research into how energy becomes matter and how information is transmitted between the mind and the brain. This has been postulated by quantum physicists as a possible explanation of how we could communicate with God and how God could communicate with us through prayer and meditation.[4]

When we try to discern these positive script #2 messages, we open ourselves to a comforting, hope-generating experience. The Bible says it this way: "Whether you turn to the right or to the left, your ears will hear a voice behind you, saying, 'This is the way; walk in it.'"[5] The skeptical reader may assume these messages are brain-generated, perhaps from an evolutionary process in which some people are predisposed to think they can hear God giving them direction and advice. However, as we saw earlier, our brains change *in response to* prayer and meditation; people don't pray and meditate because of certain anatomical features of their brains. My personal experience has been that these guiding and reassuring script #2 messages have been helpful, and I have been disappointed only when I failed to heed them. Remember, good scientists modify our hypotheses based on evidence. So I encourage you to listen for these messages and see what you discover. They may even help convince you that A > SKD is true in your own life.

Properly understood, script #2's mind-down thoughts and direction help you switch roles from simply reading the script—even if you don't like it—to *writing and interacting with the script* that directs your mind to change in ways that help you.

Before moving on, let's examine one other process we often perceive to be "thoughts."

Script #3. Remember Jesus' statement in John 10:10: "The thief comes only to steal and kill and destroy. I came that they may have life and have it abundantly" (ESV)? From it, we formulated the equation A > SKD (abundance is greater than steal, kill, and destroy).

> **Mind-down thoughts and direction help you switch roles from simply reading the script to writing and interacting with the script.**

If you accept the premise that your mind and brain are not the same thing, and if there is a God who can communicate with your mind as the Bible says through a mechanism theorized by researchers, then the possibility also exists that some messages you hear come from an enemy whose intent is to steal, kill, and destroy your life.

Christians believe that this enemy is Satan, popularly called the devil. But whether you believe in the literal existence of such a being (as I do) or not, I would wager that you have heard a voice in your head that doesn't sound like yours.

This voice feels accusatory, provoking shame, fear, or other negative emotions. Its messages include, *You are worthless. No one could love you. You're the worst person ever; God could never forgive you for that.* Sometimes, this voice sounds alluring and points out all the ways you deserve to feel a particular way or do a particular thing. *It's okay! What's the harm? You deserve it! No one will get hurt.*

So this script #3 thinking is prompted by the false, enemy voice from our A > SKD equation. And whether you believe it's the devil or your diagnosis (maybe it's just anxiety, repressed trauma, guilt, or some other brain-related phenomenon), you can recognize that it's different from the automatic thinking as described by script #1 thinking. And even if you can't make yourself believe that script #3 and script #1 are actually different events in your brain, it is helpful to think of them differently, because listening to and believing script #3 messaging usually harms your life, while script #1 messaging is often irritating and limiting but not necessarily destructive.

A good way to differentiate between script #2 and script #3 messages is the following test. When you're considering something that you want to do, even if it's not been helpful to you in the past, listen for the difference between these two voices:

> *Remember last time? You'll feel better tomorrow if you don't do that tonight* (script #2).
> *Live in the moment; you deserve it! You'll feel good tonight if you do that* (script #3).

In summary: Script #1, brain-side inputs tend to be negative or sometimes just self-protective. Script #2, mind-down thoughts are encouraging, warning, or executive, helping you figure things out and make progress. Script #3 messages are all about shame, blame, or temptation.

Understanding these different types of input is helpful in ensuring that your mind has top-down control over your brain. It also enables you to switch into the empowered position of self–brain surgeon. You can then manage your thoughts in helpful ways by harnessing your brain's ability to make structural changes at the mind's direction.

You cannot manage something if you are unaware of it, so it pays to accept that not everything you think is true. Knowing that thousands of times a day you hear multiple types of scripts that all *feel like true thoughts* should convince you of the importance of learning to discern the true ones and recognize and challenge those that are false.

If you want to become healthier, feel better, and be happier, you need to believe that not every automatic thought you have is true. But learning to discern the nature and source of a thought is the key to taking control and beginning to write your own script.

Relevant Neuroscience

Automatic thoughts stem from deeply embedded neural circuits formed by past experiences and conditioning. Many of these are based on outdated or incorrect assumptions. By exerting cognitive control through the prefrontal cortex, you can challenge these automatic thoughts and develop healthier mental habits.

Guiding Scripture

> We demolish arguments and every pretension that sets itself up against the knowledge of God, and we take captive every thought to make it obedient to Christ.
>
> 2 CORINTHIANS 10:5

As the apostle Paul says, it's wise to "take every thought captive" and investigate your automatic thoughts before you respond to them.

Questions for Reflection

1. What automatic thought do you frequently have?
2. How often do you react as if you're obligated to believe that thought? How do you act on it?
3. How has that helped you? How has it sometimes harmed you?

14

The Fourth Commandment
I Must Believe That My Mind Is in Charge of My Brain

*Consciousness simply cannot be reducible
to physical processes in the brain.*

SHARON DIRCKX
Am I Just My Brain?

The extent to which you believe that the structure of your brain determines your behavior and your future, and that it can be broken but not repaired, *is the measure of your capacity to make progress in your life.*

In the brain-out worldview, your brain simply generates the concept of "you" so that your sense of self is an illusion produced by neuronal activity. This belief system, if followed to its logical conclusion, means that ultimately your life has no purpose beyond the evolutionary aims of survival and reproduction. Free will is illusory as "your" decisions are yours only insomuch as your brain tricks you into thinking you intended to make them. Ultimately everything you *think that you think* is predetermined by your genes and is the undirected result of natural processes. This eliminates any real meaning or purpose to your life, since even these concepts are just electrical events bouncing around in your head like so much "sound and fury, signifying nothing."[1]

Brain-out thinking is why assuming our "identity" is rooted in such factors as personality type and trauma is so tempting. If uncontrollable and unchangeable things like genes, parents, and trauma can create or modify our brains and thus produce our personalities and behaviors, then we're not responsible for how we react to difficulties. Identity becomes an excuse for how we are destined to see the world, interact with others, and feel about our future. Identity is something, then, to post in our profiles so people know how to treat us: "I'm an Enneagram 8; you better not challenge me." After all, the way we're going to respond to them is fixed, and we can't change it. This leads to assumptions like "I'm just living my truth," but we become progressively more frustrated when our "truth" never seems to lead to our flourishing.

The brain-out perspective—which has been so widely adopted by neuroscientists and systemically metastasized across the Western world over the past three centuries—seems to me to be the source of much of our floundering. Even many people of faith have been infected by the defeating belief, *This is just how I am*. As a result, they settle for lives they think are limited by the structure or function of their brains and genes, with only a distant hope that God will someday make it all better.

I've watched the eyes of many such believers brighten once they realize that the choices they make can, in fact, change their brains and improve their lives. The findings from neuroscience line up repeatedly with the Bible's prescriptions for how to flourish here on earth. It turns out that you don't need a miracle to change your life; you just need to master the process God built into all of us, which allows you to change your brain by changing your thoughts.

That perspective shift then allows you to use your baseline characteristics and the ways your life has shaped you, not as excuses, but as *insights* to help you map your path forward. Knowing how you are inclined to react gives you a responsibility to manage those inclinations *and* enables you to use a mind-down perspective to change any responses that are not helping you.

In fact, even the most ardent atheist or committed skeptic can understand the value of taking control of their thoughts, thanks to quantum physics and neuroscience. Even if you believe that your life is largely determined by the activity of the neurons in your brain, changing the way you think about those "why?" and "what now?" questions we discussed earlier has the power to radically transform your quality of life. Regardless of your underlying belief systems, to find meaning you must first decide that your life *does matter* and that you have a real purpose.

The observer effect from quantum physics is real. The way you choose to interact with the world changes the behavior and reality of everyone in it. So there *is* a purpose to your life, since how you interact with everyone else (even yourself) ultimately creates a different reality than what would have occurred without your choices.

In case you're discounting this because you think quantum physics and neurobiology are not relevant to each other, let me say this: Your brain is made of cells, proteins, and other bits of material, all of which are made up of molecules, right? And molecules are made of atoms and subatomic particles (protons, neutrons, electrons, gluons, quarks, etc.). Quantum physics describes the behavior of particles more accurately than classical physics does, which is why those smart folks in the early 1900s came up with it in the first place.

So if *you* are made of atoms, and the math of how atoms behave shows that using your mind—your attention, your perspective, and your choices—changes the behavior of your physical brain and the brains of the people with whom you interact, then it's clear you're here to make a difference. Your brain is not the boss of you; it's waiting for you to direct its behavior. You, then, are not your brain; you are your embodied *mind*.

The outmoded belief that your brain is a supercomputer that creates your reality is fading fast for those who honestly assess the evidence. From a self–brain surgery perspective, the internet provides a better example. You (your mind/soul) are the server: the master computer that is connected to, receives input and feedback from, and ultimately directs the host computer, which, in this analogy, is your brain and body. Your brain just wants to serve you by automating things and running the programs you've consented for it to run, freeing your mind to run more important programs.

Your brain is not the boss of you; it's waiting for you to direct its behavior.

Having said all of that, you need to recognize that an unhealthy brain will harm your life. If the computer on my desk has a bad hard drive, then the server's ability to interact with it will be hindered. No matter how much information there may be on the internet, the server will be unable to present that information to my computer. So, if my powerful desktop Mac is damaged or I fail to maintain it properly, the wealth of information available on the internet server will do me little good. In the same way, recognizing that the brain is the organ through which your mind interacts with your body and the world should lead you to optimize your brain health.

And since the brain is the organ your mind uses to direct your body, communicate with others, store your memories, and run your physical life, it is imperative that you take good care of it. You need to provide your brain with proper materials to do that work and to protect it from harm in any way that you can.

This is a twofold process. As we've seen, harmful thinking can worsen the chemical and functional environment of your brain, but we also must acknowledge that your mind cannot interact properly with your brain unless its physical structure is sound.

If your brain doesn't work right, you won't work right. And even though you, as a self–brain surgeon, know that your mental activities are separate from and have controlling influence over your brain activities, if the brain is physically injured, unhealthy, or lacks proper nutrients or blood flow, the mind cannot function properly either.

To that end, we must love our brains, as my friend Dr. Daniel Amen says, by bathing them in the proper thought environment *and* providing them with the nutrients they need to grow, change, and improve throughout our lives. This obviously includes *not* doing things we know to be harmful to the brain's structure and function.

Dr. Amen has written extensively about the brain side of a healthy thought and emotional life, and his work in functional imaging has transformed the treatment of disorders like ADHD by focusing on how the structure of the brain affects its function.[2]

For now, I offer a few guidelines for loving your brain from the perspective of someone who sees firsthand what behaviors lead to problems:

1. **Wear a helmet if you're on something with wheels.** I'm the guy who has to tell someone's spouse that they died because they weren't wearing a helmet while riding a bike or hoverboard "just that one time." It's awful when the surviving spouse realizes how easy it would have been for their loved one to stay alive and well.

    Studies indicate that the use of bike helmets reduces the total number of deaths and serious injuries by 34 percent.[3] And don't think that helmets are just for kids. Interestingly, children are slightly *less* susceptible to major head trauma than adults, partly because of greater brain resilience in childhood, but also because they can't go as fast as adults and don't fall from as great a height. So don't be one of those parents who makes their kids use helmets but thinks grown-ups don't need one. Kids' brains are soft and easily injured, and you need to protect them. But you need to protect *your own* brain as well!

2. **Avoid substances like alcohol that are known to be toxic to the brain.** I don't want to be a party pooper, but the scientific answer to how much alcohol is excessive is "any." A large review study published in *The Lancet* in 2018 concludes that even small amounts of alcohol intake are associated with health risks and that there is no detectable health benefit to alcohol use at any dose.[4] The World Health Organization bluntly states, "When it comes to alcohol consumption, there is no safe amount that does not affect health."[5]

Alcohol is a direct neurotoxin.[6] It is so damaging to nervous system tissue that when we perform brain surgery, we do not allow any type of alcohol to be close to the patient in the operating room because it kills neurons. We want to avoid accidentally getting it onto an instrument that might touch the brain.

Since neurosurgeons recognize that allowing alcohol even to touch the brain's surface damages its cells, it doesn't make sense to put alcohol into your bloodstream either. Alcohol is quickly metabolized to the substance acetaldehyde, which easily crosses the blood-brain barrier and is even more toxic to neurons than ethanol. That said, if you're going to consume alcohol, drink reasonable amounts infrequently, eat food when you do, and avoid putting yourself (or your brain) into any dangerous situations since alcohol may leave you less in command of your brain's function.

Of course, substances like nicotine,[7] marijuana,[8] and illicit drugs[9] are also bad for the brain.

3. **Give your brain good nutrition and the proper supplements.** Everyone should follow a healthy diet composed largely of whole foods. Furthermore, most people should take a good multivitamin,[10] omega-3 fatty acids (fish oil),[11] a probiotic,[12] and vitamin D.[13] (Be sure to check with your doctor before starting a new supplement or vitamin.)

Love your brain by protecting and providing for it. Doing so will benefit your mind as well, so together they can lead you to a fuller, more flourishing life.

Your mind is running the show, provided you're willing to learn the procedures and take up the practice of self–brain surgery on your own behalf. The limit on your flourishing is determined by how much you're willing to take responsibility for it yourself.

Relevant Neuroscience

Your mind is distinct from your brain and literally has creative control over your brain's structure. You can take top-down command of the process of neuroplasticity, allowing you to direct your brain's functions and override instincts or patterns that don't serve you. This means that you are more than your biological hardware. However, since the hardware of your brain must work properly in order for *you* to work properly, you have a responsibility to appreciate its capacity for growth and deliberately engage in activities that promote healthy brain function.

Guiding Scripture

> God has not given us a spirit of fear, but of power and of love and of a sound mind.
>
> 2 TIMOTHY 1:7, NKJV

Remember that you have a brain that responds to your mind and is designed to heal and grow in ways that help you. You can learn to use your mind to direct your brain—and to adopt a healthy lifestyle to keep it strong.

Questions for Reflection

1. Have you ever blamed your genetics, upbringing, or past experiences for "breaking" your brain and as an excuse for believing that this is "just how I am"? Explain.

2. How does knowing that your mind is in control and that you have a brain that will respond to your mind's direction empower you to work to change any assumptions that limit you?

3. Which of your habits or behaviors are not good for your brain? What changes could you make to better love your brain?

15

The Fifth Commandment
I Must Believe That Self-Brain Surgery Is Not a Metaphor;
It Is the Mechanism of Transforming My Life

This is not metaphor. This is miracle made material.
ANN VOSKAMP
Loved to Life

In the past few decades, technological advances have fundamentally changed the way we seek knowledge. Our patience for learning has dwindled—we google answers in seconds, skim brief articles, grab bite-sized solutions to solve the problem at hand, and move on. As a result, we often "know" a million things about a million topics—without deeply understanding any one of them.

This shift in how we consume information has, I believe, contributed to the reason so many people remain stuck despite having access to more mental health tools, self-help strategies, and therapeutic techniques than ever before.

Henry considered himself a modern Renaissance man. His phone buzzed constantly with updates on world events, scientific discoveries, and trending topics. At parties, he could talk to anyone about anything, rattling off insights from YouTube videos and social media posts. If you mentioned a popular book, he could summarize its key points but would never divulge that he skimmed the "five-minute bestseller" website every night at bedtime.

But even though he seemed to know everything, he didn't know why he felt so stuck, adrift, and increasingly anxious. It felt like the more information he crammed into his brain, the less any of it seemed to help, like he was feasting on facts but starving for substance.

One night, Henry woke from sleep feeling like he was coming out of his skin. Heart pounding, he fumbled for his phone in the dark. "Quick fix for anxiety," he typed, desperate for relief. A three-minute guided meditation popped up. He followed the instructions, hoping for peace. It worked—until it didn't. Ten minutes later, his mind was racing again. It happened over and over all night, and everything he tried—journaling, tapping different points on his body for a few seconds at a time, and several other surefire hacks to relax his nervous system—just left him feeling worse.

After a few nights like this, Henry felt overwhelmed. The facts and techniques that once made him feel in control now felt scattered and meaningless, like puzzle pieces he tried to assemble, only to realize they were all from different puzzles.

Henry had spent years gathering bits and pieces, but they never fused into anything that truly changed him. He was stuck in the same cycle so many of us are—mistaking knowledge for wisdom, collecting answers instead of creating change.

Perhaps you don't relate to Henry's unrelenting quest for knowledge, but like him, you turn to your phone or laptop for the latest hack on controlling your son's ADHD, hosting a civil family Thanksgiving dinner, or losing five pounds fast. When we feel stressed, we hunt for a quick fix—a breathing exercise from an Instagram post, a verse from our Bible app, a neuroscience hack from a podcast, or a grounding technique from therapy. While these tools may help momentarily, they rarely produce deep and lasting change. That's because snagging bits of advice from various sources to manage today's stress does not rewire the brain for real, long-term change. We might be 10 percent happier today, but tomorrow we're 11 percent more convinced that real change is impossible.

What Henry needed—and what we all need—isn't more information. It's real transformation. Having a head full of scattered hacks, clever quotes, and quick fixes might offer momentary relief, but it won't rewire your brain. You don't need another tip; you need a new way of thinking, a process of using your mind to structurally change your brain and your life.

> You don't need another tip; you need a new way of thinking, a process of using your mind to structurally change your brain and your life.

Before I show you why self–brain surgery is the mechanism of that change and not just another catchy metaphor, let me give you one last analogy to bring this idea into focus.

In particle physics, when protons interact at low energy, they do not reveal deeper forces or hidden structures. But when particles are accelerated to near light speed, they collide, and a massive amount of energy is released. New particles emerge, new insights are discovered, and science advances in ways that were previously unimaginable. In a similar way, cherry-picking pieces of Scripture, science, philosophy, and psychology won't unlock the life-changing power released when they are fully integrated. When you understand how your mind, brain, and body are designed and how they are meant to work together, you activate a radical transformation in your life.

And that brings us to the central promise of this book: Self–brain surgery is not a metaphor—it is the mechanism by which your mind physically changes your brain and enables you to flourish. When you choose to practice self–brain surgery—from the empowered perspective that you are no longer bound by the brain you inherited from your parents, nor by the traumas and tragedies you've endured—you unleash the full force of your God-given ability to learn, grow, and heal. This is not wishful thinking. It is the neuroscience of transformation, the power of faith in action, and the key to breaking free from the patterns that have held you back.

Take another look at the diagram on page 108, which is designed to help you think of the first four commandments as steps leading up to a platform. You took the step of committing to avoid malpractice against yourself, and with steps two and three you acknowledged that not everything you feel or think is trustworthy or needs to be reacted to. After completing step four, you are now armed with an understanding that when you choose to think of one thing and not another, you are taking command of the literal restructuring of your brain, and with God's guidance, co-creating your new reality. You can move forward into the rest of your life knowing that, even if hardship arises (as it surely will), you are equipped to handle it.

You've made a fundamental change—the switch from patient to doctor—and you are prepared to learn the last five commandments you need to embrace your transformed, fully realized life. It's worth repeating: Self–brain surgery is not a metaphor. It is the scientific and biblical key to changing your life. And it is how you can retrain your brain to hope by default; partner with God to create a healthier, stronger mind; and break free from the limitations of past trauma, negative thought patterns, and unhealthy habits.

Standing on the elevated vantage point you've reached through these first five commandments, you are no longer a passive recipient of life's circumstances—you are an active architect of your mind, your brain, and your future. You have left behind the illusion of helplessness and stepped into the power of intentional transformation. You are no longer simply thinking differently—you are becoming different.

Now, with the scalpel in your hand, you are ready to master the final five commandments—the principles that will not only cement your transformation but equip you to thrive. The days of feeling stuck, overwhelmed, and powerless are behind you. From here on, every thought you choose is a step toward the life you were meant to live, and the puzzle will finally start coming together.

 Relevant Neuroscience

When you intentionally change your thoughts, you are physically altering your brain's structure. This isn't metaphorical—it's the proven science of neuroplasticity.

- According to Hebb's law, "neurons that fire together, wire together."[1] Every thought you focus on strengthens the neural pathways associated with it. This means that when you continually dwell on negativity, anxiety, or limiting beliefs, you reinforce them, making those patterns easier to default to. But when you intentionally practice new thoughts, you rewire your brain, making hope, resilience, and confidence your new default state.

- The reticular activating system (RAS) acts as your brain's filter, deciding what gets your attention. When you train your mind to focus on solutions rather than problems, gratitude rather than despair, and faith rather than fear, your RAS begins seeking evidence that supports your new mindset and reinforces a powerful feedback loop of growth and transformation.

- Epigenetics shows that our thoughts influence gene expression. When we adopt an empowered, hopeful mindset, we activate genetic expressions that promote healing, resilience in times of stress, and overall well-being. These changes can even be passed on to future generations.

Guiding Scripture

Do not conform to the pattern of this world, but be transformed by the renewing of your mind.
ROMANS 12:2

You will keep in perfect peace those whose minds are steadfast, because they trust in you.
ISAIAH 26:3

Science has now proven that transformation begins at the level of thought. Renewing your mind is an active, ongoing process—one that literally reshapes your brain.

Furthermore, a steadfast mind—one trained in self–brain surgery—produces peace, resilience, and stability, even in times of hardship.

Questions for Reflection

1. In what ways have you cherry-picked solutions instead of fully integrating faith, neuroscience, and self–brain surgery?

2. How would your thought life change if you truly believed you were the surgeon of your own mind?

3. How does the biblical principle of renewing your mind (Romans 12:2) align with modern neuroscience?

16

The Sixth Commandment
I Must Love Tomorrow More Than I Hate How I Feel Right Now

Being happy and stress free, dealing with the root cause of stress rather than numbing the symptoms is the only sure way to find relief.
ANNIE GRACE
This Naked Mind

Anesthesia is a critical part of my neurosurgery practice. Without the help of my colleagues who safely and reliably keep people comfortable and still during invasive procedures, it would be impossible to do most of the things I need to do to help my patients get well. Surgery is simply too painful to be tolerated unless we can numb the area we're working on or put the patient to sleep for the duration of the procedure.

This is perhaps the biggest difference between the surgery I perform in the operating room and the self–brain surgery you're here to learn: Anesthesia is not allowed in self–brain surgery.

The problem with choosing a numbing agent to cover up what's hurting or frustrating you is that there is no local or regional anesthesia capable of making you not feel one thing and still be able to feel everything else. If you turn your brain off with things like alcohol or Netflix or pornography or comfort food, you can't feel the rest of your life either.

You have to feel it to heal it.

This is one reason the Bible warns against using alcohol to excess: "Don't be drunk with

| *You have to feel it to heal it.*

wine, because that will ruin your life. Instead, be filled with the Holy Spirit."[1] When we're intoxicated, we cannot use our frontal lobes to help us make good decisions, and we cannot communicate with God because we've anesthetized the interface between mind and brain. Being able to think clearly or hear healing words from God allows us to actually feel and deal with what's troubling us.

Choosing a numbing behavior instead of addressing our discomfort creates another dreadful problem: the tomorrow tax. This penalty is assessed when you push a problem off to another day. That's because avoiding it creates another problem—a hangover, financial stress, or relationship issues. You then have to deal with the new complication while still being sad, frustrated, or whatever feeling you were trying to numb in the first place. And while you're dealing with the headache, the debt, or the stressful conversation, you're in a worse position to handle your original problem. This is the tomorrow tax: what you must pay tomorrow for not dealing with your problems today in a healthy way.

Jesus said that each day has enough trouble of its own.[2] I would humbly offer a corollary: Each day also has things it needs from you, and paying a tomorrow tax can keep you from showing up to accomplish them. It can also put you in the wrong frame of mind tomorrow so that you miss things that might have helped you heal or experience a breakthrough.

Often when the tension or anxiety builds because you're frustrated with yourself for paying the tax again and realize you're no closer to figuring out a solution to your pain, you may feel like you're about to come out of your skin. Before you know it, you're binge-watching another series, downing a bottle during another night you won't remember, or ordering a bunch of items online that you don't need. And you know that the sound you're hearing is the tax man on his way to get you again tomorrow.

In self–brain surgery terms, it's time to remind yourself: *Don't treat a bad feeling with a bad operation.*

Numbing behaviors do not help you make progress, even though your brain's reward pathways can be conditioned to convince you that they will. You need to love tomorrow more than you hate how you may be feeling right now, because with the light from another sunrise you can be one step closer to becoming healthier, feeling better, and being happier again. No one ever wakes up and wishes they'd had one more drink the night before. No one dreams longingly of the Cheetos they didn't eat or the money they didn't spend, but almost everyone has had a moment of clarity in which they rejoiced that they made a better choice.

When you treat your bad feelings with the correct operations, you make progress and you begin to believe that healing and hope are possible. You rewire those reward circuits to start wanting to feel the full experience of life, which you've previously numbed yourself from in your attempts to avoid feeling the things that hurt.

You can't just numb the hard stuff. Anesthesia is not an option for self–brain surgeons because you and I are here to change our minds, not turn them off.

Love tomorrow more than you hate how you feel right now, and you'll start to come alive again.

Relevant Neuroscience

The brain often seeks immediate relief from discomfort (through emotional "anesthesia"), but this is driven by short-term survival instincts. By focusing on future benefits, you engage the brain's executive function, allowing yourself to endure temporary discomfort for long-term gain and strengthening neural circuits associated with patience and resilience.

 Guiding Scripture

> Don't worry about tomorrow, for tomorrow will bring its own worries. Today's trouble is enough for today.
>
> MATTHEW 6:34, NLT

Avoid paying the tomorrow tax by being willing to deal with uncomfortable feelings and situations today. That way, you can heal and grow, which will ensure better tomorrows.

 Questions for Reflection

1. What form(s) of anesthesia, or numbing techniques, have you chosen to use in the difficult areas of your life?

2. How has the tomorrow tax affected you?

3. How can you remind yourself to choose a good operation instead of a bad one when you feel lousy, frustrated, or stuck?

17

The Seventh Commandment
I Must Stop Making an Operation Out of Everything

You can be the air traffic controller of your mental airport. You occupy the control tower and can direct the mental traffic of your world.

MAX LUCADO
Anxious for Nothing

Before we start each surgery in my operating room, I ask my team a question: "Do you all want to make an operation out of this?"

They robustly reply in unison, "No!"

I have done this in ORs in Texas, Alabama, Wyoming, Nebraska, Iraq, and Germany. But it started in Pittsburgh.

My former professor, the late Peter Jannetta, was a world-famous neurosurgeon who was a pioneer in cranial nerve surgery for devastating diseases such as trigeminal neuralgia. As he watched his trainees perform brain surgeries, he'd notice things we were doing that made the procedures unnecessarily complex. He would lean over my shoulder and say, "Come on, Warren! Don't make an operation out of it."

It was his way of saying not to make things unnecessarily hard—a reminder to be more efficient and plan my moves in advance so I'd be safer, quicker, and more effective as a surgeon. I've honored Dr. Jannetta by asking my team that question each time we operate, which has evolved into a joke when they remind me not to make my cases longer than they should be.[1]

Since we lost our son Mitch, I've been on a long journey of trying to figure out what happens to people who get immobilized in their lives. This is because I was stuck for so long in grief and hopelessness from the trauma of Mitch's death. I needed to heal, and I needed (as a good doctor) to try to find ways to help others heal too. After all, Lisa and I realized that Luke 12:48—"To whom much is given . . . much will be required" (NKJV)—applies both to the blessings *and* the burdens of our lives. God brought us out of the furnace of suffering through his mercy, so we felt obligated to shine a light to show others the way out.

Sometimes part of the reason we get stuck is that we're making things harder than they have to be.

That path has led me to many amazing discoveries, but perhaps none were more surprising than this one: Sometimes part of the reason we get stuck in anything (grief, anxiety, depression, ADHD, performance barriers, bad habits, or floundering in general) is that we're making things harder than they have to be.

Here are three of the many ways you can "make an operation" out of your healing or any barrier in life:

1. **You forget that your painful or even devastating situation is not the only thing that is still true in the world.** Your TMT (The Massive Thing) is so big, so hard, so painful, or seemingly so insurmountable that you forget to zoom out a little and see that you still have people who love you, that there's still some light and beauty in the world, and that God is there helping you.

2. **You may focus excessively on the physical symptoms you associate with your pain.** Grief hurts our bodies, so you may begin to believe that you're broken instead of remembering that you are designed to heal,[2] or you may fixate on your anxiety and tell yourself, *That's just how I am*. Focusing on how you feel rather than on the fact that your mind is in charge of making your brain and body work better can keep you from moving forward. This is much like the quantum physics phenomenon called the Quantum Zeno effect. Basically, the more we observe something from a particular perspective, the more likely it will freeze in that position until we change how we're looking at it. So if you keep telling yourself that you're anxious, you'll continue to feel anxious.[3]

3. **You begin to worry that your life is now going to be less than it should be.** You focus on the past and mourn the future you expected, and you forget that you are still living the story that will determine your future. Nothing in the past actually has the power to write your future story unless you choose to put down the pen and stop writing the new one. Trauma can change the title of the chapter you thought you were in, but it creates only the future you let it create.

Look, friend, we all know that life is hard. Jesus promised us it would be (see John 10:10; 16:33). But self–brain surgery draws on the miracle of neuroplasticity and the foundation of faith so that we can plant our feet on something solid after life knocks us down. It allows two things to be true at the same time. Yes, the devastations and frustrations are real, but so are the penetrating light, joy, meaning, and purpose that life is *still* full of.

So when it feels impossible to move past whatever has you stuck, zoom out and look for places where you've focused on the problem so much that you've forgotten it's not the only thing that's still true.

Take it easy on yourself. The healing will come, in time. Go through your difficulty (you have to), but do not believe that you will always be in the most painful parts of it. Your story isn't over; remember that you get to keep writing it.

It's time to stop making an operation out of everything.

Relevant Neuroscience

Chronic stress activates the brain's amygdala and hypothalamic-pituitary-adrenal (HPA) axis. This is your body's stress response system, which produces cortisol and keeps you in a heightened state of alert. Over time, "making an operation" out of everything wears down cognitive resources. Learning to rest and avoid unnecessary overreactions allows the brain to recalibrate and restore balance, improving cognitive function and mental health.

 Guiding Scripture

> *In quietness and trust is your strength.*
> ISAIAH 30:15

When you make things too hard and are stressed by the process of trying to change, transformation often becomes impossible. But there is an unexpected remedy: Taking it easier on yourself often leads to breakthroughs.

 Questions for Reflection

1. What are some ways in which you've made an operation out of your own progress?

2. What are some areas where you could use a quieter approach in your life?

18

The Eighth Commandment
I Must Not Perpetuate—or Start—Harmful Generational Thought or Behavioral Issues in My Life or Family

We either pass on our healing, or we pass on our hurting.
GINA BIRKEMEIER
Generations Deep

Since 1953, when Watson and Crick discovered the structure of DNA, humans have been enamored with the idea that genes determine most aspects of our lives. This idea, called genetic determinism, became widely popular and is still often repeated in media headlines like, "Researchers discover the gene for dyslexia!"

The dogma of genetic determinism has a firm hold on the public imagination, but there is one problem: It's not true. It is now clear that the old idea of a particular gene having ultimate power over how your life plays out is fundamentally incorrect, and that is very good news.

Assuming that a molecular lottery has control over your quality of life removes you—your choices, beliefs, actions, and faith—from any position of power. But beliefs like *It's not my fault; I got it from my dad* are true for only a very small number of things about you, like your eye color and some medical conditions, such as Huntington's disease and cystic fibrosis.[1]

What *is* true—and can be stated without controversy now—is that your genes play only a small part in how long you're likely to live, what your baseline personality may be like, and what diseases or other issues you may be susceptible to.

The truth is, genes aren't the card game; they're just the deck. The player can win even with a hand that's not as "good" as someone else's if they play their cards right.

Molecular biology has now conclusively shown that what's important is *not* which genes you have or don't have, but rather whether those genes are switched on or off. When and how that switching process, known as genetic expression, occurs is what determines the outcome of your life. And here's the good news: Gene expression is not a fixed process, but rather one that changes constantly throughout your life. Environment, experiences, diet, activity, and even beliefs and attitude play huge roles in genetic expression. This is why identical twins do not have the same lifespans or personalities. They have the same genes, but they are different people. This means that your decisions, beliefs, and behaviors have more power to change your future than your DNA does.

Your decisions, beliefs, and behaviors have more power to change your future than your DNA does.

Fascinating research on animals and humans has shown that experiencing trauma or pain makes epigenetic changes in DNA expression that can adversely affect how stress is handled, leading to increased production of stress hormones like cortisol. These changes can be passed on to offspring for multiple generations, which means that some of the ways you feel inside at baseline and your responses to stressful situations are programmed into you by your great-great-grandparents.[2]

You may think it sounds hopeless when you learn that you may be anxious or more likely to be depressed because your grandparents didn't process hardship well, but here's the good news: These epigenetic changes can be reversed and normalized in one generation by learning to think differently. Studies of prayer, meditation, and various mindfulness practices and therapeutic techniques[3] have shown that people can unlearn inherited trauma responses and other maladaptive epigenetic switches and that their children can be born with normal stress responses.

Amazingly, you don't even have to wait a generation to see the effects of using self–brain surgery to unwind epigenetic influences in your life. Multiple studies have shown that just making the *decision* to start engaging in cognitive therapy, seeking help, or mentally rehearsing the improvements you hope to make starts the process of improving brain structure and function within hours![4] When

Air Force Thunderbird pilots mentally rehearse their aerobatic performances or gymnasts imagine their routines before they mount the pommel horse, their brains immediately begin making synapses to accomplish those incredible skills, which improves their performance.[5] When you imagine yourself getting better and mentally rehearse how you can break free from the generational issues you started with, your mind directs your brain to begin the process of setting you free from them in real time.

The old assumption that if our dad was an alcoholic, our mom was abusive, and our entire family was sickly, then we will be too, is no longer believable on a scientific level. We know that the vast majority of genetic starting points and potentials can be positively influenced or completely reversed in a single generation, largely by changing how we think and the choices we make.

This is so important in terms of your mental health, because the less control you believe you have over how your mind and brain work, the less hope you will feel that change is possible. So if you came to this chapter sad, sick, stressed, or stuck in some area of life because "I was born that way," it's time to reclaim your God-given power.

It's time to change, my friend. Just as God said when he laid out the limits of the ocean, let's tell those generational issues, "This far you may come and no farther; here is where your proud waves halt" (Job 38:11).

You have vast control over your own gene expression, and you can begin to exercise it in the length of time it takes you to read this sentence. Genes are constantly being turned on and off in your body, and you can harness the power of Hebb's law ("neurons that fire together, wire together") to make those switches work for you. When you make purposeful decisions to improve areas of your life, the changes will begin to groove new synapses in your brain. Over time, it will become easier to "be" the kind of person you feel called to be, not the one you once believed you were fated to be.

You can't use your genes as a reason to blame some prior generation for what's hurting you now. But you *can* use the power God gave you to more positively express those genes to help yourself get better.

And better beats blame, doesn't it?

Most importantly, if everyone in your family line was anxious, stressed out, depressed, or dependent on alcohol, you may believe that your kids have to struggle with those things too.

But again, it's epigenetics to the rescue, because those outcomes can be avoided in this generation if you are willing to change your mind. Start with you, and everyone around and after you will begin to be imprinted by the positive changes you're making. Future generations will start with different genes switched on or off because you took the time to reprogram them.

It's time to realize that *how you are* does not have to determine *who you are*, because almost everything about *how* you are (your personality type, your typical mood, or how you deal with adversity) is the result of gene expression rather than the genes themselves. And *who* you are is determined by the choices you make, including your decision to practice self–brain surgery and become intensely involved in improving the quality of your life. Once you know you're not stuck with the way things have been—even in your own DNA—you can take advantage of the fact that you were designed to change when you choose to.

I need to say a word to the believers here. There is a passage in the Old Testament that people often use to suggest that God punishes children for the sins of their fathers: "I lay the sins of the parents upon their children; the entire family is affected—even children in the third and fourth generations of those who reject me."[6] A fair reading of the rest of the story, however, shows that God clearly holds us individually responsible for our own behavior.[7] So what gives? I believe epigenetics are at play here, and God (millennia before people could have understood a direct statement about molecular biology) is not threatening that he will punish people's grandkids if they sin. Rather, he is warning us to be aware that the way we live affects the lives of later generations. It's not a threat; it's a compassionate warning: Be careful how you live because your kids can be hurt by your choices.

How you are does not have to determine who you are. Nature gives you a starting point, and nurture can affect how you feel and behave down to the DNA expression level. But learning to think differently makes real-time changes in your gene expression, your brain's structure and function, and how your life plays out going forward. You are literally a new person every time you think differently about your own life.

Nature and nurture can tell you how things start, but they don't have to control how you end up.

Relevant Neuroscience

Behavioral and thought patterns are often passed down through family environments, creating deeply ingrained neural pathways. Neuroplasticity offers the ability to break these cycles if you consciously choose new behaviors and teach them to the next generation, altering the inherited brain wiring.

Guiding Scripture

> *Be very careful, then, how you live—not as unwise but as wise.*
> **EPHESIANS 5:15**

How you live, including the way you choose to use your mind to make decisions, impacts not only you but everyone else as well, including future generations.

Questions for Reflection

1. What attitudes and issues have you assumed just run in your family? Which would you most like to change in your generation?

2. How does the way you currently live affect your family, and how might it impact generations to come?

19

The Ninth Commandment
I Must Believe That I'm Getting Better at What I'm Doing

Understanding our capacity to systematically alter our own neurobiology requires welcoming such concepts as choice and effort.

JEFFREY M. SCHWARTZ AND SHARON BEGLEY
The Mind and the Brain

Your brain is constantly running a consent-to-automate sequence, seeking your mental permission to mechanize things so that you do not have to spend as much mental energy to process them. This system is designed to free up mental resources for you by turning whatever you give your brain permission to automate into a synaptic program that becomes more deeply engrained and less conscious over time.

This consent-to-automate process is a good thing, but there are two problems:

1. Your brain does not really care what you tell it to automate; it just obeys your direction.

2. Most people are never aware that they are able to direct the process in ways that help them rather than hurt them.

All your habits, everything you think is "just the way I am," every routine reaction to stress, every interaction with other people, and the way you speak to yourself internally are the result of this automation process, and each of these things can be changed by taking control of the process.

But to change in ways that are helpful requires you to be aware of and attentive to the ninth commandment: I must believe that I'm getting better at what I'm doing.

For example, every time you call yourself an unkind name, you are giving your brain permission to automate the little voice (script #1 thinking) that calls you a loser or tells you that you'll never be able to do whatever you so desperately want to do. Before long, you've accepted a label you placed on yourself, and that internal belief becomes a part of your identity. Notice that you could have easily rejected that negative self-talk, biopsied those thoughts, and transplanted a healthier label for yourself. (Maybe something like, *I am made in God's image, for a purpose, and am learning to transform my mind. I'm not a loser.*)

On the other hand, when you make a healthy food choice instead of reaching for the sugary snack you always regret the next day, you can feel proud that you are making progress. Your brain rewards you with dopamine, and the next time you're tempted, new wiring will remind you how good it feels to burn more high-quality food for your brain. If you keep making that choice, it will become easier over time because you're getting better (literally, in terms of the structure of your brain and its function) at what you're doing.

It's a very simple, but not always easy, process: Anything you repeat becomes easier to do again in the future, and over time the old habit/circuit diminishes.

> **Anything you repeat becomes easier to do again in the future, and over time the old habit/circuit diminishes.**

Not knowing about the process is the biggest barrier to making it work for you. But don't feel bad if this is a new concept for you. You were born into a family system where things were done a certain way, a particular worldview was presented to you as reality, and the rules of how you were supposed to think and act were set in place before you were even aware of these expectations. Before you could speak, you developed numerous brain habits that you've likely always assumed were the normal ways humans behave. It's not until someone teaches you that these things are learned and that unhelpful habits can be changed, that you begin to see the power of self–brain surgery.

Again, you're after an approach to life that helps you become healthier (emotionally, physically, spiritually, financially, etc.), feel better (in all areas), and be happier (more resilient, fulfilled, purpose-driven, and successful), right? Knowing that you get better at whatever you decide to do, and realizing that some of the things you "do" are mental events, will lead you to this breakthrough: *Some things are holding me back because I've been "getting better" at continuing to think they're true, but I am not obligated to keep getting better at believing them.*

And *that* breakthrough enables you to look yourself in the mirror and declare, "Today is the day I stop giving my brain permission to automate things that do not serve me well."

If you're sad, sick, stressed, stuck, or tired of settling in your life, take another look at the graph that shows what it looks like when you assume other people are reaching some level of achievement that you're not.

CONCEPTS ABOUT AND APPROACHES TO LIFE

Deciding to begin getting better at making new brain habits, taking control of your brain's consent-to-automate function, and directing more of those automations to help you are powerful steps you can take to improve your own life curve.

Be aware, though, that the corollary to our ninth commandment is this: *What got you here won't get you there.*

If you realize that something needs to change, then you have to make the synaptic connections and believe that in order for something to improve, *you* have to change something. Otherwise, your brain will keep running the plays you've previously permitted it to run, even if you were unaware that you'd given permission.

But now, you know that you're getting better at what you're doing, so as a good self–brain surgeon, it's time to get better at the things that will help you progress toward your goals.

Becoming better is better than staying broken.

Becoming better is better than blaming something or someone else for what's hurting you.

Becoming better is better than the bitterness of believing that "this is just how it is for me."

Better is better.

Relevant Neuroscience

Focusing attention on the things you want to change creates and strengthens synaptic connections, harnessing the power of Hebb's law ("neurons that fire together, wire together"). Believing in that change reinforces it by activating the brain's reward system, increasing your motivation. Each time you repeat the process, you make your brain more efficient, and you gain confidence that improvement is not only possible but achievable.

 Guiding Scripture

> I am certain that God, who began the good work within you, will continue his work until it is finally finished on the day when Christ Jesus returns.
> PHILIPPIANS 1:6, NLT

According to the apostle Paul, whenever God starts something, you can count on it being completed. Your brain is wired to reinforce positive changes, and it's just waiting for you to direct that God-given process for your own good.

 Questions for Reflection

1. What are some things you've "gotten better at" and permitted your brain to keep doing without realizing that they were not helping you?

2. What is something you want to get better at that will help you, and how are you going to change your self-talk or behavior to begin "getting better at getting better" starting today?

20

The Tenth Commandment
I Must Understand That Thoughts Become Things

My thoughts are all a case of knives,
Wounding my heart
With scatter'd smart, . . .
Nothing their furie can controll,
While they do wound and prick my soul.

GEORGE HERBERT
"Affliction (IV)"

You see it so clearly now: Not every thought you think is true. Not everything you feel is a fact. Some traits you thought were ingrained by genetics or personal history are actually just responses you've permitted your brain to turn into synapses, which means you are no longer required to keep them if they're not helping you.

But here's something critical to note: Although not every thought or feeling that pops into your head is true or requires a response, *every thought you decide to think and act on turns into a real thing in the world.*

Let's take a brief detour into quantum physics and acknowledge that your observation and interaction with something influences what becomes real—and that includes your mind-brain interface. In the quantum world, all potential outcomes exist in a wave of possibility until the observer makes a choice, collapsing all those possibilities into a single reality. Similarly, before you respond to a thought, an entire field of mental, emotional, and behavioral possibilities is available to you. Your attention—what you choose to focus on—determines which of those possibilities becomes real in your life.

Imagine you are an archer, carrying your bow at your side. On your back is a quiver full of arrows, each of which is equally sharp and available for your use. Until you actually pick one, they are all just potential arrows you could choose to shoot if you want, but none of them has a more "real" mark on reality because they are all harmlessly positioned in your quiver.

However, once you select a particular arrow, nock it in your bow, and draw back the bowstring, you are turning a potential event into reality. Once the arrow is aimed, energized, and released toward your target, you have made a real event out of all those possible events, or even the possibility that you could have chosen not to shoot an arrow at all.

The same is true with your thoughts.

Think of all the possible things you could think, feel, say, or do in the next moment. You have only so many moments in your life, and you are about to choose one of them to turn from possibility into reality.

So what happens when you choose a particular thought out of all that possibility?

Draw a mental arrow out of your quiver, and imagine this example:

- The interface between mind and brain converts energy into matter as a potential event and becomes a wave-to-particle collapse in your mind. In other words, once you choose to focus on one thing, among many possibilities, that thought manifests as a single, definitive particle in your brain.

- That particle interacts with other nerve cells via synaptic connections within the vast neuronal network. As each neuron fires, its axon sends its signal to a synapse with another neuron or cell. In this process, energy is turned into electricity.

- When the axon's signal hits the synapse between the receptors in your pituitary gland, neurotransmitters are released. At this point, the electrical event has become a chemical event.

- The chemical event then becomes a biological event, as hormones are released by the gland in response to the nerve impulse. Those hormones enter your bloodstream and wind up stimulating your adrenal glands to release cortisol, the stress hormone.

- That biological event then becomes a physiological event, when the cortisol molecules cause blood pressure and heart rate to rise, and you begin to feel anxious.

- The physiological event, over time, causes an epigenetic event, and genes are tagged with methyl and acetyl groups to down- or up-regulate their transcription and cause chronic stress-related events to harm your body. Those tags are then passed to your offspring so that they are born with an abnormal stress response.

- The epigenetic event has now changed your family's ability to handle adversity, making them, at baseline, less resilient and more uneasy in life.

Everything started when you chose a thought from all the possible thoughts you could have chosen.

A thought became a particle.
A particle became electricity.
Electricity became neurochemistry.
Neurochemistry became biology.
Biology became physiology.
Physiology became epigenetics.
And epigenetics became history for your family.

All of this happened because thoughts become things.
Realizing that you are not obligated to choose any one arrow—or thought— over another gives you power to choose the one that is most helpful to you in any moment. This carries responsibility, though, because when you release a thought (especially when it turns into words or actions that affect others), it is as unchangeable as the arrow in flight. You cannot take it back, and it takes tremendous work to reduce the impact of a harmful thought that has impacted another person. The famous 5:1 Rule in neuroscience is that it takes approximately five positive statements to counteract one negative remark.[1] So calling your spouse a loser or telling your child they're stupid will leave a mark in their minds they will never forget, no matter how many times you say, "I didn't mean that."

> **When you release a thought, it is as unchangeable as an arrow in flight.**

Keep the arrow metaphor in mind and think of the sutures, tourniquets, and trauma surgeries you'd need to provide for people if you frequently let errant shots fly. Be careful with your thoughts, because when they turn into words that hurt people, those wounds are just as real.

Once you understand that a chosen thought has the incredible power to turn into something real in your life, you begin to see both the importance and the opportunity in developing a practice of careful thought selection and application. Just as good surgeons carefully select their instruments and procedures, careful self–brain surgeons choose their thoughts wisely.

Why?

Because thoughts become things.

Relevant Neuroscience

Thoughts are electrical impulses that shape the brain's structure over time through synaptic plasticity. Repeated thoughts become ingrained in neural pathways, influencing behavior, emotions, and even physiological and genetic responses. The mind can literally shape the brain and, by extension, your external reality.

Guiding Scripture

> *We take captive every thought.*
> 2 CORINTHIANS 10:5

You and I need to be careful when determining which of our thousands of automatic thoughts deserve a response. We then need to develop a safe method of expressing them.

Questions for Reflection

1. Do you believe that thoughts are harmless unless you act upon them? How has your understanding changed as you've read this book?

2. How does knowing that thoughts become things change your level of responsibility for learning to biopsy your thoughts and take them captive?

3. How would your life improve if you never shot a harmful thought arrow? How might it help your family, work, and community?

PART 4

The Operating Room

> *By developing the ability to focus our attention on our internal world, we are picking up a "scalpel" we can use to resculpt our neural pathways, stimulating the growth of areas of the brain that are crucial to mental health.*
>
> **DANIEL J. SIEGEL, MD**
> *Mindsight*

21

Operating Your Mind as a Self-Brain Surgery Specialist

Continuity of training is the great means of making the nervous system act infallibly right.

WILLIAM JAMES
Psychology: The Briefer Course

Just as you have begun learning about various approaches and techniques to use in self–brain surgery, I had acquired a lot of basic skills by the time I became a neurosurgical resident. As a medical student, I learned intubation from anesthesiologists; suturing from emergency department physicians and obstetricians; critical care from ICU doctors; and amputations from orthopedists. General surgeons had taught me to hold a scalpel, and I had learned to use a drill from an otolaryngologist.

I'd also been schooled in medicine's standards of care and best practices, much like you've been introduced to the reasoning behind the ten commandments of self–brain surgery. You have learned a lot, but you may still be unsure how to apply this information. The aim of my residency training program was to turn me into a safe and effective neurosurgeon, and this part of the book is designed to turn you into a successful self–brain surgeon. Finally, you're ready for hands-on training. It's time to operate!

But just as I still had much to learn in the operating room back then, you won't be on your own just yet. Almost every time I went to surgery as a resident, a professor would say something like, "Why do you grip the needle holder like that? Do it like this instead." Or "You're holding the scalpel like an orthopedist, like it's an extension of your arm. Hold it like a pencil or a fine paintbrush instead, so that the fine motor control of your hand muscles will give you precise control as you're cutting."

The fact that our residency program had fifteen or more professors at any one time created another wrinkle: Sometimes two neurosurgeons would teach me different "right ways" to do the same thing. One day Dr. Whiting would critique how I held a Penfield #4 dissector, a blunt-tipped metal instrument used to gently move tissue during surgery. The next day, Dr. Quigley would say, "Don't hold it like that; do it this way."

I had to be reminded during my residency that the techniques and approaches I knew and used were not always best suited to the operation at hand. What kept me from being endlessly frustrated was something Dr. Maroon told me: "I designed this place so you guys would learn a dozen different ways to do everything." That led me to see the entire training process as an opportunity to become a resilient and agile surgeon who could quickly pivot from one technique or approach to another when a case became challenging. I no longer felt hurt every time someone corrected me for not doing something their way.

As you become a specialist at managing your own mind, you will need to do as much unlearning as learning since some of your current practices will not help you perform your own self–brain surgery. You've spent decades developing habits and patterns for what you think, feel, believe, and do—for how you operate your mind and brain. Whether you knew it or not, you've been practicing self–brain surgery all your life.

That's why we started in "The Office" instead of "The Operating Room." We were already colleagues, but you needed to consider the various approaches before you could begin operating. Now it's time to learn some specific procedures to assist you in your practice. As your professor, I'm obligated to treat you to some degree like I was treated during my residency so that you'll get the most out of training and be armed with everything you need.

The overarching goal here is to introduce you to a new set of tools, strategies, and procedures you can use to help manage your mind, brain, body, and life. Everything you learn will become part of your skill set. You can then determine which option is the most appropriate for the situation at hand. For the record, Dr. Whiting and Dr. Quigley are both tremendous surgeons who taught me many of the techniques I still use today. But I don't hold the Penfield #4 dissector exactly like either of them taught me to; I have my own way, and it works for me.

Becoming a master practitioner requires humility; a thirst for learning new techniques, approaches, and operations; and a willingness to change even long-held ideas when you discover they are not working for you. You will inevitably find some occasions when you'll want to learn a new way of holding the instrument. We call it practice because it takes a lifetime to master the process of, as William James said, making our brains "act infallibly right."

If that sounds discouraging, take heart: It's not because you've been doing everything incorrectly all along; it's just that now you're learning a specialty. In the past you let your brain operate you; now you're changing positions and entrusting your mind with a new role.

We're going to make a surgeon out of you, my friend.

Making the Diagnosis

In the old days, neurosurgeons sometimes operated in an attempt to discover the nature of a patient's problem and then decide how to fix it. Based on a patient's symptoms and their physical examination, surgeons would take their patients to the OR and literally just look around to try to spot the tumor or other issue. Naturally, this led to all kinds of trouble. Some people even died from infection or other complications even though nothing had actually been wrong with them. Fortunately, thanks to modern imaging technologies like CT scans and MRIs, brain surgeons no longer perform exploratory surgery.

Imagine if you came to my office and told me you'd been having headaches for two weeks. If my response was, "Okay. Let's go to surgery. I'll open your head and try to find the problem," would you be filled with confidence that I was the right surgeon for you?

No. The proper response to your headache would be for me to do some diagnostic work.

Brain surgeons don't perform exploratory surgery.

We do not operate based purely on symptoms; we need data to make the diagnosis. Remember the SOAP progress note that you last worked on in chapter 2? The data you will learn to collect in this part of the book will be recorded in the "objective" part of the SOAP progress note, and that is the kind of information I seek after you've told me about your headaches. I do an exam and find you to be a little weak in your right arm. Let's say you've already had your labs checked, and we've ruled out allergies or other common causes of headaches.

We've now moved from something purely subjective (you telling me that your head hurts) to something objective (my unbiased exam finding of arm weakness). Now we need pictures. In neurosurgery, imaging provides the most important objective information.

Symptoms + exam findings = indication for imaging

Imagine I send you for an MRI scan, and a spot is found in your left frontal lobe. Because that lesion is in a location that could account for both arm weakness and headaches, we *finally* have a reasonable single issue that may be the source of your trouble.

We have progressed from symptoms (purely subjective) to exam findings (objective) to imaging findings (potentially explanatory). But even after all that, if I told you, "Okay, it's probably a brain tumor. Let's do chemotherapy and radiation," how would you respond? I hope you'd recognize that my offer to treat the problem with possibly harmful chemotherapy and radiation would still be inappropriate because we do not yet know the true nature of the spot we see on your MRI.

It could be a brain tumor, yes. But it could also be a benign cyst, an infection, scar tissue from an old injury, or something else that is not even causing your symptoms.

We do not make a treatment plan based on what *might* be wrong.

We don't operate based on what you think or feel (symptoms), and we don't react to things *we see* until we know what they really are.

We need more information, and we get it from tissue.

Symptoms + exam findings + imaging findings = indication for biopsy

Our next step is to perform a biopsy of the suspicious area we saw on your MRI scan. A biopsy can be done in a very minimally invasive way, with little risk. We put you to sleep, and I make a tiny incision in your scalp using a computer guidance system called Stealth. I drill a small hole and pass a biopsy needle through your brain and into the lesion, following the path I planned with the Stealth navigation software. Once the needle is inside the spot we're after, I can use it to sample the tissue, which I withdraw carefully and send down the hall to the pathologist.

When the pathologist calls into the room to tell me the true nature of the tissue we've sampled, I now have a diagnosis.

Look at all the progress we've made:

Symptoms + exam findings + imaging findings + biopsy results = diagnosis

With the diagnosis, I can formulate an appropriate, safe, and effective plan to help you deal with the problem.

If the pathologist determines that you have a brain tumor that should be removed and we agreed beforehand to do so if that was the finding, we can proceed with surgery right then. You're already in the OR and anesthetized. But some types of brain tumors (like central nervous system lymphoma) should be treated with chemotherapy or radiation alone, and surgery is not appropriate. Some other diagnoses require no treatment at all, or perhaps only antibiotics or steroids. We simply cannot decide how to treat a problem without obtaining data first.

But once we have the diagnosis, we are empowered and obligated to make a plan that addresses the real issue in the most effective way possible.

Diagnosis → treatment plan

The same progression is necessary in self–brain surgery.

You no longer want to ignore the problems that have left you sad, sick, stressed, stuck, or constantly settling. You have realized the folly of anesthetizing yourself every night, only to pay the tomorrow tax the next day because you treated a bad feeling with a bad operation. That would have been like me offering you brain surgery based only on your symptoms with no diagnostic work.

If you want a good outcome for your patient (yourself), you must carefully identify your symptoms, investigate them with a thorough examination and imaging, and then biopsy the suspicious findings before you react to them. You can know how to perform dozens of operations, but if you're treating the wrong problem, none of them will help and all of them could hurt you instead.

So in your quest to become a safe and effective self–brain surgeon, you will start with two diagnostic procedures—the Whole-System Scan and the Thought Biopsy—and build everything from there. Although it will take some time to get good at this, mental imaging will soon become second nature. Be encouraged as you remember that what you do, you get better at. And making the right diagnosis will inevitably lead to better outcomes when you operate on any issue in your life.

22

The Whole-System Scan

Worry and anxiety are interrelated, but where worry resides mainly in our minds, anxiety is worry we wear in our bodies.

JENNIFER TUCKER
Breath as Prayer

The Whole-System Scan is a procedure done prior to general self–brain surgery. You'll want to use this scan daily at first. Eventually, it will become an almost-constant part of your life and self–brain surgery practice, and you can use it anytime you are stressed, worried, or hurting somewhere.

The scan will help you identify the source of your symptoms and discover issues that will require biopsy or treatment. This powerful mindfulness technique is sometimes called body scanning. It will help you identify and bring awareness to what you feel in your body, which can reveal areas of stress and discomfort, as well as your emotions.

Studies have shown that regular body scanning can reduce stress, anxiety, and depression and improve overall mental health and physical well-being. Mindfulness-based stress reduction (MBSR) techniques can improve chronic stress,[1] pain,[2] anxiety, and depression,[3] and they can help reduce the stress associated with chronic disease and PTSD. Brain imaging shows that regular body scanning leads to improvements in interoception (the ability to perceive one's own internal state) and emotional regulation.[4] The practice can also reduce PTSD symptoms in combat veterans[5] and trauma victims. Finally, your brain literally gets better at scanning yourself the more you practice this, in accordance with our ninth commandment.

David, the most famous king of Israel and a prolific author who wrote most of the psalms, made this a regular practice: "Search me, God, and know my heart; test me and know my anxious thoughts."[6]

Running the Whole-System Scan while seeking God's help to reveal and manage areas you may have been unable or unwilling to examine before is a powerful way to begin understanding yourself more fully. Determining what is wrong is the first step to making it right. I understand that finding time to run this scan daily, or even once, may seem impossible. If so, I have some good news for you: First, even if you don't do the scan perfectly, your investment of time will pay off in the form of increased peace and contentment. Second, as the ninth commandment teaches us, over time the scan will become automated and seem as easy as breathing.

Determining what is wrong is the first step to making it right.

How to Conduct the Whole-System Scan

Running the Scan

1. Choose a place and time when you can be alone. When you are learning the Whole-System Scan, it helps to practice in a quiet environment. (Once you understand how to perform the scan, you will be able to do it in any situation.) I use my morning quiet time for this. I get up early while the house is still and the only sounds I hear are the owls outside and my racing thoughts. You can use the Whole-System Scan report template on page 287 to summarize what you discover from this procedure, which will provide objective data for your SOAP note and a record of your progress over time.

2. Take a moment for a time-out. Before starting any procedure in our neurosurgical practice, everyone on the team stops what we're doing to make sure we're performing the right surgery on the right patient in

the right location. Take a moment to remind yourself you are about to perform a Whole-System Scan for the purpose of better understanding your thoughts, feelings, pains, and other issues. In your mind, move from patient to doctor, remembering that you can participate in your own healing. The time-out makes sure you are focused, present, and intentional about why you're here and what you're doing.

3. **Close your eyes and imagine yourself sliding into an MRI machine.** Don't worry if you feel claustrophobic in a real MRI; this one is open and safe and doesn't produce all the clacking sounds. You can go into the machine feetfirst or headfirst. You choose.

4. **Mentally prepare for the scan.** Imagine that the machine is going to scan every part of your body, as well as whatever you're thinking about.

5. **Focus your mind on each part of your body, one area at a time.** Start from your head and move down to your toes (or vice versa). Notice anything you feel, like warmth, tension, tingling, numbness, pain, or relaxation. Don't try to diagnose it here; just notice it and mentally see it coming up on the screen as if you are a radiologist reading the scan: *There's some stiffness in my left shoulder*, etc.

6. **If you find discomfort or tension, make a mental note of it.** If you'd like, you can also write it down. Try to observe what comes up, but don't try to change it yet. Just give yourself permission to fully experience and identify what you are feeling. Remember, you have to feel it to heal it.

7. **Use the power of your breath.** In your mind, connect your breath to any area that is tense or hurting. Feel the tension, and then gently direct your breathing toward it. Imagine that each inhale brings relaxation to that spot, while each exhale releases some of the tension. In this step, you are proving to yourself that your mind has controlling influence over your body by directing your parasympathetic nervous system to activate the "rest and digest" response and override stress, just as it is designed to do.

8. **Stay focused.** Keep your mind anchored to your body and continue running the scan. Notice any thoughts or emotions that arise as you focus on specific areas. As you scan your brain, mind, and spirit, recognize the types of thoughts you have, and see them on the mental screen as if the scanner could detect them.

The statements and questions below may help you begin to identify thought patterns and feelings that are causing you distress.

Mind

- Identify areas of limited cognitive flexibility or tendencies to resist new perspectives or approaches.

- Search for places or situations where you may behave as if your brain is in charge; as if change is impossible because "that's just how I am"; or as if you are defined by genetics, personal history, or upbringing.

Brain

- Note any recurring thoughts. Are they excessively negative, accusatory, shame-provoking, or fear-inducing?

- Do you notice a tendency to become more anxious when certain thoughts appear? Do you find yourself worrying about situations that are unlikely to happen or that are out of your control?

- Do you tend to think through your feelings in a calm manner (suggesting you can switch to frontal lobe involvement), or are you more likely to panic or ruminate on the worst-case scenario (suggesting a more automated limbic response)?

Spirit

- Notice if you feel disconnected from your purpose or God, and whether this disconnection contributes to any feelings of aimlessness or despair.

- Do you feel a potential for more abundance in your life if you engage your mind on a spiritual level? When you pray or meditate, does it cause an increase in hope and gratitude?

Body

- As you scan your body, notice the sensations you experience and see them in your mind as if the scanner could see them.

- Document any physical symptoms you feel, like evidence of stress (tight muscles, racing heart, tightness in your chest, rapid breathing, sweating, etc.), and what you tend to be thinking about when you feel those things.

- Recognize when you feel the urge to go into "fight or flight," or if you're becoming more able to activate your parasympathetic nervous system to help you relax. This is where mind meets body. As you think and feel certain things, and gain control of those thoughts and feelings in your mind, you will become aware that your body will follow. Become comfortable and confident in your ability to think your way into improving how your body functions.

Document any imaging findings you see and use your breath to treat anything that feels uncomfortable. We will soon learn how to biopsy those thoughts and feelings that need attention.

9. **Scan for thoughts and feelings that reveal any struggles with relationships, addictions, or grief.** In addition to revealing the thoughts that are hurting you, the scan will help you recognize any attitudes, moods, sensations, or issues that may predispose you to having trouble with others (being easily offended that day, avoiding certain situations or people, etc.) or with your work. It will also reveal things that may leave you more vulnerable to resuming bad habits or abusing substances.

For example, when you take the time to run a Whole-System Scan, you may remember that tomorrow is the anniversary of a great loss you've suffered, and thus your emotions and thoughts may be fragile. This might put you in danger of not making good decisions or using numbing behaviors; but running the scan will remind you to be wary and help you stay on track.

10. **Be willing to accept whatever the scan shows without judging yourself.** It's an imaging finding, and you're going to take care of any issue it revealed. As you finish scanning each part of your body and mind, accept and let go of whatever you've noticed.

11. **Remind yourself that you can deliberately breathe tension out of your body.** Now, focus on your heart, and notice that as you control your breath you can lower your heart rate by choosing to do so, engaging the power of your mind to control your physiology. As you intentionally use your mind and breath to relax your muscles and calm your heart, you will gain confidence in the power of self–brain surgery.

12. **Spend a few more moments scanning your mental state.** Is anything else bothering you? What kind of mood are you in? Is there unresolved conflict or anger somewhere that you may be able to connect to the tension or discomfort you felt in your body? Think ahead to your upcoming day. Is there anything that you're anxious about? A meeting or encounter you will have with someone who is hard for you to be around?

13. **Consider experimenting with prayer.** Ask God to be with you as a guide as you explore your bodily sensations, pains, tension points, brain, and mind. Explore any ways in which you could change your perspective about the things you feel or are thinking about. Can God help you "re-story" some of the people or situations you're concerned about? Remember, the research shows that prayer and meditation enlarge your hippocampus over time, making your brain more emotionally resilient and less likely to become anxious.

Completing an Imaging Report

A good radiologist makes a thorough report of the imaging findings and suggests potential diagnoses and necessary follow-up. Be honest with yourself as you list what you identify from your scan and suggest possible reasons for what you are feeling. Examples include the following:

1. **Areas of cognitive overload:** Identify tendencies toward overthinking or excessive worry, linked to an overactive default mode network (DMN) or limbic system.

2. **Challenges to emotional regulation:** Evaluate difficulty managing emotions, possibly due to diminished prefrontal control.

3. **Physiological stress or pain:** Highlight signs of stress-related symptoms or chronic pain that may benefit from targeted interventions.

4. **Potential for growth:** Note strengths or opportunities to improve neuroplasticity and emotional resilience.

Soon you will learn specific procedures for treating the conditions you found. But the Whole-System Scan should become a daily, almost constant procedure you run to explore what you feel and make the correct diagnosis, which is the only way to get to the right treatment plan.

See page 287 for a template of the Whole-System Scan report you can use whenever you run this exercise. (The template includes a final section where you can list the specific self–brain surgery operations and other tools you use to address your situation.) You can add the findings to the objective portion of any SOAP note, augmenting your subjective thoughts and feelings with hard data from your imaging procedure.

If there are any complex thoughts or feelings you still need to understand or manage, it's time to take a more thorough look at them. We will need tissue to do that, so let's learn the Thought Biopsy next.

23

The Thought Biopsy

We are taking every thought captive.
2 CORINTHIANS 10:5, NASB

The Thought Biopsy is a targeted self–brain surgery procedure designed to help you analyze the complex or recurring thoughts and feelings you identified during the Whole-System Scan. Now that you've slowed down and zeroed in on the internal chatter and sensations that are making your life more difficult, the biopsy will allow you to assess the nature, origin, and impact of your thoughts, separating fact from feeling so you can follow up with constructive action. This procedure can be used as part of the basic self–brain surgery procedure; in recurring issues requiring multiple operations; and to address acute trauma and emergency situations such as panic and anxiety attacks. As with the Whole-System Scan, you'll want to perform the Thought Biopsy daily. Eventually it will become an automated, constant part of your life and practice.

Discerning the true nature of your thoughts and feelings and then responding appropriately are the goals of this operation, which can help you determine your treatment plan. Though it's called the Thought Biopsy, it will help you become a master investigator of your thoughts *and* feelings to discern what they are and where they're coming from—in other words, what script is running and what past event or situation your hippocampus is prompting you to remember. This will ensure that you make a rational and helpful response, feel more in control, and have a better outcome.

Psychiatrist Jeffrey Schwartz illustrated that intentional interruption of harmful (he called them maladaptive) thought patterns is a powerful way to leverage neuroplasticity to work on your own behalf. He coined the term *directed mental force* to describe the ability to use your mind to drive structural changes in the brain,[1] which is essentially the definition of self–brain surgery. This has been shown to increase the physical size of brain areas related to emotional resilience,[2] proving that self–brain surgery is not a metaphor but the mechanism of how we can get better at getting better through repeated intentional intervention on our own behalf. Psychologist John H. Flavell and his colleagues called this metacognition,[3] or as my friend, the writer and pastor Max Lucado, says, you should "think about what you think about."[4]

Centuries before the concept of neuroplasticity was first proposed and studied, the apostle Paul declared, "We demolish arguments and every pretension that sets itself up against the knowledge of God, and we take captive every thought to make it obedient to Christ" (2 Corinthians 10:5). Developing a discipline of investigating every thought empowers us to be in control of our emotional and cognitive lives rather than constantly reacting to them.

How to Perform the Thought Biopsy

Remember that you have over six thousand thoughts per day, and they are largely untrue and generally negative. Earlier we identified three different scripts that produce messages that come into your mind that may feel and sound like *your* thoughts. Thus, developing a discipline of critically examining your thoughts gives you a powerful method of spending time and energy only dealing with thoughts that are true and that require action.

As I described in chapter 21, when I perform a brain biopsy in the operating room, I send a tissue sample down the hall to the pathologist, who runs various tests to get to the correct diagnosis. And you can do something similar with your thoughts and feelings. The Thought Biopsy is a reliable method for you to biopsy and identify thoughts and feelings so that you can make a plan for responding in ways that help your life.

Resolve to never take action on a thought or feeling without questioning its validity first. Take comfort in knowing that the more often you practice the Thought Biopsy, the better you will get at it until it becomes automatic.

Resolve to never take action on a thought or feeling without questioning its validity first.

First, you'll need to identify the thought you wish to analyze; for example, *I'm never going to be good enough.*

Once you decide to biopsy a particular thought, run these tests on it:

Emotional Impact

Describe the feelings this thought provokes, such as shame, sadness, or hopelessness.

Cognitive Origin

The following steps will help you consider where that thought originated.

1. Reflect on the thought's source.

   - Does it stem from a specific past experience, belief, or fear?

   - Ask yourself, *When is the first time I remember thinking this thought?* Is it likely to be a brain-side, script #1 input (automatically negative, usually untrue, labeling, limiting, etc.)?

   - Does it feel more like an objective, mind-generated script #2 thought (*Maybe I could get better results if I put in a little more effort*) or even an input from God (*I will be with you and help you, even when you feel weak and ill-equipped*)?

   - Does it feel more accusatory or excessively tempting, such as script #3, enemy-generated thoughts (*You're terrible and will never amount to anything!* or *Go ahead and cut some corners! No one will know. You deserve to get ahead!*)?

2. Is the thought based on fact, assumption, or distortion? You might write down something like, "This thought comes from a childhood memory of being criticized for not achieving high grades."

Cognitive Distortions

Consider whether the recurring thought leads you to view the situation inaccurately because of any of these distortions:

1. Catastrophizing: *Everything's falling apart!*
2. Overgeneralization: *I failed at one thing, so I think I'm a failure at everything.*
3. All-or-nothing thinking: *If they don't love me, no one will ever love me.*
4. Personalization: *They didn't text me back. No one ever thinks about me and what I need.*
5. Psychic thinking/mind reading (believing you can know the future or read someone's mind): *This is never going to get better. My partner is incapable of changing.*

Three Thought Tests

Once you decide to biopsy a certain thought, continue to test it by asking the following three questions.[5]

1. **Is it true?** This seems so simple, but have you ever had to apologize to someone for reacting to something you thought they said or meant and then realizing you were mistaken? Have you ever fired off an angry text and then realized that what you were offended about wasn't even real? If so, you probably recognize that you would have been better off to first ask, "Is it true?"

2. **What if the thought or feeling is *not* true?** If the result of your biopsy shows that the thought or feeling is untrue, then tell yourself, *I am not giving any power or time to an untrue thought or feeling ever again.* You can immediately reject the thought, and soon you'll learn how to perform a transplant so you can choose to think a true one instead. Quickly filling your mind with truth is helpful. I use Scripture for this, so I can challenge untrue thoughts with true things God has said. When I feel worried about my future, for example, I remind myself of God's words in Jeremiah 29:11: "I know the plans I have for you . . . plans to give you hope and a future."

a. You can label the untrue thought like a pathologist labels a tissue sample, and learning to properly identify categories of untrue thoughts helps you automate that process and more quickly eradicate them.

b. Soon you will see the labels on thoughts before they even rise to the top of your consciousness, and they can be easily swatted away. You will begin to hear yourself say things like, "Here we go again. My brain wants me to feel like I'm not smart enough, but I don't have to think that way about myself."

c. Realizing that thoughts can be labeled and discarded is a powerful tool for self–brain surgeons because it builds confidence in the second and third commandments (feelings are not facts, and not every thought you think is true). The more aware you are that your brain frequently lies to you, the better you become at recognizing the false thoughts and feelings before reacting to them as if they were true.

3. **What if the thought or feeling *is* true?** Follow up by asking more questions of the thought:

   a. *Is this thought necessary for me to think about?* Some true thoughts relate to things outside your control. Recognize that you are not obligated to think about these things. You can decide to think about something else, pray about the situation instead of worrying about it, or make a note to address it at a more appropriate time.

   b. *Is this thought going to help me or someone else, or will my thinking about it make the situation any better?* If you realize that spending mental or emotional energy on that thought will not help anyone and will not improve the situation, it is not beneficial for you to think about.

   c. *Is this thought capable of harming me or someone else?* Let's say you have a thought like, *If I have a few drinks, I won't have to feel this pain right now.* When you biopsy it, you realize that this thought is true—if you drank, you definitely would turn off parts of your brain (and thus, the pain) and not have to emotionally deal with it. But because you are thinking about your thinking (using metacognition), you know that there is a penalty for using anesthesia on your emotional pain. You remember the sixth commandment and decide that you love tomorrow more than you hate how you feel right now. Instead of ruminating on how much a drink would reduce your current pain, you decide not to treat a bad feeling with a bad operation. Instead, you go for a walk and call a friend to talk through what you're feeling. The next day, you feel better because you're not paying the tomorrow tax, and you've made synapses that will help you remember more easily and more quickly that drinking doesn't solve problems for you.

Sometimes you have a true thought that is from script #2 thinking—a real thought that was generated in your mind or that is a nudge from God to think about a particular thing or person. Learning to use metacognition to interrogate why you're thinking about something or someone can prevent you from simply assuming that the thought is inconsequential. These are not automatic thoughts; they are assignments or even missions.

When a person pops into your head and your first thought is how much you dislike them, or that snappy thing you plan to say to them at work tomorrow, a self–brain surgery approach allows you to take a moment and think about why you're thinking about them. Pause for a second to pray that you could see that person through God's eyes and respond to them like he would.

As you reframe your thinking in this way, it allows space to interact with that person empathetically. As a result, you may learn that they are going through a difficult time, which explains why they've been behaving poorly toward you. Even if you never learn the real story, you have shifted your frame of mind from being angry to deciding to be kind and compassionate, or at least more discerning of how you spend your emotional energy.

At other times when a thought pops into your head, you know with crystal clear conviction, *This is something I'm supposed to do.* These thoughts inspire artists, authors, inventors, and engineers. They often convict you to do what's right.

They may wake you up in the middle of the night—for instance, you just know you're supposed to call the friend you had an argument with and apologize. Such thoughts may come from the conscience. Even if you are not a believer, you recognize that sometimes you just know something. That is script #2 thinking, and whether you conclude that the thought is inspired or just some kind of neuronal activity, recognizing and taking action on these true thoughts can change the world, your life, and your family.

Learning to biopsy your thinking helps you remember that you are not just your brain. You can decide to investigate a thought or feeling to determine if it is true, necessary, helpful, or possibly even a message from God that you need to respond to. You can learn to recognize untrue thoughts and transplant accurate and helpful ones in their place before you take action. As you get better at the Thought Biopsy, you will begin to more carefully wield the power you have to turn thoughts into real things in your life and the world. You will start to recognize that the things you believe to be true start out as thoughts, and that reacting as if every thought or feeling you have is true has harmed your life in numerous ways. And then, since you are a dedicated self-brain surgeon, you will remember and follow the first commandment: *I must relentlessly refuse to participate in my own demise.*

Master the Thought Biopsy and you will finally feel in control of the voice in your head. It is the foundational procedure of self-brain surgery and a necessary building block to every other operation you need to become healthier, feel better, and be happier.

Complete a Thought Biopsy Report

Keeping a journal of your recurring thoughts and how they appear when you examine them closely will help you begin to apply the correct labels to them. Just as time slowed down for Neo in *The Matrix*, the never-ending stream of thoughts in your head will seem to slow down, and you will recognize how often you hear automatic negative and untrue thoughts, which you previously accepted without question. You will now see how often you worry about true things you cannot control or have no business worrying about. You will conquer the process of taking your thoughts captive and feel the freedom of knowing that you are obligated only to respond to true thoughts that are necessary, helpful, or missional.

You can include this Thought Biopsy report in the assessment section of your SOAP note, as it provides a deeper understanding of the thoughts driving your emotions and behaviors. The insights gained here will help guide the next steps in your self–brain surgery plan. Going back over these reports can reveal huge progress in your life when you realize how far you've come in mastering your own mind.

24

Basic Self-Brain Surgery

Choices are real. You are free to make choices about how you focus your attention, and this affects how the chemicals, proteins, and wiring of your brain change and function.

DR. CAROLINE LEAF
Switch On Your Brain

Ann heard the beep, indicating that her call was going to voicemail *again*. "This is Olivia. Please leave a message."

She pushed the button to end the call, which felt like a digital representation of her life since she and her husband, Walt, had moved to Montana: shut off, unanswered, alone. *Why doesn't she ever answer my calls?* Before the move, Ann thought, she'd had a great life. Her best friend, Olivia, lived just across the street, and they met for coffee or a walk nearly every day to commiserate over life's frustrations and celebrate its joys. They'd even started a neighborhood book club that was still going strong. Along with her job managing her husband's medical practice, Ann had felt fulfilled and enjoyed her life. But then it happened: Walt landed a position as the medical director of a hospital in Missoula, and his dream of transitioning out of practice and into hospital management was coming true. The problem was, it wasn't Ann's dream.

Ann loved Dallas, and she loved Olivia and the other friends she'd made in the fifteen years they'd lived there. Now her days felt empty and small, particularly because it seemed that Walt was working all the time. To make it worse, they'd sold their home in Texas but hadn't yet found a new place. For now, they were in an apartment. Everything here felt like a step backward—she had no job, no friends, no house, no life. Their kids were grown and spread all over the country, and all of Ann's friends were sixteen hundred miles away. Ann fought back tears. *Olivia doesn't even have time to talk to me. Was she ever really my friend?*

Ann's chest felt as empty as the walls in the apartment, which she hadn't bothered to decorate since she wasn't sure how long she and Walt would live here. After placing her phone on the end table, Ann sat down on the sofa and sank into the cushions. She leaned her head back and felt her neck muscles tighten. An icy chill ran up her spine. *I don't have a purpose here. My life used to matter, and now I'm trapped in this frozen place, and Olivia and everyone else back home have already moved on.*

Her heart began to pump so hard that she could hear her pulse in her ears. *It's starting to happen again.* She felt like someone was beginning to squeeze her insides, and the pressure in her chest and head were mounting. *How can I feel completely paralyzed and ready to run away at the same time?*

She looked at her watch: 4:45 p.m. Something had to change, because the panic of being all alone in this place made her feel like she was losing her mind. Then the thought *It's five o'clock somewhere* popped into her head. She thought about the bottle of wine in the refrigerator. Maybe a glass or two would help calm her down. Walt had *another* board meeting tonight. She knew he wouldn't be home before she went to bed anyway, so what difference did it make?

Ann started to stand up and walk into the kitchen, but something stopped her. She remembered a podcast she'd heard the week before. Some ladies at the church they'd been visiting in Missoula had invited her to lunch a few weeks ago, and while they were nice, she hadn't felt a real connection. But one of them told her about a group she was in with several other empty-nest moms who were trying to redefine their lives. They'd been listening to and discussing a podcast about "self–brain surgery." Since then, Ann had listened to a few episodes and found it interesting.

Now she teetered between two choices: Open the wine bottle and tune out, or stay in the moment and try to work through her hurt. Lately, she'd gone with the wine more often than she wanted to admit to herself, let alone Walt. But on some level, she knew it wasn't *really* helping. It just seemed to push the problem off until tomorrow, with a bonus headache and cloudy thinking the next day to go along with still feeling so lonely that she wanted to scream.

She opened the podcast app on her phone and went to the show notes to recall how to scan her body and mind when she felt a panic attack coming on. She closed her eyes and tried to relax into the sofa, breathing in deeply and willing her racing heart to calm down. Soon she was locked into the rhythm of her breath, focusing on identifying what she felt in her body. *Tight neck muscles, clenched gut, tingling skin . . .* One by one, she directed her thoughts to breathe into those feelings until she could make them relax.

Once Ann felt the wave of panic begin to fade, she turned her attention to her thoughts. The podcast called it a Thought Biopsy, and she could appreciate the reference since Walt had often talked about biopsy results in the practice they used to run together. She identified the thought, *Olivia doesn't have time for me. She's moved on. Maybe she wasn't really my friend after all.* Rather than allow that thought to loop endlessly through her brain, she decided to try the biopsy procedure for herself.

Is this thought true? Ann opened her eyes and checked her recent calls and texts. Olivia had not answered three of her calls in the past four days, and she hadn't responded to a few of her texts. To her surprise, Ann noticed that she had not answered four calls Olivia had made to *her*. She'd also ignored several texts from Olivia. Ann was shocked. Olivia had made most of those calls and texts in the evening, and Ann realized that she hadn't answered because she'd already been in bed. One thing the wine had been good at was helping her fall asleep quickly.

The biopsy revealed a sobering truth to Ann: *Feelings are not facts.* Olivia *had* been trying to reconnect, so maybe Ann needed to change her mind. That's when she remembered the next step from the podcast—self-brain surgery. After you run a Whole-System Scan, gain control of how you feel inside and out, and biopsy whatever thought is bothering you, it's time to operate. Like Ann, you can use your mind to take charge of your brain.

Operating Instructions

It's time to learn the steps to the basic self-brain surgery operation, which can help with most anything we struggle with. This is an appropriate place to remind you that good surgeons recognize when they need to call for a consultant—whether because their patients need expertise they do not possess or their current approach is not working. So be sure to seek professional advice if you are struggling! These techniques are meant to guide how you approach the moment-to-moment interaction between your mind and brain, not replace the help and oversight of your physician or therapist.

In appendix A, you will learn multiple variations on this operation, and you can apply those to a variety of different situations. But all of the procedures follow the same basic plan, which we're going to learn now.

Types of Surgery

Self–brain surgery operations, just like the "real" brain surgeries I perform in the hospital, fall into two categories: general/elective and emergency/trauma.

General/elective. General and elective cases are for those times when a patient has a problem but it's not a life-and-death emergency. We have time to plan and discuss it, run diagnostics, seek second opinions, and schedule the surgery when it's convenient for the patient. In self–brain surgery, these procedures are targeted at everyday issues that can keep you stuck, frustrate you, or cause other nagging problems.

Emergency/trauma. Emergency and trauma procedures are used when the problem is so significant that the patient won't survive or could suffer permanent harm (such as nerve damage or stroke) if we fail to act quickly. Likewise, sometimes things happen that require immediate attention (like having an anxiety attack; being offended; feeling overwhelmed; or experiencing a traumatic event, acute grief, or loss). Certain self–brain surgeries will give you tools to attack these problems and clear your mind so you can function effectively in your life.

Emergency and traumatic situations *require that you have a plan in place* for what you will do *if* a crisis happens (like the panic attack that starts whenever your boss calls on you in a meeting, or the tsunami of outrage that threatens to overwhelm you whenever your spouse seems to belittle you). Remember, you don't rise to the occasion; you fall to your preparation.[1] My patients are often prescribed a course of prehab: therapies and medications designed to make them as strong and prepared as possible before surgery. Likewise, we all benefit from developing a good perspective on suffering before we're hit with a big life challenge. We'll then be less likely to get stuck on the question "Why?" and better positioned to ask, "How do I begin to move forward?" For believers, an important part of prehab is getting to know our gracious God and his good promises, which are found all throughout Scripture. Developing a good theology around suffering doesn't mean we won't hurt when trouble comes, but it will make it far easier to trust in God's goodness and presence even when we can't see him.[2] Having a planned response is a wise choice that will enable you to practice effectively on your own behalf no matter what happens.

Pre-Surgical Steps

Before deliberately beginning a self–brain surgery, how do you ensure that it will be effective? Let's review the essential steps to follow every time, whether you want to address something in everyday life or an urgent issue that must be handled immediately.

When your patient (you) has a problem:

1. Admit to yourself that something is hurting or bothering you, limiting your performance, or in some other way keeping you stuck.

2. Make the patient-to-doctor switch and remember that you have the tools and training to do something on your own behalf to make it better.

3. Take a thorough history and perform a good examination of the patient (you).

4. Perform appropriate testing (Whole-System Scans and Thought Biopsies) to make the diagnosis.

5. Document your findings and plan with a SOAP note:

    a. Chief complaint: State very clearly the reason you are here today for self–brain surgery. Use one word or a short sentence to bring the situation into clear focus.

    b. Subjective: Acknowledge the things you think and feel, and remember that thoughts and feelings are not always accurate.

    c. Objective: Identify things that *are* true—the data you collected from the Whole-System Scan and your Thought Biopsy—and view them from the perspective of a wise and compassionate physician who will tell you the truth and show you what needs to be done.

d. Assessment: Sum up where you are and what you've learned about the problem, and reconcile any gaps between the subjective points and the objective data you can trust.

e. Plan: Synthesize all the concerns and data into a workable plan to address the problem and make it better.

Treatment Plan

After detecting disordered thoughts and feelings, you can begin the disciplined process of self–brain surgery to remove and replace them with true and healthy ones, and direct your brain to automate more useful patterns in the future. Over time, your brain becomes more reliable at presenting true thoughts, automating useful responses to the events—real and imagined—in your life, and influencing positive epigenetic regulation of your gene expression so that future generations are better at handling stress. Through processes such as emotional contagion, limbic resonance, and the phenomenon of quantum entanglement, you can even improve the well-being of people around you.[3] (See "The Two-Patient Rule" on page 224 of chapter 26 and the list of suggested books in appendix E for more information.)

> The disciplined process of self–brain surgery will enable you to remove and replace disordered thoughts and feelings with true and healthy ones and to direct your brain to automate more useful patterns in the future.

When you perform a self–brain surgery operation to intentionally change a thought, challenge a feeling, or transform a brain habit, here are some of the cellular and molecular changes that will happen in your brain:

- *Purposeful decision and directed attention*: As you willfully direct your attention to a new thought or action, this directed mental focus produces activity in specific neuronal circuits, such as the prefrontal cortex (in charge of decision-making and executive functions) and hippocampus (responsible for emotional regulation, memory retrieval, etc.).[4]

- *Activate and repeat:* The neurons in these networks begin to fire together and send signals through synapses. As you keep running the new thought or behavior, synaptic plasticity is activated—the process in which new synapses between neurons strengthen or weaken based on demand, in accordance with Hebb's Law: "Neurons that fire together, wire together."[5]

- *Microtubules lay the tracks:* Microtubules are the structures inside your neurons that provide framing and guidance for axons and dendrites, guiding and helping them grow and strengthen connections in frequently used pathways. More frequent firing of a pathway promotes the release of neurotransmitters like dopamine, serotonin, and glutamate, which help deepen and reinforce new patterns by enhancing neuronal communication.[6]

- *Synapse formation and pruning:* Almost immediately (within a few hours to days), new synaptic connections begin to form in response to you directing your brain to change a thought or behavior.[7] The more you focus on the new thought, the more the connections stabilize; but it can take several weeks of repetition to form a connection deep enough to persist.[8] At the same time, old connections begin to be physically cut up and removed in a process called synaptic pruning. Literally, your brain destroys some old connections and uses the same materials to make new microtubules and synapses over time.[9]

- *Myelin coating:* Those old synaptic highways begin to fade, and you begin to add a structure called myelin to the new ones. Myelin is the coating on nerve cells that increases the efficiency of their firing.[10] It is important to note, however, that traces of the old patterns persist, just like the remnants of old highways or wagon trails are sometimes discovered by archaeologists after having been long overlooked. Those old highways can be reactivated if you slip back into old thought or behavior patterns. Remember, your brain basically does what you tell it to, so when you direct your attention and focus to something, almost immediately your brain will begin laying the tracks to make that thing easier to think about or feel.

Self–brain surgery, then, as we learned in the fifth commandment, is not a metaphor; it is the mechanism through which changing your mind changes your brain and your life.

With that understanding, when you choose to operate via self–brain surgery, you are doing exactly what I do in the operating room with my patients:

- We are choosing to make structural and intentional changes in our patient's brain
- for the purpose of improving the function of the organ
- to help our patient become healthier, feel better, or be happier, and sometimes to save their life.

This means that every self–brain surgery operation you perform has three objectives:

1. Identify a harmful, false, or unhelpful brain habit.

2. Sever the sick or unhelpful synapse that has been serving that brain habit's ability to keep presenting you with negative, harmful, unhelpful, or untrue thoughts or feelings.

3. Transplant a better thought, feeling, or response in place of the sick synapse, and then repeat it long enough for your transplant to "take" and to begin wiring into your brain (via repurposing microtubules, myelinating axons, forming new connections with dendrites, and improving the neurotransmitter environment around the new network) while the old network begins to fade.

That's the entire self–brain surgery process, no matter what specific issue you are dealing with. It works for thought problems (negativity, unforgiveness, lousy attitudes, self-esteem issues), unhelpful emotions/feelings (anxiety, chronic stress, fear, loneliness, sadness, depression), maladaptive trauma responses, chronic pain, performance issues (settling for less than you're capable of, being defined by limits, falling into bad habits, lacking motivation), and anything else that relates to how your thoughts and feelings can limit your ability to live the way you want or need to.

While we'll lay out the basic procedure in this chapter, note that there are other proven therapeutic approaches that allow the mind to take control of the brain. In appendix A, I outline specific procedures for a host of common issues, but every one of them can be handled through the following steps.

The Operation

1. **Choose your approach:** You must choose the approach that best suits the needs of the patient and the problem at hand. If you assume, *Nothing can help me*, that is likely to prove true since your attention and decisions impact the reality of your life. Otherwise, choose the approach with which you feel most comfortable, remembering that good surgeons change approaches when they need to make better progress. You might think, "Maybe *something* can help me" if you don't want to make an operation out of an issue and just want to "fix it." You can skip the neuroscience and scriptural information in each procedure and go directly to the instructions, but if the procedure does not seem to be working, remember that you can (and should) change approaches.

    "Maybe science can help me" will take you deep into the neuroscience behind each procedure—whether basic self–brain surgery or the targeted operations in appendix A—and you will begin to understand how your mind, brain, body, and life will benefit from it on a deeper level. Sometimes, though, even understanding the science of an operation will leave you with more questions and a deep sense that you're not experiencing the level of breakthrough you need. This may lead you to the "Maybe God can help me" approach, and there are Scriptures and guidance in each operation to help you find the answers you're looking for.

    Whatever approach you take, put yourself in a good position by practicing these procedures when you are rested, in a healthy frame of mind, and able to slow down and focus. Remember that anesthesia is not allowed in self–brain surgery: You have to feel it to heal it.

2. **Position the patient (yourself):** Knowing what to do and how to do it is not enough. You have to place the patient on the operating table in a way that will allow you to reach the problem safely and not cause other problems. If I need to operate on your frontal lobe, I can't get there if I position you on your belly.

    Trying to make good decisions about your thinking will not succeed if you are inebriated or overly tired. Some self–brain surgeries cannot be done in a noisy environment, while you're driving, or while you're in the early stages of grief or trauma. Safe positioning means that you apply the right operation at the right time and that you are situated mentally, physically, and emotionally for success.

3. **Perform a time-out:** My surgical team and I pause before each operation to state the patient's identifying information, the reason we are there, and what our intended goals are for the case. It is our last safety check before we pick up the scalpel.

    Here's an example of a good time-out for self–brain surgery: "I am here because I am feeling anxious. I am tired of my brain making me feel this way so often, and I know that feelings are not facts. I have the tools and training to make it better, so I am going to perform this operation with the goal of taking charge of my feelings by allowing them to inform me rather than instruct me."

4. **Perform a proper exposure:** As we learned in chapter 9, a good operation is only as good as the exposure. You cannot fix a disc herniation without making an incision that will properly expose it. In the same way, with self–brain surgery you must clearly lay out the problem (especially to yourself) if you want to make it better. You have to name it to know it, and you have to feel it to heal it. You cannot expect to manage something you are not willing to fully acknowledge and expose, even to yourself. Be willing to call it out and confess it (at least to yourself and to God, if not to others) so that you are also willing and committed to dealing with it completely.

5. **Perform the appropriate self–brain surgery operation:** Once you've performed a Thought Biopsy and identified a harmful brain habit, thought pattern, unreasonable fear, shaming/labeling voice, etc., then you must take the mental scalpel and sever the sick synapse. Visualize yourself cutting the neuronal connection between the thought/feeling/memory/trauma response you've always had and your typical reaction to it—the reaction your brain and body are telling you that you "have to" take. You have chosen to cut the link between stimulus and response, and now you are ready for the transplant.

6. **Visualize yourself choosing a donor organ to put into your patient:** You would not choose to give your patient a new lung that is full of cancer or a new kidney that is wrecked with disease. As a compassionate physician, you would choose the healthiest organ you could find to give your patient the best quality of life possible. In the same way, you will want to choose the healthiest and best thought, feeling, or response you can find to transplant in for the severed synapse.

7. **Complete a careful closure:** After my team and I complete a procedure in the OR, we are very careful to close the wounds in a way that will minimize scar formation, heal beautifully, and cause the least amount of pain possible. In self-brain surgery, we can sometimes get stuck in the OR, overfocusing on our problems and never getting back to living our lives; or we might abort procedures without truly addressing the reasons we were there in the first place. But if we want the best outcome, we will finish the operation and learn to put ourselves back together again so that we can heal.

Be kind to yourself postoperatively, reinforcing the new positive changes you told your brain to make and being careful to give the new transplant the best possible environment in which to grow, strengthen, and become part of your life going forward. After I perform surgery on patients in my practice, I always have them work with a team of physical and occupational therapists for a few weeks. This postoperative therapy is critical to help a patient recover from surgery, since it is easy for someone to reinjure themselves if they try to heal alone without a good plan. The rehab team, along with the patient's family or caregivers, become a vital community of supporters for my patient so they can step back into their lives as fully as possible.[11]

Every surgery leaves scars, but we can learn to see those as evidence of our movement toward wellness rather than as ongoing wounds. Remember that we do not go to surgery just to look at the problem; we are there to take decisive action to make it better. But once we've done that, we need to close the case and get on with life. And we all need to rehab ourselves—continually working on reinforcing healthy thought patterns, developing better brain habits, and leaning on our community of people who want to help us flourish.

That is the basic self–brain surgery operation, and it will radically transform your life. You can, like kidney transplant patients, get off the daily dialysis of dealing with the stream of negative thoughts, bad brain habits, and other issues that have kept you sad, sick, stressed, stuck, or settling in your life.

When Ann worked through these steps, she realized that she'd been using alcohol to numb the pain of loneliness. She also identified the thoughts that had been robbing her of contentment and peace. She'd been displaced from her home and was in an unfamiliar place. She had less time with Walt, and she'd lost the purpose she'd gotten from helping run their business together. She felt adrift and did not know what her life was about anymore. To make it worse, she was losing touch with her best friend.

She decided to call Olivia and was surprised to hear her pick up.

"Hey, Ann, I'm so glad you called." Ann could hear pain in the soft sound of Olivia's voice.

"You don't sound good," Ann said.

Olivia sighed and said, "I haven't taken your calls for a few days because it seemed like you were ignoring mine. I thought maybe you'd made some new friends in Montana and didn't need me anymore. I was just sitting here missing you, and when you called it made me so happy but embarrassed at the same time. I'm sorry!"

They spent the next half hour catching up and agreed to keep in touch every day. Ann realized after the call that she'd been telling herself a story that had never been true. Her brain and body had been living in that false story, and she had been using alcohol to anesthetize herself against the pain of a wound that was entirely self-inflicted. She didn't have the *same* purpose she had before, but she still had *a purpose*: She was here to support Walt in his new career, to support her friend Olivia, and to make a difference in her new community. She just had to take her thoughts captive and manage her mind to see things from a different perspective. And now she had Olivia as part of her rehab community to help her keep her thought life healthier going forward.

She looked around the room and had another thought: *I need to do something about these empty walls.*

What worked for Ann will work for you now that you know how to operate to become healthier, feel better, and be happier.

Writing the Operative Report

As you know, I advocate good recordkeeping as a way to track both your problems and progress. In fact, by keeping a record of the procedures you perform, you are documenting progress as surgeons do. The operative report—op report for short—is an instrument you can use to track the following details:

Diagnosis: The problem identified from your Whole-System Scan or Thought Biopsy that requires treatment. For example, Ann might write, "I feel lonely and isolated."

Procedure: The specific self–brain surgery procedure used, including details about how you applied it. Ann might record, "After acknowledging my loneliness and challenging the false belief that Olivia had forgotten me, I positioned myself for connection by reaching out to her, and now we text or call each other at least several times a week."

Outcome: Improvements in your mood, thought patterns, relationships, and other aspects of your life as a result of this procedure. Ann might summarize, "I feel reconnected to Olivia, which has made me more interested and confident in reaching out to women in my church and neighborhood so I can build new friendships. I'm no longer tempted to numb myself in the evenings."

Use the op report template on page 289 to keep track of your own progress.

You're now ready to incorporate the technical skills you've learned into "The Practice" so you can continue to learn and grow as you overcome whatever challenges arise in your life. You'll be able to devise your own operations, using the guiding principles of the ten commandments of self–brain surgery. Over time your approach and method will become your own, just as I practice a bit differently from the professors who taught me so well.

Our time in "The Operating Room" concludes with you graduating from training. I will leave you with a few thoughts on how to prepare to practice, and then you will complete your board examination to become a full-fledged self–brain surgeon.

25
Completing the Training Program

Dwelling on negativity won't suddenly have positive results. It only brings more negativity into your head. You can't buy happiness with the currency of unhappiness.

JAMES ALTUCHER
Choose Yourself!

Congratulations, my friend. You've done it! You've reached the end of your training, and it's nearly time to enter "The Practice."

When I finished my residency, Dr. Maroon and the other attending neurosurgeons hosted a fancy dinner in Pittsburgh to celebrate the completion of my training. I was honored as, one after the other, my professors and fellow residents got up to congratulate me, gently roast me, tell stories of my time there, and encourage me that I was ready to practice on my own.

I thought it was interesting that the same professors who had been giving me a hard time for six years—seemingly criticizing my every decision, critiquing my techniques, questioning my diagnoses, and generally busting my chops every day—stood there and complimented me. To a person, they said some version of, "Lee is the best surgeon I've ever trained."

I was smart enough, however, to remember that I'd heard them say the exact same things to prior chief residents at every year's graduation party. It's been over twenty years now, and whenever I ask my patients about any neurosurgeries they've had, they always tell me that their neurosurgeon was said to be "the best one in America."

Perhaps I was just raised to be humble, or perhaps I had enough small-town imposter syndrome in me to never let the praise go to my head, but hearing patient after patient echo what my professors said to every one of us at graduation allowed me to connect the dots and see the game that was being played. *Neurosurgeons need to believe they are the best, or they have no business opening up your head.*

If your surgeon believes that another neurosurgeon across town is better than they are, then you definitely would want them to refer you to the other surgeon, right?

Graduation

As you graduate from training and head out into practice for yourself, remember: No one in the world can be better than you at managing your mind. That is true, because *literally no one else can perform self–brain surgery for you.*

We tell every graduate they're the best so we can give them the audacity needed to perform life-and-death brain surgery. It's a psychological trick to boost their self-esteem.

In your case, it's true. No one else can do this job for you.

It's up to you.

The good news? You're well trained and entirely capable, and the system is built to respond to your direction. You've learned to take every thought captive, to challenge your automatic negative beliefs, and to use the tools of self–brain surgery to reorder your mind and rewire your brain. Now it's time to put everything together.

> No one in the world can be better than you at managing your mind.

As you move into the "The Practice," the final part of the book, you will be able to catch yourself when negativity creeps in, use the skills you've learned to rewrite the story, and choose hope even when life feels overwhelming. But before you step fully into practicing self–brain surgery, there's one last challenge: It's time for your board examination.

Taking Your Board Exam

Neurosurgeons take two final tests before they're allowed to call themselves board-certified by the American Board of Neurological Surgery. Before graduating from residency, they must pass a written exam, which has been called the hardest examination in the English language. And then, after they have been in practice for a minimum of four years, they appear in person before a panel of their peers and undergo an oral examination.

In the oral exam I took, we were questioned about real cases. Could we evaluate scans and hear patient stories, know what questions to ask, and make the right diagnosis? Were we able to suggest an appropriate treatment plan (whether surgery or something else)? Could we defend our choice and anticipate potential complications?

The oral examination is brutal, uncomfortable, and somewhat traumatizing. I know multiple excellent surgeons who failed it once or twice before finally passing. I had to take my orals a month before I deployed to the Iraq War, and it was definitely the most stressful time of my life up to that point. Thankfully, I passed, so that was not hanging over my head while I was at war. I had a colleague in Iraq who was scheduled to take his oral examination one week *after* he got home from the war.

Fortunately, *your* board examination is much simpler, but no less important. It's designed to help you evaluate your readiness and reflect on the key principles you've learned. And unlike my oral exams, there's no pressure—you score yourself, and you have unlimited chances to pass. Even if you do not pass, all you have to do is go back and read the relevant sections again until you are ready to begin your practice.

These five questions are your opportunity to pause and consider everything you've learned. They're a chance to remind yourself why this matters—and to embrace the transformation you're stepping into. This is more than a test; it's a commitment to yourself. By answering these questions, you're declaring that you're ready to take charge of your mind and step boldly into the life you want to create.

Here is your board examination:

1. Do you believe that you are not just your brain and that your mind is in charge?

2. Do you believe that you're not stuck with the brain you have—and that your mind is constantly reshaping your brain with every thought you choose?

3. Do you believe that changing your approach when something isn't working is a sign of strength, growth, and wisdom—not weakness or failure?

4. Do you believe that following the ten commandments of self–brain surgery will help you become healthier, feel better, and be happier?

5. Do you believe that you cannot change your life until you change your mind?

If you answered yes to all five questions, then congratulations—you're ready for "The Practice." Now it's time to take everything you've learned and put it to work. Remember, you have the tools, the training, and the support you need. It's your time to create the life you've always imagined. Let's get after it!

PART 5

The Practice

We are not controlled by events or people, but by our perceptions of them.

DANIEL G. AMEN
Change Your Brain Every Day

26
Rewiring for Radical Transformation

The practice is not the means to the output, the practice is the output, because the practice is all we can control.

SETH GODIN
The Practice

The little boy was dying, and it was up to me to save him.

My very first day as an attending neurosurgeon, I checked into the neurosurgery clinic at Wilford Hall Medical Center in San Antonio, Texas, then the Air Force's largest hospital. I walked up to the colonel in charge and introduced myself. He told me that he'd been waiting all summer for me to arrive and that he was going on vacation. He handed me the beeper—we still carried beepers back then—and left the hospital.

I was alone and in charge, and I didn't even know where the operating room was.

Five minutes after the colonel left, the beeper went off.

The call was from the emergency department, informing me about a three-year-old patient in a coma. I asked our unit secretary how to get there, and I ran to see the boy. The brain scan showed that he had a large tumor in the cerebellum—the back part of his brain—that was causing massive swelling and hydrocephalus, a buildup of cerebrospinal fluid. When I examined him, he was completely unresponsive, and both of his pupils were extremely dilated. He was actively dying and had maybe an hour left.

To add more pressure to the situation, both of the boy's parents were medical professionals who worked in the hospital, so they understood exactly how sick their son was.

I told them, "He has to have surgery right now, or he's not going to survive."

His mother said, "Are you a pediatric neurosurgeon?"

"No," I said, "but I've done this before, and he doesn't have time for us to fly him to a children's hospital. We've got to operate now."

The boy's parents looked at each other and nodded. The dad said, "Go, Doc. Save our son."

On the elevator ride to the operating room, I had a serious internal panic attack. My first operation as a practicing neurosurgeon was not going to be a simple elective spine surgery but an absolute emergency brain procedure on a little boy. Every possible anxious thought and feeling flooded into my mind at the same time:

You're not a pediatric specialist.
You have never operated in this hospital before. What if they don't have everything you need?
He may already have permanent brain damage; you might not make a difference for him at all, or it might be too late already, and you'll get blamed for his death even though it's inevitable.
You're not good enough to do this alone.

That's when I remembered my cell phone.

I took a picture of the boy's scan and sent a text message to my mentor in pediatric neurosurgery in Pittsburgh. Here's how the conversation went:

(me) John, this is a three-year-old with a big cerebellar mass, hydrocephalus, coma. I'm alone here and I'm not sure what to do.

(John) Remember your training, Lee. See the case in your mind. What's going to happen first when you open?

(me) The brain is going to swell out at me.

(John) Yes, so what do you need to do first?

(me) Have the anesthesiologist hyperventilate him. Give him steroids and mannitol to reduce swelling while I'm positioning and opening him and have a drain ready to remove fluid and depressurize the brain quickly.

(John) Right. Once the brain is soft, take a breath and slow down. You know how to remove cerebellar tumors; I've seen you do it well dozens of times before. Don't let the setting or the intensity of the situation make you forget what you know. You can do this.

Minutes later, I stood over the boy in the operating room. I thought through John's guidance and pictured everything I expected to encounter. Then I took a deep breath and asked the scrub tech for the scalpel.

I hesitated for a moment as the weight of the situation started to build. Just then, Dr. Jannetta's voice popped into my head: *Don't make an operation out of it, Lee.*

The case actually turned out to be very routine. Everything played out just as John said: The brain swelled out, which I handled by placing a drain to remove excess cerebrospinal fluid. The tumor was easy to separate from the boy's normal brain tissue, and I sent it to the pathologist, who called into the room as I was closing the case to tell me there was no cancer. The tumor was a benign growth called pilocytic astrocytoma, which is curable with surgery.

Postoperatively, the boy's pupils were back to normal size. Within a few days, he began to wake up, and he eventually made a full recovery.

I texted John with an update.

(me) The boy is doing great. Thanks for your help!

(John) I just reminded you of some things you already knew. Good job.

I think about that first case often, especially whenever I'm faced with a patient who has a scary problem I haven't encountered before. When in the Iraqi tent hospital seeing wartime trauma that was far more devastating than what I'd encountered in civilian hospitals, my brain would tell me, *You don't know what to do.* I would respond by mentally replaying the conversation with John, envisioning what I was likely to encounter in the coming operation and reorienting my mind to the true things I could control.

I've learned the power of reaching out to steady myself with something true—a quick call to an old professor, a review of evidence-based best practices or my own case logs, a breath prayer to regain control of my physiology and steady my hands. I overcome overwhelm with action as I remember that I am a well-trained surgeon who can do something about the problem on behalf of my patient.

Then I stop contemplating and start operating.

Your First Case as a Self-Brain Surgeon

There is a comfort to the training environment.

You develop a routine of seeing patients, rounding with professors, and operating with ever-increasing levels of participation and responsibility. Every day for years, you develop skills, add knowledge, and gain the trust of those in charge of shaping you into a competent and safe surgeon capable of practicing independently. The rhythm of taking a risk—speaking up when the chief resident asks a question or venturing to make a diagnosis or deciding to take someone to surgery for the first time—becomes more comfortable as you relax into its design: *This place was created to shape me for success; I'm safe here.*

But with the comfort and safety of routine also comes a slowly building pressure, the tension of knowing that every day in the training program is bringing you one day closer to its end. I knew that there was a day coming, after the speeches and the applause had faded and the ink had dried on the diploma, that I would walk out the door for the last time as a fully trained surgeon.

Then the rhythm and routine of training would be gone. No one would be asking me questions in a controlled environment anymore. Yes, there would be patients whose problems needed diagnosing and whose tumors needed removing and whose bleeding had to be stopped. But no one would automatically be there to say, "Are you sure about that?" when I was deciding whether to operate or to treat something more conservatively.

Building the Practice

Some situations took me by surprise. Not long after my residency ended, I was discussing a potential surgery with a patient who asked me a very simple question: "How long after surgery will I be in pain?" I was dumbfounded, because I realized that in the entire time I'd been a resident, I'd never seen a patient in the office *after they'd had surgery*. Our program was essentially all done in the hospital, where we performed operations and took care of folks until they went home. But after surgery they came back to see the attending professors, so the residents never saw them again. Now that I was in practice, the professors were not there, and the patients were *my* patients.

It took me some time to learn the art of postoperative care—how to advise people about safely returning to work and other activities and what to expect after the procedure—not just what the books said, but what happened after *I performed that operation on a particular person*. I figured out quickly that you become skilled and comfortable in practice only by actually practicing.

> **The only way to become skilled and comfortable in self-brain surgery is to actually practice it.**

Eventually every neurosurgeon must learn to manage their patients and their practice independently. This does not mean that we have all the answers or never need outside help. It means that we develop the skills to manage our practices and make good decisions for our patients. Sometimes those decisions look like involving a consultant, referring a patient to another surgeon with different skills, or transferring a patient to a hospital with greater resources.

The mark of a skilled surgeon is that they know what they know, they know what they do not know, and they have a firm grasp on their capabilities and weaknesses. They are humble enough to ask for help when needed, they are laser focused on their patients' needs, and they are committed to the training and principles they have learned and accepted as the standard of care for their practice.

And the same is true for self-brain surgeons, my friend.

Facing the Unexpected

The first few times you perform self-brain surgery, the setting or the intensity of the situation will try to make you forget what you know. And as life inevitably brings you situations you haven't previously seen—traumas, dramas, tragedies, and massive things that feel so overwhelming—your brain and body will initially react in the ways you've consented them to automate so many times before.

You'll feel panic or uncertainty when faced with an overwhelming thought, a painful emotion, or a trigger from your past. Doubts will flood your mind:

I don't know how to handle this.
What if I mess it up?
What if it's already too late to change this part of my life?
This is just who I am. Why should I try to change now?
Maybe I'm not strong enough.

But here's the truth: You're ready.

You are well trained, equipped with everything you need, and mentally prepared for what's going to happen when you start operating. Equally important is that you now know what will happen if you *don't* operate: Things will stay the same or get worse because the default process is also a type of self–brain surgery. And you've learned that default leads to decline and that choosing not to change is choosing to stay the same.

So when you're scared or your brain feels like it is swelling out at you with its relentless presentation of racing thoughts, powerful emotions, or painful memories, remember your training. You committed to change when you chose training over staying sad, sick, stressed, and stuck. Reach out to steady yourself with something true as you decide to exert the mind-down control you've learned to trust. Recall the ten commandments of self–brain surgery, and *you will overcome overwhelm with action*. No matter what you've gone through and what unhelpful responses you've developed, your brain will respond when you direct it to develop and automate healthier responses.

Your brain wants to help you break limiting habits, unlearn maladaptive reactions, and become healthier, feel better, and be happier. And it will do so when you start practicing every day and improve at what you are doing. The questions you ask yourself will surprise you at first, as many of my patients' questions surprised me: "How long will it be before I start to feel better?" "When will I finally overcome this habit?" "Will my grief really lessen over time?"

But as surprising as the questions were, my immersion in self–brain surgery *had* given me the tools to discover the answers. I followed a daily discipline of using my training, adhering to the standard of care, and applying the techniques and approaches I'd learned. Then I slowly started to see it: My brain rewired over time so that hard things became easier, uncertainties became settled knowledge, and fears became confident assurances that I knew what I was doing and had the tools I needed to do it successfully.

And you will experience this too.

As you practice, your brain will rewire over time (via neuroplasticity) so that "getting better" will become the default. You will automatically biopsy thoughts and feelings and spend less time reacting to them before examining and transplanting them when needed. You will recognize when you need a consultant—whether a therapist, this book, or guidance from God—to help you with a challenging case or issue that you're facing.

Getting Up to Speed

When I first began to practice, things came at me fast.

In training, there was always someone around with more experience than me, reminding me that, yes, removing that tumor might be a good idea, but had I noticed that the patient had so many other medical problems that they would never survive surgery? On my own, the information I needed to make a good decision for my patient felt hopelessly jumbled in a sea of details: things that could be checked, tests that could be ordered, rules I was supposed to follow, and a nagging sense that I hadn't even considered some other important factors.

Every time I saw a patient, I had to remember to check the labs, read the scans, obtain the patient's consent, book the surgery, file the insurance paperwork, and then, well, *actually perform the operation*. It felt overwhelming—learning to process everything I needed to know, make all the decisions, notice crucial things, and still have enough confidence to perform well in the operating room.

This was because, in those early days, I did not yet have a firm paradigm for deciding what I was going to think about when I needed to think about it. Once I understood what information was mission-critical to safely care for my patients—and then developed a system for tracking and processing that—my practice became easier. I made checklists to remind myself of the order in which I obtained information, how I valued the quality of that information, and the steps I took to decide what needed to be done and how to do it safely. I first put those lists on paper, but over time they became a part of the flow of information in my mind, and I experienced a *Matrix*-like vision of things slowing down so I could see the whole picture at once, make good decisions, and feel less stressed and worried about missing something.

As Iain McGilchrist points out, "Things change according to the stance we adopt towards them, the type of attention we pay to them, the disposition we hold in relation to them."[1] In other words, what you choose to notice and how you relate to it changes everything. Once I'd developed a paradigm that guided me and kept me focused in the office and operating room, my ability to care for patients was transformed. The same principle can revolutionize how you care for your own mind.

Remember the story of the surgeons who came to observe Dr. Fukushima perform surgery? They had been trained to operate from a particular bias and set of procedures, but they learned that other doctors were achieving better outcomes by changing their practice. They boarded planes and flew from all over the world because they wanted something better for their patients.

The same is true for you.

You've spent your entire life processing your thoughts, emotions, and reactions to daily events according to a worldview that was imprinted on you by your genetics, upbringing, and circumstances. You may have believed that *This is just how I am*, or *This is how we do things around here*. You may have even thought, like the young professor who told me there was only one correct way to clip an aneurysm, that it would be impossible for you to think, feel, believe, or perform differently, despite having seen other people live a version of life that felt more abundant than yours.

But something wasn't working for you. You picked up this book and started training in self-brain surgery. Now you're ready to practice on your own. You are armed with a vast amount of knowledge and understanding of how to make the patient-to-doctor switch and manage your mind, brain, body, and life. I do need to warn you: In your practice, things come at you fast.

- You know that thoughts are not always true and that feelings are not always facts, but you will still hear all those thoughts that sound like you and feel all those feelings that feel so true.

- You know that you can perform different operations to change your brain and get it to automate more helpful behaviors, but you will still often find yourself engaging in old reactions and habits before you even realize it.

- You know that other people do not have the power or ability to break or change you unless you give mental consent to internalize their actions and program your reactions, but you will still feel like they "made" you feel or behave the way you did because of something they said or did.

These things will frighten and frustrate you unless you remember that the only way you get good at practicing is by actually practicing. Also remember that change—even when it's positive—is often scarier than the comfort and familiarity of staying the same. Your default mode will keep trying to play its familiar scripts, inviting you to slip back into the smallness, sameness, and perceived safety of your old life. But you will challenge these scripts by remembering that the risks of accepting the practice are so much better than the long failure of staying put.

You Don't Go It Alone

Perhaps the most helpful insight I had when I moved from training to practice was that I could still call my old professors for advice. In my first few years out of residency, I would call them or share images with them, tell them my ideas and plans, and seek confirmation that my thinking was clear (or get alternative ideas when needed).

In the same way, remember that you're never practicing alone. You have this book, which you can reference any time you need it. If you're open to the "Maybe God can help me" approach, you can use prayer and meditation to seek God's guidance in your decision-making and performance.

Equipped with the tools and training you've received, you can begin to make checklists and strategies to prepare for the battles ahead. You can remind yourself that under stress, you won't rise to the level of your ideal intentions but will fall to the level of your preparation.

Like a quarterback calling the play before the snap, you can decide in advance how you will respond when the pressure comes. For example, you replace self-doubt with gratitude, reframe failures as opportunities to grow, and focus on what matters most: the mission-critical thoughts that align with your goals, values, and purpose.

You recognize that the mental noise of past failures, limiting stories, and old traumas will always try to intrude. But now, you know better. You've trained for this, and you have help when you need it—from this book, from your faith, and from the people who care about you.

The truth is, when you learn to take control of your mind, you have the potential to change others' lives as well. We're all patients *and* self–brain surgeons, but because of the knowledge and experience you're acquiring, you can positively affect others with every mental action you take. Let me show you how.

Self-Brain Surgery Never Stops with You

No one practices self–brain surgery in a vacuum. Every thought you choose to act on, and the way you use your mind to interface with your brain, affects the people around you. Every act of self-healing or self-harm ripples outward, altering the brains, bodies, and even futures of those around you—sometimes in ways you can't see.

That's where the two-patient rule comes in.

The Two-Patient Rule

Scripture teaches that our thoughts and actions really do affect others, either helping or harming them:

> *As iron sharpens iron,*
> *so one person sharpens another.*
> PROVERBS 27:17

> *A cheerful heart is good medicine,*
> *but a crushed spirit dries up the bones.*
> PROVERBS 17:22

And science backs this up, from the wiring of our emotions to the edges of quantum possibility.

Let's explore how the two-patient rule plays out in three sectors—the immediate, the distant, and the lasting—and consider what it means for your own self–brain surgery practice.

Some of these connections may seem strange, fringe, or too mysterious to believe.

But remember: Science advances by first noticing a phenomenon, then forming a hypothesis, and then testing it until it can be verified or refined. These insights reveal the wisdom of the two-patient rule, even if the science isn't fully worked out yet.

When you keep seeing the same patterns over and over, faith and science together can help you understand them—and use them to your advantage.

Thus, I give you the two-patient rule so that you can practice self–brain surgery with full awareness that it's never just about you.

Nonverbal and Local Effects—Wiring Minds Together

Your brain doesn't exist in isolation; it's built to connect.

When you shift your mindset—say, from despair to hope—your brain's plasticity kicks in, reshaping synapses. But that's just the start. Those changes leak out—through your face, voice, posture, and even the energy of your presence—and others feel it.

Limbic resonance: the syncing of minds. You've felt this before—the Debbie Downer effect. Someone walks into the room, and suddenly, the air feels heavy. This happens because the limbic system, which governs emotions like fear and joy, tunes into the emotional states of those around us.

Studies show that within milliseconds, we unconsciously mirror others' expressions via mirror neurons[2]—specialized brain cells that help us interpret and respond to social cues. If I steady my amygdala (the emotional part of my brain) by taking a deep breath before knocking on the examination room door, my patient and her family might feel less tense—without even knowing why.

Mirror neurons and limbic resonance likely also explain the phenomenon of emotional contagion. This is when we "catch" emotions from others—joy sparking joy, stress spreading like wildfire—as our brains mirror their expressions and our limbic systems sync up, diffusing feelings like a subtle vapor.[3]

Your mood and mindset operate on those around you.

Heart coherence: the electromagnetic influence of emotion. Research has shown that our hearts emit electromagnetic fields that influence others nearby, and studies have found that people sync heart rates when in close proximity—even in the next room.[4]

This effect is strongest when we are coherent—when we regulate our heart rate variability through mindfulness, gratitude, or prayer. I see this in the OR: When I calm myself by deep breathing to activate my vagal nerve and slow my heart rate, my surgical team moves more smoothly. My self-brain surgery broadcasts calm.

Hormones and chemical signaling. Even subtler signals affect us. A 2009 study showed that our stress pheromones, the chemical signals we release in sweat that others can subconsciously detect, can make the people around us anxious—even when they don't realize why.[5]

Likewise, optimism changes body chemistry in ways that others unconsciously detect—lifting their moods before a word is spoken. Unlike the Debbie Downer, the optimistic person always seems to brighten the room just by arriving. What's inside us spills out—for better or worse.

Nonlocal and Potential Effects—Beyond the Room

Could the two-patient rule stretch even farther—across miles or unseen dimensions? The science gets fuzzier here, but the hints are intriguing.

Quantum entanglement and prayer. In physics, quantum entanglement links two particles so a change in one instantly affects the other, no matter the distance between them.

Some speculate consciousness might work similarly. It's unproven but intriguing. The Global Consciousness Project uses a global network of random number generators, devices built to record sequences of random data. During events like 9/11 or mass prayers, they've shown unexpected deviations from randomness, hinting that shared attention might nudge physical systems. Interpretations differ, but it's worth pondering: Can focused intention ripple out?

Scripture says yes—interceding for others has potent results: "The prayer of a righteous person is powerful and effective" (James 5:16).

Could quantum entanglement hint at how God ties our prayers to others or prompts us to act for them? Science can't confirm it, but as a believer, I've seen "coincidences" that defy dismissal. For example, one day while driving to work, I felt a sudden urge to pray for a friend and then call him. He answered, "I was just praying someone would call. I'm in the ER with my daughter—it's bad. I'm alone and scared. Thanks for calling."

Lasting Effects—Echoes Across Time

The two-patient rule isn't just immediate or spatial—it's generational.

Epigenetics: inheriting more than DNA. Epigenetics reveals that stress, trauma, or healing can alter gene expression—and that these changes pass down through generations.

A 2010 mouse study found that stress altered methylation (a chemical tag that silences genes), making offspring more anxious—an effect that may last for multiple generations.[6] In humans, studies of Holocaust survivors reveal similar imprints: trauma-altered methylation in survivors and their children, with hints it may ripple to great-grandchildren.[7]

When I retrain my mind for resilience, I don't just change myself—I subtly reshape my children's epigenome. The good news, as you now know, is that they can use self–brain surgery to reverse those effects, assuming they have the knowledge and desire to do so.

A Call to Operate

I've treated patients facing brain cancer, trauma, or other devastating loss—and watched them emerge stronger. But what's more striking? Their families grew stronger too.

That's the two-patient rule in action.

So here's my challenge: Operate with intention. Wield every thought like a surgeon—not just for yourself, but for the second patient. For more on how to teach self–brain surgery to your children or grandchildren, see appendix C. If you're mentoring, counseling, or caring for other adults, appendix D will help you pass on what you've learned to them. Remember that when you practice self–brain surgery, you *will* impact other people—some of whom you may never even meet.

Jesus said, "Let your light shine before others" (Matthew 5:16)—your self–brain surgery is part of that light.

Make it shine brightly.

The Work of Radical Transformation

Your life is about to change dramatically. I'm not promising it will be easy. Transformation never is.

What is the first step? Start small. Identify one thought or habit you want to change. When it arises, pause, reflect, and apply what you've learned. "The Practice" begins today. You've done the work. Now, you are reordering your mind and reshaping your future.

It may be easy to slip back into old thought patterns, which are like ancient wagon tracks carved deep into the ground. Emotional reactions will resurface, and you may feel the tug of old coping mechanisms—the ones that numbed you, distracted you, or kept you stuck.

Not everyone around you will celebrate your transformation. Your friends and colleagues are used to how you work. They've grown comfortable with your style and the results you usually get, especially if theirs were better than yours. When you start making progress in your own life, someone else is inevitably going to think that your new approach is weird or scary, or that it threatens them in some way. As a result, some relationships may shift, and group dynamics may change as your patterns do. But here's the difference: You are now equipped to respond in ways that reflect your values, not your fears or past conditioning. And because the two-patient rule is always in effect, you may even motivate others to begin changing the way they think.

Transformation begins with awareness. When frustration or despair rises, pause, breathe, and biopsy your thoughts. Then it's about action—small, consistent steps that create change. Choose gratitude over grumbling, courage over fear, and hope over despair. Trust the process, the design of your brain and mind, and the power of self–brain surgery to create lasting change.

You see the truth now, so you are equipped to bring unproductive thinking—particularly the script #3 language that the enemy whispers to you—down to size.

When you do, your reaction might be like that of the ancient Israelites when they saw the powerful king of their enemy cast down. Now that the ruler who had once caused them so much suffering had been defeated, he no longer seemed invincible:

> *Everyone there will stare at you and ask,*
> *"Can this be the one who shook the earth*
>   *and made the kingdoms of the world tremble?"*
>
> ISAIAH 14:16, NLT

This passage captures the way you can view your disordered thinking once you've taken control of your mind and brain. The thoughts that once terrified you, the feelings that felt so consuming, the inner voice that was so negative, the reactions that seemed hardwired—they were never as powerful as they seemed. Now when those thoughts arise, you'll recognize them for what they are, shake your head, and think, *Really? I used to believe those had control over me?*

You're a fully equipped self-brain surgeon now. *You* decide what your thoughts, feelings, and experiences mean. You choose their weight and value, and you determine what to do about them. Your mind is in control, and you have tools, training, and guidance whenever you need them. As Jeffrey Schwartz and Sharon Begley write, "It is the life we lead that creates the brain we have."[8]

This is the beginning of your radically transformed life.

EPILOGUE

How Self-Brain Surgery Saved My Life

*You'll discover that you are a potent creator, and
that your thoughts lead to things.*

DAWSON CHURCH
Mind to Matter

"Leave the door open, please," my patient said as I walked into the exam room. I looked at the woman, who was sitting in a chair facing the door. Her arms were crossed and her shoulders slumped, and she was bouncing her left leg repeatedly.

"Of course," I said. "Is it hot in here? We can adjust the temperature if you'd like."

She shook her head and looked down at the floor. Quietly, she said, "No, I just get really nervous."

Sitting to her left was another woman, older, with a kind face. She stood and shook my hand. "I'm Caroline, Jennie's caseworker. She's living at our group home, a place for women who have been abused, incarcerated, or addicted. While they're with us, they learn new skills and get back on their feet. She's been through a lot, and she doesn't like closed spaces."

I sat on a stool and said, "Hi, Jennie. I'm Dr. Warren. Do you mind telling me why you're here to see me?"

She nodded slowly and finally looked up. Her eyes darted back to the open door as if to check whether it was still open, and she said, "He hurt my neck, and my arm is numb. I'm dropping things and . . ." Her voice trailed off and she started to cry. She looked back down at the floor and whispered to Caroline, "Will you tell him?"

Jennie reached out her left hand for Caroline to hold, and when Jennie extended her arm, I saw part of her story written in needle marks along her forearm. Caroline held Jennie's hand and spoke. "Five years ago, Jennie was assaulted by her boyfriend. She was four months pregnant at the time, and the trauma caused her to miscarry the baby. She's been mostly living on the streets since then, but recently she spent three months in the county jail for solicitation. She didn't have any other way to feed herself and her addiction. She came to our halfway house a month ago. She's trying to make progress in her life, but she's in a lot of pain and can't seem to hold anything with her right hand. Can you help her?"

The visit unfolded from there. I tried to examine Jennie, which took some time since she was so skittish that she could hardly let me touch her to check her neck and arm strength. She slowly warmed up to me and allowed me to test her hand and arm, which were both very weak. I noticed, along with the needle tracks, that she had lost some of the muscles in her hand to atrophy, a sign of long-standing nerve injury.

I showed Jennie her MRI scan, which revealed a large, ruptured disc in her neck that was pressing on her spinal cord.

"This is why your arm is weak," I said as I pointed at the screen. "You'll need surgery to fix it, and there's a good chance your strength will improve."

She stared at the scan for a few seconds and said, "Improve? Do you mean it might not be okay?"

"I mean that I can't guarantee it will get back to normal. You've lost a lot of muscle in your arm. Surgery will help with the pain, but it's been that way for five years since—"

Jennie cut me off, "Since the day he killed my baby. Since the day," her breath stuttered, and she paused for a beat. She looked back down at the floor and crossed her arms again, then continued, "Since the day he killed me too. I haven't been alive since then, and I never will be."

We concluded the office visit with Jennie agreeing to have surgery. She went down the hall with Caroline to meet with Lisa, who scheduled our surgeries. I went to see other patients. This was about six weeks after Mitch had died. Lisa and I had already been to San Antonio to meet Scarlett. Then we'd returned to work after my sleepless night, when the pastor's reading of Psalm 126:5-6 seemed to make an impossible promise. It was hard to believe then that, if we would be willing to plant the seeds of our work while we wept, someday we would harvest with joy as God grew a crop out of our faithful willingness to continue living life even though it hurt so badly.

A few days after returning to work, we'd gone to the research center in our office building to observe study participants in the functional MRI scanner and discovered that we can change our brains by changing our thoughts. That day was the beginning of my articulation of the ideas you've learned about in this book, and it was Lisa who tied that together with Philippians 4:6-8, which tells us that gratitude is the secret to overcoming anxiety. By then I realized that self-brain surgery was as mechanistic and real as the surgery I perform in the OR. But it was Jennie who showed me the consequences of continuing to live unaware that change is possible and available for all of us—including me in my broken, bereaved state and Jennie in hers. I wish I could tell you there is a happy ending to her story.

There isn't.

The day came for Jennie's surgery, and she was a no-show. We called the halfway house, and Caroline told us the bad news. Jennie had run away, gotten high, and overdosed. She hadn't survived.

In the following months, Jennie's death became the shadow that sharpened my resolve to teach others what she never had the chance to learn. I began to see my patients in a new light. I'd always cared about them, but now *I could feel with them*. It was different because I was different. In the first days and weeks after Mitch's death, I was a dead man walking, moving forward out of necessity to care for and comfort my family while not losing my business or dying of grief myself. But all these moments coalesced into something that started to make the shifting sands of sadness under my feet feel a little firmer.

I saw how Jennie's anguish—the physical pain from her injury and the emotional devastation from being abused and losing her child—consumed her to the point that her addiction had more pull than the hope of healing I offered her with surgery. That led me to examine myself, and I began a transformation that took years to fully realize. But it started with Jennie—broken and literally killed by the pain of loss and her attempts to stop feeling it—and the realization that her story could easily have become *my story* if I didn't carefully steward my life following Mitch's death. I wasn't an addict, but grief has a powerful way of taking over your life, and it can be just as deadly as heroin if you lose hope.

Over the next few years, I pondered and internalized those truths. I began to feel a burden to share the things we were learning. I began to write a weekly newsletter that is now read worldwide and books that told our story, which I'd mined for helpful lessons. That led to my podcast, now heard weekly in over one hundred fifty countries, where I tie neuroscience and faith together to help people see a path forward, whether something has hurt them or they're seeking a higher level of performance.

Then something surprising happened.

Lisa and I were having coffee and checking our emails together one morning a few years ago, and I received a devotional that I read every day. The devotional message was a lesson from Psalm 126: "Those who sow with tears will reap with songs of joy" (verse 5). The steam from my coffee warmed my face, but inside I felt something warmer that's hard to explain in words. An idea was dawning inside me, something that felt like new life being created as the overwhelming truth of that promise filled my mind. I said to Lisa, "It's really true!"

Lisa looked up from her iPad and said, "What's true, honey?"

"Like the psalmist said, when you plant seeds even when you're suffering, you'll later see the harvest and rejoice."

"Explain that," she said.

I almost couldn't believe it, how so much truth was dawning on me at once. "We couldn't imagine having the strength to go back to work after Mitch died, remember? The pastor gave a message on this same psalm, but its promise felt out of reach."

She nodded, "Of course. We cried all the time, even between patients during those first few weeks back."

"Yes. But today we're harvesting with joy. Look what's happened!" I started to cry then, the tears that come when you're remembering something hard that has a different flavor now. "We were so broken we didn't think we could even make it through the first day, but somehow we did. God kept giving us the strength. We never failed to make payroll. Our business, our other kids, and our marriage made it through. We're helping people all over the world by telling our story. And, somehow, even though it doesn't make sense because we're still so sad about losing Mitch, we're happy again. It's a different happy, but it's just as real."

Lisa thought for a moment, then took my hand. "You're right. It *is* a different happy, but it's deeper too. We've been through something impossible together, and we made it. It's amazing!"

Lisa and I have fought the good fight of survival, recovery, rekindling of faith, and restoration of hope, but we had to change our minds first. We had broken thoughts, and we believed for a time that life would always feel heavy and impossible. But because we learned the truth that thoughts become things and that we had the power, by God's good grace, to create different things in our lives by creating them in our minds first, we made it through, despite sowing with tears.

So my message to you as your training ends is this: It is worth it to change your mind, my friend. It is worth it to choose a thought that leads to flourishing over the one that triggers a well-worn but sick synapse that produces anxiety, numbing behaviors, and the repetition of troubles that begin as thoughts and end up as unwanted feelings or actions.

You are already practicing self–brain surgery, but now you have learned that you can make the patient-to-doctor switch and make the system work for you. I pray that you will practice this lifelong discipline to heal, help, and make whole the parts of you that came to this book looking for answers. I hope that this practice will lead to a higher level of satisfaction and flourishing in every area of your life, as well as in the lives of the other patient-surgeons around you and those who come behind you. It's not always easy, but you do not have to be afraid. You can overcome fear by training and practice, and you have an incredible gift: God did not give you a spirit of fear, but of power, of love, and of a sound mind.[1]

I'm so grateful for the time you have invested in this book and for the opportunity to have provided you with this training. Self–brain surgery saved my life. It saved Leonid Rogozov's life, and it can save or improve yours. So go: Practice, get better at getting better, and come back to these pages when you need a refresher course.

But never forget: You can't change your life until you change your mind.

And the good news is, you can start today.

APPENDIX A

Tactical Self-Brain Surgery Procedures for Specific Problems

The fifteen specific microsurgeries that follow are designed to help you manage many common challenges. You can come back to this section any time you're dealing with one of them, as part of your lifelong self–brain surgery practice. (For a review of how to perform the Whole-Body Scan, the Thought Biopsy, or the basic self–brain surgery operation, please refer to part 4, "The Operating Room.")

Note that, just as we learned in our discussion of the various approaches surgeons take to accomplish their operations, the procedures you will learn here are not the only ways to manage these various issues. If you try one of these operations and are still struggling with the issue, see a therapist or your doctor. (This is especially recommended if you are dealing with major depression or feel suicidal.) They will have other tools and techniques you can use to make progress. The important thing is that you keep trying to become healthier, feel better, and be happier. These operations can be part of your overall strategy to reach those goals, but don't forget to seek professional help if you need it.

You will notice some repetition of key ideas if you read straight through this section. That is because some operations for different problems have similar neuroscientific mechanisms, but I want the procedures to stand alone when you need to reference them for a specific issue. In each appendix, I point to the neuroscience and relevant Scriptures that illustrate why these microsurgeries are effective. Whether or not you share my faith, however, these operations will provide practical help as you seek to address specific pain points.

You can use the example progress notes and reports in appendix B to track your progress.

When You Feel Sad or Depressed

Procedure: Microsurgery for Your Mood

WHEN TO USE

- When your Whole-System Scan and Thought Biopsy have revealed that you're feeling down, emotionally sluggish, or somewhat sad

- When you feel depressed, but you can't really figure out why; when you feel a lack of joy or are somewhat numb

- When you can't seem to make yourself do things you want or need to do, leaving you more depressed when the list of things you haven't done gets longer

- When you have decided you need to perk up, but you haven't been able to

Important note: This operation will not be enough if you are struggling with major depression[1] or feeling suicidal. If this is your situation, seek professional help.

TIME-OUT

You have chosen your approach and have positioned yourself to get better, and now it's time to operate. Take a deep breath and pause to recognize and expose your current mood without judging yourself. Remember that feelings are not facts, but they *are* important signals that need to be addressed. You are here to perform self–brain surgery because those depressed feelings do not have the power to define you or your day's potential, and you are ready to change them.

GOALS AND BENEFITS

- To incrementally improve your mood and regain a sense of control by purposefully taking small, practical actions

- To experience a lighter emotional burden, clearer thinking, and increased resistance to the inertia of depression

- To gain confidence that you can reverse low mood without overwhelming yourself

- To be empowered to attack this day on your terms without your mood holding you back

RELEVANT NEUROSCIENCE

Tactical engagement in small, positive activities has been shown to stimulate increased dopamine and serotonin production, two neurotransmitters that are vital in regulating mood and motivation. When you focus on being grateful that you can use your mind to *choose* to feel better by engaging in small but intentional actions, you fire up your prefrontal cortex. This begins to reverse the effects of low mood by wiring in positive reward pathways, increasing your sense of well-being, and enhancing your mood.[2]

GUIDING SCRIPTURE

Those who sow with tears will reap with songs of joy. Those who go out weeping, carrying seed to sow, will return with songs of joy, carrying sheaves with them.

PSALM 126:5-6

This is such an important passage because it is a reminder of the blessings you receive when you push through a sad or depressed mood and *do something anyway*. Even though you didn't feel like it, you did what you needed to do and did not let your brain boss you around. This results in three primary blessings. The first is that your nervous system rewards you by rewiring your anterior cingulate cortex (involved in willpower and motivation) to make it easier for you to do something you do not feel like doing the next time.[3]

The second blessing is the dopamine and serotonin release you get from forcing yourself to take action when you do not feel like it. You feel proud of your accomplishment and begin wiring in the desire to be rewarded by doing it next time since you are *getting better at getting better*.

The final blessing comes after you've paid the bill, visited the doctor, made the phone call, or taken the other step you dreaded. That's because, at some point, you will be gifted with the stunning realization that *If I hadn't done that, this other thing would have happened that would have made me feel even worse!*

You will "reap with songs of joy" because you recognize that you overcame your feelings and were rewarded with feeling better, accomplishing more, and banishing the guilt you felt when you were avoiding doing what needed to be done.

TECHNIQUE

1. **Make the gratitude shift.** Write down three small things you're grateful for. (The act of writing engages your brain more deeply than just thinking about something.) This will force your hippocampus—which acts as a one-way

switch that determines where a thought or emotion will travel in your brain—to get your frontal lobes engaged and bring reason and rational decision-making to the situation. Your mood will also start to improve. Gratitude journaling has been shown to increase happiness and satisfaction over time.[4]

2. **Lead with actions, and feelings will follow.** Count down from five and then stand up, stretch, and take a brief walk around your house or office if you can. Do five standing squats or some other light physical activity, since even short bursts of movement stimulate endorphin and dopamine production, the chemicals that elevate your mood. You will feel better from moving even when you don't feel like moving, and the reason you don't feel like moving is mostly because you haven't been doing it.[5]

3. **Prioritize social connection.** When you're feeling depressed or sad, that's a signal that your neurochemistry is off, and you will likely feel a strong pull toward isolation and being alone. To overcome this feeling, you need to connect with other people. Even sending a text message to someone, just to say good morning or hello, has been shown to significantly improve mood.[6]

4. **Perform microsurgery to manage your mood.** Don't focus on the massive list of tasks you have been putting off because you did not feel like working on them. Doing so will reinforce your feeling of "stuckness" and worsen your mood, as you will start hearing those negative thoughts telling you it's never going to get better. Choose one small task and do it immediately. Make your bed, unload the dishwasher, pay that bill, send the text, take out the trash. You will immediately have a sense of accomplishment, and the momentum will begin to build in your mind as you realize that the job you've been putting off is not overwhelming after all. Such microwins start to stack, and before long you will be convinced that feeling better happens *only when* you take action, never from just waiting for your mood to improve.[7]

5. **Adjust your attitude.** Aggressively attack negative self-talk and labeling thoughts, knowing that *they arise from your negative mood rather than from reality*. When you hear your brain tell you, *You never get anything done, so you must be depressed*, you say to yourself, *No. I haven't been very productive lately, and that is making me feel depressed. I can change that with self-brain surgery.*

OP REPORT

Write down your feelings before and after you perform this microsurgery. After the operation, has your mood improved, even a little? Use this procedure anytime your feelings seem to be making you procrastinate or avoid other people or activities you need to do or usually enjoy. Track your progress over time.

When You Have a Chronic Illness

Procedure: The Persistent Problem Palliation

WHEN TO USE

When facing a chronic illness that doesn't go away and requires ongoing physical and emotional accommodations

TIME-OUT

In medicine, surgeries meant to alleviate symptoms without curing the underlying issue are called palliative operations. Similarly, when illness persists, we move from expecting a cure to embracing a perspective change. This shift acknowledges that while prayers for healing may feel unanswered, faith is not reliant on the outcome but rooted in ongoing trust in God's provision for what is ultimately best.

When you focus solely on the problem, you reinforce it in your brain's pathways, making it more entrenched. But you can choose a mindset that promotes peace and hope instead. Take a deep breath, accepting the reality of your condition without allowing it to define you. Exhale, releasing expectations of a quick fix, and turn your focus toward amplifying mental pathways that support wellness, joy, and purpose—even when your body is unwell.

Remember, you're not giving up on seeking healing or believing it's possible. Two things can be true simultaneously: You can grow stronger and more resilient through pain, and you can wire your brain and body to foster a positive, nurturing inner environment that may promote healing.

GOALS AND BENEFITS

- To nurture a mindset of peace, resilience, and purpose within the framework of chronic illness

- To reduce mental suffering, promote a greater sense of meaning, and increase the ability to adapt in a way that builds hope and inner strength, allowing you to flourish despite physical limitations

- To foster inner abundance and peace and enable you to hold on to hope, faith, and purpose even amid pain, fatigue, limitations, and unpredictability

RELEVANT NEUROSCIENCE

Chronic illness can shift the brain toward a limbic (threat-detection and stress) response, amplifying feelings of fatigue, worry, and low mood. Practicing acceptance and focusing on gratitude engage reward pathways in the brain, helping stabilize mood and enhance resilience.[8] Reducing stress and deepening frontal circuits focused on calm and reason also promote improved immune function, making healing more possible.[9]

GUIDING SCRIPTURE

Praise the LORD, my soul, ... who forgives all your sins and heals all your diseases.

PSALM 103:2-3

In this context, *diseases* can also mean "dis-ease," referring to the mental and emotional distress that accompanies illness. Even when physical healing isn't likely, God has designed a way for you to achieve inner peace and relief from psychological distress by strengthening neural pathways that help diminish dis-ease and grow stronger through adversity.

I have posted watchmen on your walls, Jerusalem; they will never be silent day or night. You who call on the LORD, give yourselves no rest, and give him no rest till he establishes Jerusalem and makes her the praise of the earth.

ISAIAH 62:6-7

Persistent prayer is an active, faith-driven response, even when the outcome remains unseen. Isaiah encourages us to pray even when there seems to be no answer or hope, reinforcing the switch from patient to active participant in self–brain surgery. By continually praying, you are not passively waiting for help but actively engaging in a process of seeking peace and healing in both body and soul.

TECHNIQUE

1. **Accept the current reality.** Begin each day with a time of prayer or meditation, accepting the presence of your illness while rejecting that it defines you. Say, "This problem is part of my experience, but it is not my whole story."
2. **Assess your limits.** Set mental and physical boundaries for managing chronic illness. Identify your energy limits, learn to work within them, and prioritize activities and relationships that nourish your spirit and promote flourishing.

3. **Record blessings and gratitude.** Journal even small things you're grateful for, or blessings you have despite (or even because of) your illness. This practice retrains your brain to focus on positive experiences, counteracting the focus on stress that chronic illness creates.

4. **Invert inertia.** When illness creates a sense of "gravity," weighing you down, turn the tables on it. Set small, achievable goals and make yourself accomplish one or two, even if you don't feel like it.[10] This releases endogenous opioids and positive neurotransmitters, giving you a sense of reward and reinforcing the fact that your illness doesn't control every moment.[11]

5. **Rehearse recovery.** When tempted to ruminate on losses or what you can't have because of your illness, counter by directing your brain toward the things that remain good in your life. Meditate on Scriptures like Psalm 23:4 and 2 Corinthians 12:9, and engage in spiritual practices that reinforce resilience, inner strength, and connection to a higher purpose.

OP REPORT

Record those moments when you overcame the inertia of your illness, accomplished needed tasks, or reshaped your thoughts toward gratitude and resilience. Reflect weekly on your progress, noting how these practices help you treat your illness with the persistent power of prayer and purposeful action. Over time, you'll witness the impact of this self–brain surgery, which cultivates inner strength and a more hopeful outlook.

When You're Chronically Stressed or Anxious

Procedure: The Gratitude Graft

WHEN TO USE

- When you feel anxious or stressed
- When you anticipate a situation that often provokes anxious feelings
- When you find yourself worrying about things that have not happened or are unlikely to happen

Note: Do *not* use this operation during a panic or anxiety attack. See "The Anxiety Ablation" procedure on page 279 if you are experiencing an attack.

TIME-OUT

You are here to reduce anxiety and stress, and to clear your thinking about a particular situation. You do not want to feel tense, worried, or uncomfortable anymore, especially when anxious feelings arise even in the absence of an immediate cause.

GOALS AND BENEFITS

To bring more peace and relaxation to your mind, brain, body, and life by reducing anxiety, stress, or worry. *Note:* This technique is intended to support your approach to managing stress and anxiety, but if you struggle to make sufficient progress, seek professional help.

RELEVANT NEUROSCIENCE

Your hippocampus plays a key role in regulating emotions, memory, and cognitive processes. It acts as a "switching station," directing information flow between various brain regions, including the amygdala (which handles responses to fear, anxiety, and stress) and the prefrontal cortex (involved in rational thought and calmness). Beyond simple information routing, the hippocampus serves as a kind of librarian, retrieving memories and encoding new ones, and as a threat detector or guard dog, constantly scanning for potential danger.

Functionally, the hippocampus perceives a situation (even if you are simply imagining it), tries to find relevant memories of other times you've perceived something similar, and then prompts the response it is most wired to create (either down toward the amygdala to trigger a fight-flight-or-freeze fear response, or up to engage the frontal lobe's executive function to seek a rational, calm response to the situation). As we've discussed, the brain is always running the "consent to automate" task, seeking your permission to make things happen with less mental energy. Because of this feature in your brain's design, you have the opportunity to use neuroplasticity and self–brain surgery to your advantage.

Studies indicate that cultivating gratitude can reduce both stress and anxiety. Practicing gratitude strengthens your hippocampus and enhances its activity, making it more likely to switch from the amygdala-driven stress reaction toward a calmer, frontal-lobe-driven response. This happens according to Hebb's law ("neurons that fire together, wire together"), which aligns with the ninth commandment of self–brain surgery.[12]

GUIDING SCRIPTURE

Do not be anxious about anything, but in every situation, by prayer and petition, with thanksgiving, present your requests to God. And the peace of God, which transcends all understanding, will guard your hearts and your minds in Christ Jesus.

PHILIPPIANS 4:6-7

Notice how the apostle Paul advises you to let anxiety give way to gratitude. Over time, thankfulness strengthens your hippocampus, helping it become more emotionally regulated and able to engage the frontal lobe for calmness in stressful situations.

TECHNIQUE

1. **Throw the switch.** Whenever you start to feel anxious or stressed, think of one thing—anything—that you're grateful for. Since the brain can't multitask, when you keep your focus on that, your hippocampus will direct activity and blood flow to your frontal lobes. This enables you to stay calm and make rational decisions rather than being triggered by stress hormones released by the amygdala.

2. **Inhale the miracle of mindfulness.** If gratitude feels elusive in particularly challenging moments, try this: Take a deep breath and hold it briefly. Realize that with each breath, you're taking in approximately twenty-five sextillion molecules[13]—an astronomical gift that sustains you. Focus on that miracle, telling yourself, *I'm grateful I can breathe.*

   Picture the oxygen reaching your hippocampus, activating connections to your frontal lobes and helping you relax. Even if the stress or anxiety remains, you're approaching it from a controlled, calm state rather than one of panic. This practice creates new synapses in your brain that make choosing gratitude more automatic over time. You can remind yourself, "I'm thankful for this oxygen and for Hebb's law, which I can use to feel less stressed and anxious."

   In this exercise, you have effectively severed the sick synapse that used to drive you toward stress and anxiety and "grafted in" a new path of gratitude and calm. This will reinforce your confidence that you can "breathe your way" out of stress and anxiety in the future.

OP REPORT

Write down a situation or emotion that typically makes you anxious or stressed. Allow yourself to notice how it usually makes you feel. Then take a deep breath, focusing on how that oxygen is sustaining you and expressing gratitude for it. Notice if the feelings of stress or anxiety lessen. Document this experience and try this exercise with other sources of gratitude over time, noting if your overall levels of stress and anxiety diminish and if you're able to regain emotional control more quickly.

 ## When You Feel Stuck

Procedure: The Unstuck Operation

WHEN TO USE

- When you feel like you cannot make progress in your life, or you keep slipping into old patterns that are not beneficial to you

- When you feel stuck with persistent negative thought loops, you feel emotionally stagnant, or you have a sense of being unable to move forward

- When you feel stuck in grief, anxiety, or perpetual stress

TIME-OUT

You've been through some sort of trauma, tragedy, or other massive thing. Or you've just had a series of small nuisances that added up to one big quicksand pit, and you feel as if you simply cannot move forward in your life. You know that the longer you stay stuck, the better you'll be at staying stuck, and that seems unacceptable.

GOALS AND BENEFITS

- To break out of the cycle of rumination and develop action-oriented thinking that leads to progress

- To increase motivation, reduce anxiety, develop greater emotional resilience, and boost your willpower to gain traction in life

RELEVANT NEUROSCIENCE

The anterior cingulate cortex, particularly the mid-anterior region, is implicated in complex emotional processing, including grief and the modulation of willpower. Research shows that persistent activation in the anterior cingulate occurs in complex/prolonged grief, indicating a problem with emotional adaptation and regulating responses to loss.[14]

The subgenual region of the anterior cingulate is involved in emotional self-regulation, willpower, and effortful control. Choosing to engage in undesirable or difficult tasks (like making yourself do something when you feel stuck) activates the task-positive network and can reduce overactivity in the anterior cingulate, which improves focus and your ability to shift out of "stuck" and start moving ahead.[15] Just as our ninth commandment says, what you're doing now, you're getting better at. Your brain reliably listens to your mind's instructions, and it wires in more adaptive behaviors when you force yourself to start the process of change.

GUIDING SCRIPTURE

Do not conform to the pattern of this world, but be transformed by the renewing of your mind.

ROMANS 12:2

"The world," whether other people, popular opinions, cultural influences, or spiritual forces, tries to shape or conform you into believing that a particular pattern of behavior is "just how you are," or "to be expected when you've gone through what you've gone through." But the writer is clear that, to get unstuck, you must realize that your mind can be *transformed* instead of *conformed*. Your life really can change, but you have to change your mind first.

TECHNIQUE

1. **Biopsy your thoughts.** The first step to moving forward is to recognize when you are thinking, *This is just how I am; I can't change*, or *I feel like it's always going to be this way*. Such thoughts indicate that you're caught in the emotional quicksand of being stuck.

2. **Shift gears.** Your anterior cingulate is like a gear shift, and it can be stuck in neutral. To shift into drive and get unstuck, make yourself engage in a small, manageable task that shifts your thinking from the default mode network (that self-focused *Me Show* that makes you continually replay the past or worry about the future) to the task-positive network (which rewards you for doing something by making it easier to do other things). This encourages activity in brain regions associated with conscious effort and reduces subgenual anterior cingulate overactivity.

3. **Remember the second commandment.** Feelings are not facts, so when you "feel" stuck, remind yourself that you're perceiving a chemical event, and you can change that by taking action. Use encouraging self-talk to reframe the situation with statements like "I am antifragile" and "This massive thing I've been through will eventually make me stronger and is helping me build resilience."

4. **Perform microsurgery.** Small, achievable actions make a difference. Write down a short list of tasks you've been putting off and do three of them today (before you overthink it and decide they are too hard).

OP REPORT

Keep a log of the ways you feel stuck and the types of microsurgery you perform to make yourself accomplish a few small tasks. How did each procedure affect your sense of momentum and willpower? Write down any changes in how you feel and the progress you're making.

This procedure leverages the knowledge that shifting your mid-anterior cingulate cortex out of neutral and into gear can foster resilience and help you start progressing.

When You're Tired of Settling

Procedure: The Settle-for-More Shift

WHEN TO USE

- When you find yourself frustrated at the results you are getting from any area of your life, such as your relationships, work, finances, spiritual growth, health, or fitness

- When you envision a certain level of performance in your mind but never seem to be able to reach it

- When the gap between what you know you're called to or capable of and where you are feels impossible to bridge

TIME-OUT

You came to "The Operating Room" today to biopsy your thoughts and find out why you have been settling for less when you feel called to more. You intend to expose the limiting beliefs, harmful fears, disordered thought patterns, and unproductive behaviors that prevent you from reaching your goals. Once exposed, you will attack them one by one and begin only "settling for more" in your life. The Settle-for-More Shift will help you honestly assess where you are, smash comfort zones, quiet limiting stories, and overcome fear to help you break through.

GOALS AND BENEFITS

- To recognize and disrupt the mindset of complacency
- To realign your motivation with your values and God's calling
- To decide to believe God's promises rather than thinking that they apply only to others
- To shift your belief system to truly knowing that your mind and brain are powerful and capable, and that you can learn new high-performance patterns in your life
- To understand and overcome the psychological biases and fears that often produce settling
- To identify and take tangible steps toward performance breakthroughs in your life, work, or relationships
- To inspire faith-driven action with the confidence that God equips you for what he calls you to

RELEVANT NEUROSCIENCE

Sometimes we settle for less because we are more afraid of life on the other side of the limit than we are of the familiar discomfort of where we are. I call this "the slow failure of staying put."

Fear of change or of higher performance is deeply tied to the amygdala, your brain's "fear center," which is activated when you perceive a threat, even if the "threat" involves positive changes or breaking through to your higher calling.[16] Your brain has automated many of your responses because you gave it consent, perhaps throughout much of your life. This means that even if you're in an uncomfortable place in life, at least you know and understand it. Even good change feels risky to your brain. Psychologically, this is due to a phenomenon called ambiguity aversion, a cognitive bias in which people favor familiar risks over unfamiliar ones.[17]

Unwillingness to change or take risks can lead you to being frustrated at your performance, while simultaneously never trying to do anything about it. This is where neuroplasticity can either work for you or against you. You may have long-held beliefs and deeply grooved synaptic pathways that reinforce self-doubt, fear of failure, or complacency, but your brain's ability to rewire itself through intentional thought and behavior shifts can break those down and forge new ones, enabling you to think and act in alignment with your higher goals.

The default mode network (DMN) is at play in chronic settling as well. It is active during introspection and self-referential thinking, and if you do not challenge it, the DMN can default to reinforcing limiting beliefs and negative stories about your capabilities. Interrupting this cycle through intentional focus and action helps reframe those narratives.

Your brain's dopamine system plays a critical role in motivation and reward. When you set goals—even small ones—and begin to achieve them, dopamine is released to reinforce the behavior and create a cycle of motivation. Choosing to take tangible, incremental steps toward your desired performance is the key to making the reward system work for you.

As opposed to the fear-based response of your amygdala that is active when you find yourself chronically settling, your prefrontal cortex thrives on a growth mindset. The prefrontal cortex is responsible for executive functions like planning, decision-making, and self-regulation—all essential to high performance in any context. The growth mindset is the belief that you can develop your abilities and intelligence rather than believing that some people "just have it," and that maybe you don't. Neuroscience research proves that focusing on effort and learning rather than on your limitations engages the prefrontal cortex and boosts your capacity for growth and high performance.[18]

Your reticular activating system (RAS) filters the information you perceive, based on what you focus on. If you believe you're incapable of higher performance, your RAS will filter out opportunities for growth. They will still be there, but you won't be as likely to notice them. By shifting your focus to possibilities, potential, and God's promises, your RAS will help you start noticing pathways to higher performance. Remembering that feelings are not facts and that thoughts aren't always true will help you detach from these limiting narratives and take action anyway.[19]

GUIDING SCRIPTURE

[God] is able to do immeasurably more than all we ask or imagine, according to his power that is at work within us.

EPHESIANS 3:20

Forgetting what is behind and straining toward what is ahead, I press on toward the goal to win the prize for which God has called me heavenward in Christ Jesus.

PHILIPPIANS 3:13-14

These passages reveal that God is capable of more than you can even imagine and that he has a plan and purpose for your life. Faith enables you to step out of your comfort zone, shake off your limiting beliefs, and hold on to the promise that you are capable of more.

TECHNIQUE

1. **Expose the places you've been settling.** Ask yourself, *What is one thing I've settled for that I can change?*

2. **Identify the limiting beliefs.** Listen for the negative voices that say things like, *I'm not good enough*, *It's too scary*, or *It's too late for me*. Challenge them with the truth of your potential and God's promises.

3. **Switch to a growth mindset.** Choose a specific area in which you've been settling for less (career, health, relationships, spiritual growth) and a *specific and actionable* way you could begin shifting toward higher performance. For example, "I will read *The Seven Habits of Highly Effective People* this month and implement one of those habits in my life," or "I will spend fifteen minutes a day practicing gratitude, since I know that gratitude reduces fear and will help my frontal lobes be more active."

4. **See and say the change.** Visualize the "new you" who is walking in your God-given potential. Speak true things into your life like, "I am capable. I am called. God has designed me to be able to change my mind, my brain, and my life."

5. **Shift into "settling for more."** Push yourself slightly beyond your comfort zone daily. You're not trying to be perfect; you're just trying to make progress. Stop asking what you could lose if you try to change and start asking what you could lose if you don't. Make settling for less the uncomfortable outcome and settling for more the goal.

6. **Align your goals with your calling.** Ask God for clarity about your calling and for courage to pursue it. Write down what comes to mind during these moments and press into those places where God is asking you to stop settling for less.

OP REPORT

Honestly record the ways you feel you've been settling in your life, as well as the places you've felt frustrated by limiting beliefs and stories. Have you let fear keep you from breaking through in a place you feel called to?

Ask yourself specific questions. You can use a progress check like, *How many times did I step out of my comfort zone this week?*

Write these things down and track your progress over time. You'll begin to see your Thought Biopsy results improving as you develop a growth mindset, and your self-imposed limits will fall away as you learn to "settle for more."

When You Have Chronic Pain

Procedure: Repurposing Pain

WHEN TO USE

- When you have pain that has no clear cause (e.g., persistent pain after injuries or surgical wounds have healed, fibromyalgia, phantom limb pain, chronic headaches but normal brain scans)

- When you're stuck with chronic pain loops and need to unlearn the ways in which your brain has "remembered" the pain, and then create healthier pathways

TIME-OUT

As you prepare to perform the Repurposing Pain procedure, acknowledge that pain is not the enemy. Pain is designed to signal the presence of danger, but chronic pain causes the brain to create a memory circuit of the old problem, which can continue to fire even when the original issue has resolved. Once this pain loop forms, your brain perceives that the injury or problem is happening now, and unless the loop is interrupted with self–brain surgery, you will respond to it emotionally and physiologically just as you did when the injury was fresh.

While pain is a natural alarm signal, if your mind responds as if there is an ongoing and painful problem, you may feel despair and hopelessness if you're thinking, *Nothing can help me.* However, the second commandment reminds you that feelings are not facts; they are chemical events in your brain. You can address your brain's memory of pain by reprogramming those circuits and reducing the impact of pain.

Chronic pain may feel overwhelming, but neuroplasticity means that change is always possible. This procedure will guide you toward that change.

GOALS AND BENEFITS

- To reduce your brain's learned pain response and to "unlearn" the pathways that your pain has created in your memory circuits

- To wire in new pathways that are focused less on the pain and more on your brain's natural pain-relieving mechanisms

- To experience a reduction in the intensity and the emotional activation of your pain and develop a new mental reaction to it

- To begin to feel more resilient and empowered as you become convinced that you can actually train your brain to revalue the pain signals and reengage in your life more fully[20]

RELEVANT NEUROSCIENCE

Brain scans reveal that acute pain from fresh injuries activates circuits in the brain that are specifically mapped to the injured area of the body. However, chronic pain stems from a surprising shift: When pain persists without a clear cause or lingers long after healing, the brain redirects these signals into memory processing circuits.[21] Think of it as your brain rewiring itself to remember pain, even when the original injury is no longer present. This shift causes chronic pain to become "sticky" in your neuronal circuits, making it harder to manage because it is no longer confined to areas of the brain that respond to pain medication or traditional pain-management techniques.

Your brain literally "learns" to relive memories of old pains, and this memory-forming circuit begins to cascade like a snowball rolling downhill.[22] Over time, it may amplify your sensitivity even to nonpainful stimuli (like a light touch on your skin), which causes minor irritants to feel excruciating.

Fortunately, neuroplasticity—the brain's ability to adapt and change—offers a way out. By engaging in techniques that retrain memory circuits, such as visualization, mindfulness, and gratitude, you can redirect neural pathways away from the pain loop. These practices help activate areas of the brain responsible for reward, relaxation, and positive experiences. Over time, the miracle of neuroplasticity allows these new pathways to strengthen, gradually overriding the old pain circuits and offering you relief and renewed hope.

GUIDING SCRIPTURE

He heals the brokenhearted and binds up their wounds.

PSALM 147:3

God's healing is available whenever you feel brokenhearted, discouraged, exhausted, or grieved because of your pain. The psalmist reminds you that restoration and wholeness in your mind and body are possible. Your heart can heal even as you relearn new ways to manage old pains.

But we also glory in our sufferings, because we know that suffering produces perseverance; perseverance, character; and character, hope.

ROMANS 5:3-4

Your pain does not have to rob you of hope. Instead, you can rejoice that pain has the potential to strengthen your resilience, deepen your character, and help you persevere knowing that God uses your hurt to create something meaningful inside you. Just as perseverance strengthens character, your persistence in retraining your brain can build resilience and foster hope.

TECHNIQUE

1. **Acknowledge the truth.** If you have recovered from an illness, injury, or surgical procedure, the chronic pain you continue to feel is partly a learned experience stored in memory circuits. Make the patient-to-doctor switch and mentally reframe your pain as something your brain has learned rather than an unchangeable condition. Expose it for what it is: *This pain is something my brain has learned, and I can unlearn it.*

2. **Position yourself for success.** Practice this operation while sober, realizing that since the pain you feel is not happening in pain-related areas of your brain, pain medications or other numbing agents like alcohol will not help. Shift your focus to unlearning old memory circuits and seek to sever those sick synapses.

3. **Take control.** Take a moment to be grateful that, although pain can be amplified and reinforced by your brain's limbic system, you are not just your brain. Pause to breathe in for four seconds; as you do, draw in the knowledge that you can change your brain by changing your mind. Now slowly exhale for six seconds as you acknowledge the persistence of your pain while affirming your ability to change how you experience it.

4. **Transplant.** Choose a specific, pleasant memory, an uplifting Scripture, or a calming image to transplant in to replace the pain. Close your eyes, breathe slowly, and visualize this memory, verse, or image with as much detail as possible. This will activate regions of your brain related to positive emotions and relaxation and reduce your limbic system's ability to reinforce the pain.

5. **Change the task.** Remember that your brain cannot multitask. When the pain comes to mind, rob it of its power by purposefully *doing something.*

Engage in a task that requires your full attention, such as a hobby, deep conversation, or exercise. Research shows that by focusing your mind and taking action, you activate your brain's reward system and reduce your capacity to pay attention to the remembered pain circuits.

6. **Repurpose the pain pathways.** Remember that when you sever a sick synapse, the physical, structural brain parts (such as microtubules) become available to rebuild more helpful synapses. See yourself performing this surgery, cutting out harmful pain memories and using those pieces to make new and helpful circuits. Write down three things you're grateful for, focusing on what is possible despite your pain. This self–brain surgery operation will help you build positive neural pathways and shift your brain's focus away from pain and toward contentment and resilience.

7. **Remind yourself of who you are becoming.** Repeat affirmations like "I am resilient; I am stronger than this pain," or verses like Romans 5:3-4 (see the "Guiding Scripture" on the previous page) to remind yourself of the strength and perseverance being developed within you. Regularly reminding yourself of these truths builds new patterns in the brain, reducing the automatic responses to pain. One of my favorite affirmations is from French psychologist Émile Coué: "Every day, in every way, I am getting better and better and better."

8. **Practice persistent prayer.** Like the diligent, prayerful watchmen described in Isaiah 62:6, commit to persistent prayer, asking for both physical and emotional relief. Allow this practice to ground you in hope and peace, trusting that even as pain persists, you're building a stronger, more resilient mind. Remember that what you are doing, you are getting better at, and you are getting better at unlearning the pain and repurposing those parts of your brain toward your healing.

OP REPORT

Keep a journal of your pain scales and progress over time. Record moments when you successfully directed yourself away from pain or encouraged yourself with a verse, pleasant memory, or affirmation. Note the decrease in the intensity or frequency of pain and how your attitude toward it has changed. Keeping good records reinforces the rewiring process. It will help you reclaim the parts of your life that pain has impacted and strengthen your overall resilience.

When You Struggle with Negative Self-Talk and Self-Doubt

Procedure: The Self-Talk Switch

WHEN TO USE

- When you notice that you're ganging up on yourself

- When your automatic thoughts are excessively negative and you are agreeing with them, doubting yourself, blaming yourself, harshly criticizing yourself, or ruminating over things from the past that provoke shame, guilt, or other self-esteem issues

TIME-OUT

You come to this operation when you realize that you are not being kind to yourself and want to change that.

GOALS AND BENEFITS

To identify and interrupt negative or harmful self-talk by switching to empowering and constructive thinking. This will shift your brain's focus from a threat-based response to an opportunity-based mindset, improve your problem-solving, help you regulate your emotions, and foster resilience.

RELEVANT NEUROSCIENCE

Neuroscience studies reveal that repeated negative self-talk creates and reinforces synaptic circuits related to stress and anxiety. When you intentionally switch to positive or at least neutral self-talk, you harness the power of neuroplasticity to encourage new, healthier synaptic connections that wire in more useful thinking patterns.[23] This rewiring will then automate how your brain processes stress and self-perception,[24] and your baseline internal conversations will become kinder.

GUIDING SCRIPTURE

Let the words of my mouth and the meditation of my heart be acceptable in your sight, O LORD, my rock and my redeemer.

PSALM 19:14, ESV

You shall love your neighbor as yourself.

MATTHEW 22:39, NKJV

Out of the abundance of the heart the mouth speaks.
MATTHEW 12:34, NKJV

When a person speaks, his words show what is really in his mind.
LUKE 6:45, EASY

In Psalm 19, David asks God to help him not only speak things that please God but also to think thoughts that align with God's will. Jesus' teachings emphasize that loving oneself is as vital as loving others, reminding us that self-compassion is rooted in divine truth. These passages underscore that our thoughts shape our speech and actions, affirming the need to nurture positive inner dialogue.

TECHNIQUE

1. **Biopsy the comments you frequently speak to yourself.** Pause and become aware of the negative or critical self-talk. Call it what it is and label it.

2. **Run a scan.** Ask yourself, *When was the first time I thought that about myself? What was going on in my life when I decided I deserved to talk to myself like that?* Remember that negative self-talk often reflects underlying shame, judgment, and unforgiveness. And even though the feelings may seem real, they are just chemical events in your brain, not facts.

3. **Sever the sick synapse and switch it.** Visualize using a scalpel to sever the connection between that deep-rooted feeling and the self-talk that is attached to it. See yourself surgically removing the diseased negative thought and transplanting in its place a more realistic and positive (or at least neutral) phrase, trusting that this practice will make you feel better over time. For instance, replace *I never do anything right* with *I get better at what I actually do, so I'm going to stop beating myself up and instead start coaching myself to improve.*

4. **Practice every day.** Use affirmations or Scripture to tell yourself true things over and over. In accordance with Hebb's law, those truths will become wired into your self-talk over time.

5. **Stabilize the new connections.** Combine your new self-talk with a physical action—like taking several deep breaths or placing your hand on your chest—to surgically create and connect a sensory action to the new thought.

OP REPORT

Write down some of the negative things you commonly say to yourself. Physically cross out each phrase and write a note of how you transplanted a new statement in its place. Spend some quiet time reflecting on how your internal dialogue improves as time passes.

When the Biopsy Shows "I" Trouble

Procedure: The "Maybe It's Me" Mind Shift

WHEN TO USE

- When it feels like "everyone" else is being unreasonable, "everything" is bad, or "nothing" is working out for you

- When you objectively analyze your Thought Biopsy and the result is that you have "I" trouble

TIME-OUT

You are here to become healthier, feel better, and be happier. The Thought Biopsy has revealed that maybe everyone else isn't the problem this time, and you've realized that "maybe it's me."

GOALS AND BENEFITS

Once you realize that no one else can make you happy or change enough to solve all your problems, you are empowered to change yourself. This operation will help you improve your outlook, think more clearly, and break down thought loops that keep you stuck in negativity.

RELEVANT NEUROSCIENCE

Dwelling on negative thoughts creates alterations in your neurochemistry that, over time, can rewire your brain to automatically adopt a more negative baseline. If you are unaware of this self-inflicted negativity, you may falsely conclude that your emotions are solely a result of external circumstances or other people, when, in fact, you often feel the way you do because of how *you* choose to perceive situations.

Research indicates that reducing negative thinking is a more powerful way to improve emotional well-being than simply increasing positive thinking.[25] This is related to the 5:1 Rule, which posits that negative experiences, words, or thoughts are more difficult to reverse compared to positive ones.[26] While this ratio originated from studies on relationships, it has been observed as generally applicable to overall well-being, even if it's not always mathematically exact. Negativity exerts a powerful and detrimental impact on mental health, underscoring the value of shifting one's mindset to harness the brain's neuroplastic potential for positive change.

GUIDING SCRIPTURE

Do nothing out of selfish ambition or vain conceit. Rather, in humility value others above yourselves, not looking to your own interests but each of you to the interests of the others. In your relationships with one another, have the same mindset as Christ Jesus.

PHILIPPIANS 2:3-5

"Maybe it's me" and other lousy attitudes often stem from excessive self-focus, which is linked to the activity of the default mode network (DMN) in the brain. This Scripture underscores the transformative power of shifting your focus outward—from self-centered thoughts to an attitude of humility and service. Such a shift fosters a healthier perspective, reduces the hold of negative thinking, and promotes positive changes in your mental and emotional well-being.

TECHNIQUE

1. **Take a breath and reflect.** When you start to feel frustration or resentment bubbling up, pause. Take a few deep, calming breaths and mentally label the emotions you're experiencing. Acknowledge them by saying, "Maybe the problem is me, and I just have a lousy attitude. I'm going to perform a 'Maybe It's Me' Mind Shift to change my mind."

2. **Mentally cut out the lousy attitude.** Write down the specific thoughts contributing to your negative mindset. Run the Thought Biopsy questions and challenge these internal statements by asking, "Is this true?" or "Is there another way to see this?" By examining and questioning your thoughts, you can start to dismantle the patterns that keep you stuck.

3. **Transplant a healthier thought.** Once you've identified and challenged the negative attitude, replace it with a more constructive thought. This could be an expression of gratitude or a more positive perspective on the situation or person involved. Shifting your focus to what is going right can help rewire your brain toward positivity.

4. **Perspective switch.** Remember that you are both the patient and the self–brain surgeon. Ask yourself, *How would a compassionate, skilled surgeon approach this situation?* This question helps you step back, view the situation objectively, and pivot away from the self-centered mindset of "I" trouble.

5. **Commit to change.** Reinforce your shift in thinking by repeating an affirmation such as, "I am in control of my attitude, and I choose a mindset that uplifts me and those around me." Connect this to the ninth commandment of self–brain surgery by declaring, "I'm getting better at having a better attitude by practicing the 'Maybe It's Me' Mind Shift."

OP REPORT

Write down the areas or moments where you struggle with "I" trouble. Give yourself permission to realize that, just as it's unhealthy to blame yourself for *everything*, it is also unhealthy to be unwilling to take responsibility for *anything*. Sometimes our own attitudes *are* the problem, so when the biopsy confirms that *Maybe it's me*, be honest about it. Reflect on how acknowledging that you can be the source of some of your own difficulties has empowered you to change. How do you feel now that you know you have the tools to operate on your mindset and make it better?

When You Focus on the Worst-Case Scenario

Procedure: The Filter Refocus

WHEN TO USE

- When you find yourself frequently forecasting doom, worrying about worst-case scenarios, or overfocusing on negative possible outcomes to situations in your life

- When you feel paralyzed by anxiety or worry because you convince yourself nothing ever goes right for you

- When the fear of failure or a negative outcome often keeps you from trying new things or taking chances when opportunities present themselves

- When you realize that these negative, worst-case thoughts are impacting your mood, motivation, relationships, work, or decisions

TIME-OUT

You are purposefully starting this operation with the goal of rewiring your brain to change its filtering mechanism and default to "best-case" thinking. You recognize that if your default has been to imagine situations in which things go wrong, it is just as reasonable to imagine what would happen if things go right.

GOALS AND BENEFITS

- To change the way in which your reticular activating system filters what you see in the world around you; to break the loop of negative, worst-case thinking with more helpful thought patterns to present hope, workable solutions, and positive possibilities to your mind

- To free up mental energy so that you can improve your ability to problem-solve, reducing stress, anxiety, and hopelessness

- To operate your life out of reason and power rather than fear, using the same neural circuits you've previously trained to see only the negative

- To increase emotional resilience, give you a proactive approach to challenges, and reinforce a sense of agency and personal power

RELEVANT NEUROSCIENCE

The reticular activating system (RAS) is a neuronal network in your brain stem that (among many other things) serves as a sort of attention filter. It follows your mental direction (what you want to pay attention to) and gates anything from your conscious perception that does not support what you have decided to look for.[27]

The function of the RAS explains things like the famous invisible gorilla experiment, in which psychologists Daniel Simons and Christopher Chabris asked a group of volunteers to focus on counting how many times players passed a basketball back and forth.[28] After the passes were complete, the researchers asked the people what else they saw, and almost all of them had completely failed to notice the person in a gorilla suit walking among the players at various times. This is called inattentional blindness, a cognitive bias that happens when we focus intently on one aspect of something, mostly missing other obvious details in the process.[29]

By prioritizing information that aligns with your immediate focus or goals, the RAS filters out anything that is not essential to the task it has been assigned, like the gorilla. The RAS plays a role in managing your limited attentional resources, which explains why what you focus on becomes more real and other details may be completely unnoticed.

Note that the RAS does not care *what* you tell it to look for. It simply listens for mental commands and begins to amplify your awareness of supporting information. This is the basis of the Baader-Meinhof phenomenon, or frequency illusion. When you notice and pay attention to something—say a species of bird you've never seen before—suddenly you start noticing it everywhere. Most likely, the birds were always there, but you hadn't prompted your RAS to look for them.

It is important to recognize the role of the RAS in generating your mental perceptions, since you generally believe your perceptions to be "real." The truth is that your attention shapes what seems real to you.[30]

By filtering incoming information based on what the mind prioritizes, the RAS directs your attention to real-world events *or even imagined ideas or thoughts* that align with your values, beliefs, and expectations. Constantly focusing on worst-case scenarios primes the RAS to notice and amplify negative cues, reinforcing fear-based thinking.

While you cannot actually *manifest* physical realities (you can't just say, "I am going to be rich" and have a million dollars appear in your bank account), you can certainly manifest misery if you tell your RAS that you expect to fail or to have a bad day, or if you constantly envision worst-case scenarios. Your RAS will do its job and continue to show you evidence that your fears are coming true. The trouble is, those negative outcomes are not inherently unavoidable; you will simply fail to notice all kinds of opportunities to make things work out better.

Using the Filter Refocus operation can help redirect your RAS to recognize positive or constructive elements in the environment, break negative thought loops, and promote neuroplastic changes that help you see things more hopefully in the future.

GUIDING SCRIPTURE

Finally, brothers and sisters, whatever is true, whatever is noble, whatever is right, whatever is pure, whatever is lovely, whatever is admirable—if anything is excellent or praiseworthy—think about such things.

PHILIPPIANS 4:8

This passage reminds you that your brain is always listening (as my friend Daniel Amen says), and the RAS will tune your perceptions to what you tell it to look for. Better thinking produces a better perceived life, no matter what circumstances occur.

You will keep him in perfect peace, whose mind is stayed on You, because he trusts in You.
ISAIAH 26:3, NKJV

In other words, peace does not come from events, but from what (or rather *who*) you think about.

TECHNIQUE

1. **Identify a negative filter you may have installed.** Notice any worst-case scenarios that pop into your head and write them down: *I constantly tell myself that I am going to fail.*
2. **Biopsy the thought.** Run the Thought Biopsy procedure and recognize false labels, limiting beliefs, or stories that might have become filters your RAS has established to make your worst-case scenario more likely to be true.
3. **Run a Whole-System Scan.** Identify how worrying about the negative outcome is affecting your body and mental state. Do you feel more anxious or stressed when you allow the negative thought or worst-case scenario to play out in your mind?
4. **Breathe and pray/contemplate.** Recognize that you have the mental ability to relax your mind and that you are not obligated to prognosticate failure or negativity over your life. You can sever this habit, perpetuated by sick synapses you've been unaware of, when you refocus your RAS filter.
5. **Refocus your filter.** Tell yourself, *Since my worst-case scenarios and negative thinking do not always come true or turn out to have been worthy of all that mental focus and stress, I am going to decide to create a best-case scenario or a positive bias to my thinking instead.*
6. **Start looking for gorillas.** Pay attention to and write down whatever you notice or experience when you set your filter to look for opportunities, good things, and better outcomes. You will likely see doors open you never noticed before, people being kinder to you, traction developing, and hope rising in your life. Then you will realize those things were always there, but you were counting passes instead of gorillas.

7. **Keep your RAS tuned to help you.** Remind yourself of the new positive filter throughout the day, especially when you feel the worst-case scenario or negative thinking resurfacing in your mind. Add some physical cues, like tapping your wrist or placing your hand over your heart, to reinforce the new filter structurally in your brain. This will help hardwire the new thought process, allowing you to more easily bring it to mind whenever old thinking bubbles back up.

8. **Lock in the new filter.** Take an immediate action that will lead to the release of rewarding neurotransmitters in your brain and reinforce the new setting on your RAS. If your new thought is, *People are going to be nice to me today*, smile and greet the first person you see. They will most likely smile and return your greeting, and your brain will release dopamine to reward you and make your RAS reinforce the filter that is looking for kindness. You'll begin to see kind people everywhere.

OP REPORT

Record the moments when you were able to refocus your filter. Notice and write down how this shift impacted your mood, actions, or sense of control. This reflection will help reinforce the new habit, keeping your RAS engaged with your improved filter.

When You Feel Lonely or Isolated

Procedure: The Loneliness Ligation

WHEN TO USE

- When you struggle with loneliness or isolation, including the feeling of being lonely in a crowded room

- When negative self-talk convinces you that no one sees you, understands you, or cares about you

TIME-OUT

The Loneliness Ligation[31] procedure will help you reorder your thinking and recognize that feelings of loneliness are normal, driven by brain processes that can respond to self-brain surgery. You intend to rob these negative feelings of their power by applying the neuroscience of attention density and the Quantum

Zeno effect (which, together, explain that the more attention you give to something, the more likely the associated neural pathways will "freeze" in place, reinforcing that perspective). Loneliness is an experience, not your identity.

GOALS AND BENEFITS

- To reduce the emotional and physical impacts of loneliness by fostering connection (internally and externally) with yourself, others, and God

- To enhance your mood, improve your stress resilience, reduce anxiety, and improve your physiology by lowering inflammation and blood pressure through increased social interaction and connection

RELEVANT NEUROSCIENCE

Research shows that chronic loneliness activates the amygdala, the brain's alarm system, which then increases cortisol and perpetuates stress and hypervigilance. Long-term effects include heightened inflammation, immune suppression, and risks for depression and cardiovascular disease that are comparable to smoking fifteen cigarettes a day.[32]

When you fixate on feelings of loneliness, you repeatedly activate neural circuits, reinforcing these pathways. The brain adapts by devoting more resources to these negative patterns, making loneliness a self-reinforcing cycle. Sustained focus on loneliness also amplifies its presence. Redirecting attention to positive emotions or actions weakens its neural pathways, building healthier connections.

You can use the Loneliness Ligation procedure to divert excess attention away from the lonely feelings, allowing your brain to adapt and rewire based on where you direct your focus, creating an opportunity for positive change.

GUIDING SCRIPTURE

God sets the lonely in families.

PSALM 68:6

There is a friend who sticks closer than a brother.

PROVERBS 18:24

These verses affirm the value of connection, whether through biological relationships, chosen community, or with God himself, who provides for our relational needs.

TECHNIQUE

1. **Position yourself for connection.** Recognize that loneliness thrives on inaction and negative self-focus. Decide to proactively seek opportunities for connection rather than waiting for others to approach you.

2. **Expose the feeling.** Verbally acknowledge your loneliness and examine its root causes. Challenge beliefs such as *I am unlovable* by seeking objective evidence to the contrary. Make the patient-to-doctor switch: List qualities about yourself that would make someone want to connect with you.

3. **Perform microsurgery for meaningful progress.** Set small, manageable goals to engage with others daily, like texting a friend, making a brief call, or starting a conversation.

4. **Switch to service.** Channel energy into helping others. Acts of kindness activate the brain's reward circuits, reducing feelings of loneliness. Volunteer or engage in a group activity aligned with your values to meet like-minded people.

5. **Ligate loneliness with gratitude.** Start each day by listing three things you're grateful for, especially moments of connection or kindness. This gratitude practice shifts focus away from loneliness, creating room for positive emotions.

OP REPORT

Track instances of feeling lonely or isolated. Then monitor both the actions you take to combat those feelings and the effect on your emotional state. For example, write down three qualities or strengths you possess that would benefit others. Shift into action mode with an affirmation: "Today, I commit to counteracting loneliness by intentionally connecting with others in small but meaningful ways. I will reach out to one person, express gratitude for an interaction, and remind myself that loneliness is temporary. I'm creating new connections in my brain to foster community and alleviate the negative effects of isolation."

 When You're Suffering

Procedure: The Suffering Substitution

WHEN TO USE

When you are experiencing significant hardship, severe emotional pain, trauma, tragedy, or other massive life circumstances that feel overwhelming or as if they have no purpose

TIME-OUT

Acknowledge your TMT (The Massive Thing you're going through). It is devastating, and it's valid to recognize that this type of suffering can alter a person's entire life. You are here because you understand that you are not inherently fragile but rather antifragile. You believe that suffering can be transformative if it is reframed with purpose. You want to be refined, not defined, by it.

GOALS AND BENEFITS

- To shift mentally from despair and hopelessness to a mindset focused on growth through pain

- To discover moments in your story for which you can be grateful, even while navigating a redefined future

- To build emotional resilience and benefit from pain reduction so that, instead of breaking under hardship, your brain rewards endurance with increased strength

RELEVANT NEUROSCIENCE

Suffering and pain naturally draw you inward, leading to an increased focus on personal loss, perceived injustices, and anxieties about what the future may hold in the wake of a significant life event. During these periods of intense introspection and rumination, the default mode network (DMN) is activated. This network supports introspection (more formally known as self-referential processing) but also amplifies a focus on negative past or current events, and potential (often imagined) future scenarios.[33]

Making a mental shift from thinking about your loss to thinking about what you can be grateful for enhances emotional regulation, makes you feel more in control, and reduces anxiety and the perception of pain. Any kind of suffering is associated with increased physical pain, but gratitude helps release endorphins and serotonin, promoting a sense of well-being.[34]

GUIDING SCRIPTURE

Not only so, but we also glory in our sufferings, because we know that suffering produces perseverance; perseverance, character; and character, hope.

ROMANS 5:3-4

Give thanks in all circumstances; for this is God's will for you in Christ Jesus.

1 THESSALONIANS 5:18

I have refined you, but not as silver is refined. Rather, I have refined you in the furnace of suffering.

ISAIAH 48:10, NLT

These verses are reminders that suffering does not have to destroy you; instead, it can be transformative. You are designed in such a way that hardship can make you stronger and more hopeful. God created you to be antifragile—able not just to endure hardship but to emerge more empowered and resilient, knowing you can handle whatever comes next with his help. Gratitude is the gate through which this transformation passes, turning pain into purpose and growth.

TECHNIQUE

1. **Adopt the approach that** *something can help you.* You can choose to simply follow the steps of the procedure, delve into and leverage the neuroscience to your advantage, or seek God's help in mastering this process of substituting gratitude for suffering.

2. **Make the patient-to-doctor switch.** Perform self–brain surgery and address the situation. Move from helplessly believing this situation has the power to permanently define your life to seeing yourself as a wise and compassionate doctor with the ability to make a difference.

3. **Name it to know it for proper exposure.** Write down and clarify exactly what is hurting you, as specifically as you can.

4. **Shift your perspective.** Rather than thinking about *what you've lost*, think about *what you're grateful for having had.* When you focus on the ways your life was enriched by the experience or individual, you engage your prefrontal cortex.

5. **Substitute purpose for pain.** Think about potential ways you can learn from this situation and add purpose to the pain. Ask yourself, *How could I grow from this?* Consider how you could redeem this experience, possibly by using your story (or the story of the person you've lost) to inspire or help others.

6. **Focus on gratitude.** Purposefully identify and write down aspects of the situation or your life for which you are thankful, even seemingly trivial ones.

7. **Seek healthy closure.** Embrace the belief that change is possible. Remember the quantum principle that two truths can coexist—you can hold both your pain and its purpose without dishonoring either. Reiterate to yourself, *This*

will make me stronger, or *I am not fragile; I am resilient.* Spend time in prayer or meditation, focusing on gratitude and the belief that meaning can arise from trials.

OP REPORT

Reflect on and record the changes in your emotional state as you perform The Suffering Substitution operation. Notice any increase in hope, shifts in perception, or reduction in distress. Track repeated use over time to see long-term benefits in your outlook and resilience.

When You're Falling into Old Habits

Procedure: The Five-Minute Freeze

WHEN TO USE

- When you feel yourself being drawn into unhelpful habits or thought patterns you've struggled with in the past

- When a familiar situation or a stressful/painful time triggers old, unhealthy behaviors

- When you feel stuck in repetitive cycles that hold you back, whether these are related to addiction, procrastination, negative self-talk, or other habits

Note: This procedure is not designed to be the sole treatment for serious or chronic issues such as drug or alcohol dependency. You will need additional support from your recovery community and accountability partners, and professional help may be necessary. Self–brain surgery is most effective as part of a broader strategy that includes the support of others.

TIME-OUT

You come to this operation when you are ready to get off the carousel of pain, shame, and defeat caused by bad habits and addictions. You are tired of committing to change only to resume unhealthy behaviors, making promises to yourself, to others, and even to God that you can't seem to keep. When you've given in to the habit again, you find yourself starting all over. You want freedom and the success you can see in your mind on the other side of this issue, and you are ready to free yourself from this problem once and for all.

GOALS AND BENEFITS

- To identify and interrupt thought and behavior patterns that lead you to fall back into old habits
- To rewire your brain for healthier responses through neuroplasticity
- To find hope and confidence by believing you can gain control over habits that have felt like they're in control of you

RELEVANT NEUROSCIENCE

Everything you repeatedly do in your life has become or is becoming a brain habit. As previously discussed, you get better (structurally in your brain) at whatever you do because of the ninth commandment and Hebb's law: "Neurons that fire together, wire together."[35] This means that every repeated thought or action strengthens the neural pathways associated with it, making the behavior easier and more automatic over time.

The root cause of many bad habits is often tied to a failure to keep the sixth commandment—you do not love tomorrow more than you hate how you feel right now. Bad habits frequently arise as coping mechanisms, offering immediate relief but creating long-term harm. The brain's reward system, particularly the release of dopamine, reinforces these behaviors by associating them with feelings of pleasure or relief.[36]

Crucially, your brain's prefrontal cortex—the part responsible for rational decision-making and impulse control—is often overridden by the limbic system, which governs emotion and survival instincts.[37] In moments of stress or discomfort, this imbalance may lead you to prioritize short-term relief (the bad habit) over long-term well-being. In self–brain surgery terms, this is when you treat a bad feeling with a bad operation.

Over time, repeated engagement in bad habits shifts the brain's baseline functioning. The behavior becomes linked to your brain's reward system, making it seem necessary for you to feel happy or even just "normal."[38] This rewiring makes habits harder to break without intentional effort, such as introducing new, healthier behaviors to compete with and overwrite the old pathways.

By understanding these mechanisms, you can recognize that feeling the pull of old habits isn't always a moral failing, but it *is* always a biological process. Every time you repeat a habit or consciously take steps to break one, you are performing self–brain surgery. With patience and consistent action, you can perform this operation to create new, healthier patterns that support your goals and values. Even when dealing with those habits that are spiritual or moral in nature, you will have to unwire them biologically and replace them with healthier (and holier) pathways if you want to be free.

GUIDING SCRIPTURE

No temptation has overtaken you except what is common to mankind. And God is faithful; he will not let you be tempted beyond what you can bear. But when you are tempted, he will also provide a way out so that you can endure it.

1 CORINTHIANS 10:13

Do not conform to the pattern of this world, but be transformed by the renewing of your mind.

ROMANS 12:2

It is for freedom that Christ has set us free. Stand firm, then, and do not let yourselves be burdened again by a yoke of slavery.

GALATIANS 5:1

If the Son sets you free, you will be free indeed.

JOHN 8:36

These verses remind you that habits and temptations are always manageable if you value freedom over how you feel in the moment. But due to the rewiring in your brain that made the habits largely automated and linked to a sense of reward, you will have to change your mind and purposefully set out to rewire those faulty pathways into helpful ones.

When you're tempted, God promises to provide a way out. You can pause and think, *This isn't going to help me, and I can choose something different instead*—but you must remember that *life change follows mind change.* You can't think the same way if you want to live in a different way.

TECHNIQUE

1. **Prepare with prehab.** Be aware that bad habits arise from disordered thinking. That means you need to have some *ordered thinking* in place during the times and situations that often lead you to fall back into the old habit you wish to break. In a way, doing so is like taking the antibiotics and other medications we give patients before surgery to prevent infection. If

you start your day by thinking about any potential triggers you may face, you can put thoughts in place to help you keep your mind on the mission (breaking free of the habit) rather than the stress of the moment. By anticipating challenges, you activate the prefrontal cortex, strengthening its role in decision-making and reducing the likelihood of reactive, limbic-driven responses.

2. **Position yourself for success.** Many habits are hard to overcome because of choices you made earlier in the day. You are less likely to eat six doughnuts before bed if you did not buy them when you were at the store earlier.

Making one decision to avoid the temptation (resolving not to purchase alcohol or the wrong foods; not to call that person you're trying to end an inappropriate relationship with; not to go to the casino) is easier than having to make several decisions later (*Maybe just one*; *It's just a text message*; or *I'll only play the dollar slots, but I won't go to the blackjack table*). Habits are easier to break in the grocery store than they are in the kitchen when you're looking for a midnight snack.

Every decision you make earlier in the day reduces the mental strain of facing temptation later. This not only simplifies your choices but also trains your brain to associate success with proactive behaviors.

3. **Perform a Thought Biopsy and Whole-System Scan.** Examine your thinking when you are deciding whether to engage in the habit. What stories are you telling yourself about why you need or deserve whatever you're considering? What situation do you think would be more bearable if you went ahead and did it, and will that issue be better or worse tomorrow if you fall back into the habit now?

By examining your thoughts objectively, you activate your brain's anterior cingulate cortex, which is involved in error detection and conflict resolution. This helps shift your focus from impulsive reactions to intentional actions.

4. **Expose your temptations for what they are.** When you find yourself reverting to an old habit, pause and observe. Label the behavior or thought pattern without judgment, simply noticing it as a neural pathway that's been reactivated. Be honest with yourself about the narrative you hear in defense of the habit (*You deserve it, You need it, Just one more time*). Then, like a good pathologist, consider at least one alternative diagnosis. (*Actually, I use this behavior because I'm so worried about my marriage. But tomorrow my marriage is going to feel even worse because we spent another night drinking instead of talking to each other.*)

5. **Make it harder to engage in the habit than to avoid it.** Put a copy of the ten commandments of self–brain surgery in the drawer where you keep your ice cream scoop so you consciously process the fact that eating a pint of ice cream *is an act of self–brain surgery* that will make you better at choosing to overeat and worse at not overeating.

    Fill your refrigerator with healthy food choices. Delete the contact of the person you are trying to end a relationship with, so it's harder to call them. Buy a "Love Tomorrow More" wristband so you have to think about the sixth commandment every time you reach for a cigarette or a can of beer.

6. **Practice the Five-Minute Freeze.** Develop a habit of taking five minutes to think before you choose to reengage in your habit. Think about the results of your Thought Biopsy, the reasons you are making your choice, and what you will gain or possibly lose from it. Remember God's promise of providing a way out and take a moment to be grateful that you are now aware that any addiction is simply a brain habit that was formed by repetition and can be broken and replaced by repeating a new habit. It is stunning how often taking five minutes to "freeze" before engaging in the old habit will produce clearer thinking, allowing you to perform a different operation instead, so you get better at getting better.

    See the tomorrow you could have if you choose not to repeat the habit, and love tomorrow more than you hate how you feel right now. The Five-Minute Freeze leverages both mindfulness and neuroplasticity to help you change your mind about your habits and aligns with Romans 12:2 in giving you the space to pause, renew your mind, and no longer conform to the harmful habit.

7. **Flash forward to flash back.** One powerful technique to implement during your Five-Minute Freeze is to *flash forward to flash back*. Visualize previous times when you've given in to this habit or temptation and the problems or regrets that resulted the next day because of your choice. Make a list of the ways that, if you'd made a different decision *then*, you would have had less trouble the following day. Then ask yourself how you want your actual tomorrow to play out. Let the quality of tomorrow be more important than how you feel right now.

    Flashing forward to flash back activates your prefrontal cortex and the memory circuits in your brain and will help reinforce healthier decision-making pathways. This is a powerful way of learning to love tomorrow more than you hate how you feel right now.

8. **Do a postmortem.** The day after you have repeated your bad habit, take some time to honestly assess why it happened and what you were thinking when you made the choice. Avoid blaming others or your circumstances since you realize that the only person who can ultimately make you do something (or stop doing something) is you. Don't tell yourself, *The devil made me do it*, if you are the one who bought the bottle and put it in your pantry; the devil didn't drive you to the store.

Taking ownership of the thought processes that led you to act will empower you to own the changes you want to make. Do a patient-to-doctor switch and decide to provide compassionate and wise care of your patient next time via self–brain surgery.

The postmortem is like conducting a compassionate case review. By understanding the *why* behind your choices, you will empower yourself to make better decisions next time. This is an essential part of the self–brain surgery process—a time to gather insights, not criticize yourself. What thoughts led to your choice? What can you do differently next time? This reflection helps you refine your approach, turning setbacks into opportunities for growth.

OP REPORT

Record the things you struggle with and write down what your life would look or feel like if you eliminated them. Here's an example of what you might jot down:

> This bad brain habit is the result of disordered thinking when I thought the habit would anesthetize me against something I did not want to feel. Now I know that it never works out that way because I still feel the thing the next day and it just turns into a carousel of pain. What would actually help me is to be free from the habit so I can use my brain power to work on the real problem.

What is a habit you keep promising yourself you will stop, only to find yourself frustrated at how often you give in to it? Implement the steps above and then journal for a week about how you feel each day when you either do or do not reengage with the habit.

Which days feel best? On which days are you most productive? If you really want to become healthier, feel better, and be happier, does this habit help you or hurt you?

Write down a vision of what your life would look like without this habit. Describe how you would feel, how your relationships would change, and what opportunities might open up. Use this vision as a motivator to reinforce healthier patterns.

Breaking old habits isn't easy, but each step you take strengthens your resolve and rewires your brain for freedom and growth. Remember that God's promise to provide a way out is as real as the science of neuroplasticity. With patience, grace, and intentional effort, you can transform your habits and your life.

 ## When You're Grieving

Procedure: The Grief Guide Wire

WHEN TO USE

- When you are hurting over a fresh loss, facing overwhelming pain and a flood of emotions such as longing, disbelief, sadness, and disorientation

- When the wound is so deep you wonder where God is or if he even exists; doubt and shock are making you question everything you thought you knew

Note: If your grief feels unrelenting and you suspect you may be stuck in prolonged grief, refer to appendix A.4, "When You Feel Stuck," for additional tools.

TIME-OUT

Recognize that grief is holy ground, a place to acknowledge the depth of your loss and to reestablish your footing on the solid foundation of all that is still true in the world. Grief is a natural response to the loss of love and attachment, and your pain is a measure of the significance of the person you've lost. Feel the weight of the experience without judging yourself or feeling pressure (from yourself or others) to "move on." You approach this operation with the intent to honor your loved one's memory, process your emotions, and begin to explore a path forward while carrying the love and connection you shared.

GOALS AND BENEFITS

- To engage with grief in a healthy, intentional way that fosters emotional healing

- To gain awareness of the ways in which your brain can deceive you and keep you stuck, and to teach you how to operate your mind so you can move forward in hope and healing

- To find opportunities to honor your loved one's memory and keep their influence alive in your life

- To make room for joy and hope to coexist with sorrow over time, integrating your loss into a meaningful future

- To provide the tools you need to navigate the confusing maze of emotions, negative brain messages, and despair, recognizing that grief is a process rather than a problem to be solved

RELEVANT NEUROSCIENCE

Acute grief involves intense activation of brain regions tied to attachment, such as the anterior cingulate cortex and insula, which are responsible for emotional regulation and the processing of social bonds. This is why grief feels like a physical ache or yearning. The amygdala, a key structure in the brain's emotional processing center, is often hyperactive during acute grief. This can result in heightened stress responses, such as increased heart rate, difficulty concentrating, and a sense of being overwhelmed. Understanding this can help normalize these physical sensations as part of the grief process. After his wife died of cancer, the British author C. S. Lewis famously wrote, "No one ever told me that grief felt so like fear."[39]

Over time, the brain naturally begins to reorganize memories of the lost person, transitioning from raw pain to a bittersweet integration of their presence into your life story. Engaging in intentional grieving practices activates the prefrontal cortex, which helps regulate emotions, reframe painful memories, and encourage adaptive thought patterns.

Stuck or prolonged grief, where the intensity does not lessen over time, may be a sign of persistent activity in the default mode network (DMN) and the mid-anterior cingulate cortex, which contribute to rumination and a sense of being unable to move forward.

GUIDING SCRIPTURE

The Lord is close to the brokenhearted and saves those who are crushed in spirit.
PSALM 34:18

Blessed are those who mourn, for they will be comforted.
MATTHEW 5:4

Jesus wept.
JOHN 11:35

The thief comes only to steal and kill and destroy. I came that they may have life and have it abundantly.

JOHN 10:10, ESV

Because of the LORD's great love we are not consumed, for his compassions never fail. They are new every morning; great is your faithfulness.

LAMENTATIONS 3:22-23

These verses are a reminder that grief is a normal part of the human experience and that God meets you in your sorrow with compassion and comfort. Mourning is not a sign of weakness but a reflection of love and a necessary path to healing. It is inevitable that disease and death will steal people and things that you love, but Jesus shows you that even then it is possible to have an abundant life. Grieving in a healthy way is the path to embodying these truths, and doing the good work of learning to grieve well allows you to step into the renewal and hope these verses promise.

TECHNIQUE

1. **Reconsider your approach to grief.** Acute loss, especially when it is unexpected, can throw you into deep doubt. Things you thought were true are no longer true, which then makes you question everything else. If your attempts to find your way seem difficult, remember that using a different approach is often helpful. Turning to God or spiritual practices in such times can be a powerful step in your healing.

   Remember that grief is a journey; you don't have to rush through it, but you also don't have to stay stuck. You have the capability to manage your mind, brain, body, and life through this evolving process.

2. **Acknowledge your multiple roles.** If you are part of a family or group who shares this loss, recognize that you are all playing multiple parts. You will feel pressure to "be there" for others while intensely needing comfort and support from them. People naturally grieve in different ways and on different schedules, so do not compare your progress to theirs.[40]

   There is no correct speed or path to your healing. What matters is that the journey you take results in you finding your feet again with God's help. Realize that the five stages of grief, developed by psychiatrist Elisabeth Kübler-Ross, were never intended to serve as a template for how people grieve and move through major losses; instead, they were based on

Kübler-Ross's work and observations of how people handle the news that they have a terminal illness.[41] These five stages of grief have since been called into question by modern research.[42] While they remain influential in popular culture, they are best understood as one lens among many for understanding emotional responses to grief.

Be there for your people, and let them be there for you, but do not expect yourself to be on the same timeline as anyone else. Supporting others in grief does not require suppressing your own emotions; instead, it's about compassionately navigating the need to balance support for yourself and for them.

3. **Name it to know it for proper exposure.** Acknowledge the depth of your loss and name the other things you are afraid you might lose now that the person is no longer here. Accept the loss as both real and permanent, and then acknowledge that you are still here and have a life yet to live.

4. **Place the guide wire.** Just as surgeons use guide wires to help us safely navigate the placement of hardware during surgery, we can use gratitude to guide us and help us stay on the right path in our grief. Write down specific ways your loved one's presence impacted your life. List qualities, memories, or moments you are grateful for and that made your relationship unique.

   What are three things that you love about yourself that you developed because of your relationship with your lost loved one, and how can you nourish those qualities as a way of making their life continue to add value and purpose to yours?

   This guide wire will not only help you honor the one you have lost, but also allow you to focus on what you have and can look forward to—but only because of your loved one's life. What beautiful and important things can come true in the future only because of their influence and impact? This exercise will create a loss-to-legacy shift in your mind. Because your thoughts become things, they will serve as a guide in your future thinking and actions.

5. **Breathe to grieve.** When you are feeling anxious or afraid, practice slow, intentional breathing (inhale for four seconds, hold for four seconds, exhale for six seconds) while repeating a comforting phrase or guiding Scripture, or reflecting on a memory of your loved one. This activates your parasympathetic nervous system, reduces stress hormone levels, promotes calm, and helps ground you emotionally during intense waves of grief.

6. **Move closer to closure.** Spend time in prayer, meditation, or quiet reflection. Specifically work through the loss-to-legacy shift and find reasons to give thanks for the ways your loved one blessed your life. Acknowledge what you have lost but also gained by knowing them. Allow yourself to feel your emotions fully while seeking God's presence, comfort, and guidance.

OP REPORT

Reflect on how engaging with this process has impacted your emotional state. Record any changes in the way you perceive the loss, your ability to function day to day, or any moments of peace or hope you've experienced. Track your progress as you move through the stages of grief, noting any shifts in how you carry your loved one's memory and how you integrate their influence into your life.

Document moments when you took an action inspired by your loved one's influence, such as making a kind gesture, pursuing a goal they encouraged, or sharing a memory of them with others. These actions help integrate their legacy into your ongoing life story.

Write down times and places when you felt hope returning, pain lifting, or God honoring his promise to be close when you feel brokenhearted. Note what you were doing and thinking when these healing moments happened, and strive to recreate them when you're hurting in the future. Share these reflections with a trusted friend or therapist, or in prayer to externalize your progress and find additional support.

When You're Having a Panic or Anxiety Attack

Procedure: The Anxiety Ablation

WHEN TO USE

When you are feeling acutely anxious or panicking

TIME-OUT

The Anxiety Ablation[43] is designed for those times when you feel like your body and mind are out of your control, and these feelings or thoughts are interfering with your life, work, family, or safety.

Note: Remember that self-brain surgery is just one tool to help you manage your life. If you consistently struggle with anxiety or panic attacks, it is important to seek professional help.

GOALS AND BENEFITS

- To regain control of your mental state and physiology
- To gain confidence in your ability to reliably ablate anxiety and panic attacks by hijacking the brain's inability to multitask

RELEVANT NEUROSCIENCE

Mindfulness and sensory grounding techniques have been shown to reduce symptoms of anxiety, panic, and depression.[44] When you are experiencing an anxiety or panic attack, taking a physical or mental action to force your brain to engage in something other than perpetuating the anxious feelings can help you regain control. The 5-4-3-2-1 method (which I'll break down in the Technique section) is a powerful tool that robs metabolic energy from the amygdala and directs it to the areas you choose to engage.

GUIDING SCRIPTURE

Cast all your anxiety on him because he cares for you.

1 PETER 5:7

Form a mental image of robbing your anxiety of its energy and throwing it away. Your nervous system is designed to allow you to choose what you think about and feel, so engaging certain parts of your brain—instead of the ones that make you feel panicked or anxious—gives you a sense of control. You are *choosing* to direct your brain to relax instead of perpetuating the anxiety. You are choosing to be grateful that God cares for you enough to have wired this powerful ability into you.

TECHNIQUE

The Anxiety Ablation. When you feel yourself falling into an anxiety or panic attack, your tendency is to focus on the feelings (*My heart is racing, I don't feel safe, I can't be in this place,* etc.). What you pay attention to becomes more real, so the secret is to *choose to pay attention to something other than your anxiety*. The 5-4-3-2-1 method is a widely taught and effective mental grounding procedure that will enable you to ablate feelings of anxiety or panic.

- *5 Things I Can See*: Look around and tell yourself (or write down) five things you can see. Be very specific. For example: "I see a blue pen on the counter. I see the golden tinge of sunset on the leaves of that tree."
- *4 Things I Can Touch*: Notice and touch four things around you. Direct your attention to their texture, how they feel to your fingers, how hot or cold they

are. Acknowledge them in your mind or write them down. "I feel the sharp edge of my desk. I feel the warmth of my coffee mug."

- *3 Things I Can Hear*: Direct your ears to pick out three sounds around you. Again, specifically call them out or write them down. "I hear the air conditioner running. I hear a dog barking outside."

- *2 Things I Can Smell*: Notice two smells and process them. If there is nothing around you that you can smell (or if you have a cold and are congested), imagine the smell of a rose or peanut butter.

- *1 Thing I Can Taste*: Take a sip of coffee or a bite of something and mentally describe it to yourself or write it down.

Now, take several deep breaths in and out, and mentally picture what you've accomplished: You have taken command of five different areas of your brain—the occipital lobe (vision), parietal lobe (sensation), auditory cortex (sound), olfactory cortex (smell), and gustatory cortex (taste)—and directed blood flow to each of them. In the process, you have stolen power from your limbic system's ability to continue to make you feel anxious.

How do you feel now? You've just completed the Anxiety Ablation.

OP REPORT

Write down what you felt in your body and your thoughts and feelings as you were experiencing the attack. Now note how you were able to direct your mind and brain to think about certain things, in the order you chose to, and how your mind/brain/body came under your control as you did. Finish by affirming, in writing, "I chose to do self–brain surgery, and I now know that I can overcome anxiety and panic by deciding what to pay attention to and dwell on."

When You're Offended

Procedure: The Offense Obliteration

WHEN TO USE

- When you feel an intense negative reaction to something someone says or does, whether it feels strongly like an insult or criticism, or it triggers anger and puts you on the defensive

- When you realize you often blow up or lose your cool, harming your relationships

- When you are in an emergency situation and an emotional response could damage you professionally or relationally

TIME-OUT

Being easily offended—or prone to emotional outbursts—can be a barrier to strong relationships and overall emotional health. Learning to pause and respond rather than react is essential for preserving trust and ensuring you don't disrupt the critical 5:1 ratio of positive to negative interactions that make relationships thrive.

You are choosing to recognize that sometimes your responses to life events or other people do not serve your quest to become healthier, feel better, and be happier. This requires you to remember that you have an internal locus of control. Outside forces, people, or situations lack the inherent power to make you feel or behave in a certain way unless you give mental consent for your brain to automate that response.

Learning and practicing the Offense Obliteration is a choice to master your mind-brain-body interface so you respond intentionally rather than feeling as if your brain forces you into certain behaviors. By taking a time-out, you intercept the emotional escalation, reducing the likelihood of blowing up or losing your cool.

GOALS AND BENEFITS

- To remind you that your mind has top-down authority when feelings of offense or emotional overwhelm trigger intense brain responses and automatic reactions that could harm relationships or cause regret

- To regain control by severing sick synapses tied to impulsive reactions and replace them with healthier, intentional responses

- To be mindful that negative interactions create more lasting impact than positive ones, and so it's important to use caution in choosing your words

- To strengthen your emotional resilience by building new neural pathways that support measured responses, leading to long-term relational and emotional health

RELEVANT NEUROSCIENCE

Feeling offended or blowing up is a limbic/amygdala-driven response similar to the fight-or-flight reaction. This can make you feel as though you "must" lash out, defend yourself, or attack to regain control or achieve justice.

- *Amygdala hijack:* This intense emotional response overrides the rational functions of the prefrontal cortex, leading to reactive behavior you may regret.
- *5:1 Rule:* Dr. John Gottman's research shows that negative interactions are more powerful than positive ones in relationships. Blowing up could create a deficit that may weaken relational bonds.
- *Neuroplasticity:* Repeated emotional outbursts wire the brain for reactive patterns, making future blowups more likely. Choosing to pause and respond builds healthier neural pathways.
- *Empathy and perspective:* Engaging the orbital prefrontal cortex through cognitive reappraisal and empathy reduces limbic overactivity and fosters rational decision-making.[45]

GUIDING SCRIPTURE

A person's wisdom yields patience; it is to one's glory to overlook an offense.

PROVERBS 19:11

Everyone should be quick to listen, slow to speak and slow to become angry, because human anger does not produce the righteousness that God desires.

JAMES 1:19-20

[Love] does not dishonor others, it is not self-seeking, it is not easily angered, it keeps no record of wrongs.

1 CORINTHIANS 13:5

Practicing the Offense Obliteration will change your life dramatically. You will be able to choose the best response to situations that you previously believed had the power to make you react a certain way. The script will flip as the voice you hear most often becomes one of guidance and not offense. This is a gift of God's grace—the peace that comes from wisdom, self-control, and patience.

TECHNIQUE

Mastering this operation first requires that you regularly practice the Thought Biopsy before reacting to things you think or feel. You remember that you get better at what you are doing, so you resolve to get better at being thoughtful instead of getting better at being bitter.

When you feel yourself beginning to feel offended or like someone has triggered one of your automated responses, first biopsy the thought and determine what is really happening.

1. **Acknowledge the offended feeling and what triggered it.** You have to name it to know it, so realize that your normal response might be, *How dare she say that!* But now you want to manage your internal state first and choose an appropriate response, so instead you tell yourself, *I feel offended by that.*

2. **Pause, breathe, and run a Whole-System Scan.** Breathe deeply and exhale fully a few times to decrease sympathetic/fight-or-flight activity and engage your parasympathetic nervous system to help move you toward a measured response and away from an automated reaction.

3. **Make the patient-to-doctor switch.** Are you really offended by what they said, or is something else going on? Is your internal state vulnerable to being triggered because you feel unwell or you're scared or worried about something? Is there some unresolved and unrelated issue that needs to be addressed? Is the best treatment for your patient (you) to react to the offense, or is it to diagnose and operate on what is really wrong? Think back through your life and ask yourself whether running your automated offense reaction has helped or hurt you in the past.

4. **Perform a cognitive reappraisal.** Choose to turn the situation around in your mind and look at it from multiple perspectives. Ask yourself,

    - *Did they really mean to hurt me with what they said?*
    - *Is it possible that I heard it that way because of how I was already feeling, and that they did not intend it the way I took it?*
    - *Is there something going on that I don't know about that may be affecting how they behave?*

    Searching for alternative explanations for the offense creates a pause that enables you to make a healthier response. It also fosters empathy and reduces self-focused neural network activity, increases frontal lobe function, and leads to better decision-making.

5. **Choose the best response.** Sometimes the situation *really is offensive or wrong*, and it requires an appropriate response. In this case, you want your frontal lobes helping you choose the words and actions most likely to lead to a helpful resolution rather than a combative, limbic reaction that may perpetuate the issue or cause more trouble for you or the relationship in the long run.

6. **Operate.** Say to yourself, *I am in control of my own mind and brain. I can think through this situation and operate in a way that helps me and does not cause me more trouble.*

7. **Decide between offloading and unloading:**

   - *Offloading:* Express emotions in a healthy way, whether with a trusted person, by journaling, or through prayer. This is a decision to bring another person into your feelings and attempt to deepen the relationship in a healing way. It is *turning to* someone versus *turning on* someone.
   - *Unloading:* Venting anger or frustration impulsively at the offending person, risking relational damage, and creating trust issues for the other person, who may then question your real feelings for them at times when you are not offended.

OP REPORT

The next time you feel offended or on the verge of losing your cool, document the experience:

1. What triggered your response?
2. How did you feel initially, and what was your automatic reaction?
3. What techniques from the Offense Obliteration did you use?
4. How did this change your response and outcome?

Track your progress over time. Look for a reduction in emotional outbursts, a greater sense of control, and improved relationships. Celebrate the rewiring of your brain as you become less easily offended and more emotionally resilient.

Developing and practicing this procedure will help you obliterate reactivity when you've been offended, strengthen your relationships, and ensure that your emotional responses align with your goals for a healthier, happier life.

APPENDIX B

Progress Notes and Reports

The SOAP Progress Note

Use the SOAP note to keep track of your progress as you practice self–brain surgery to manage your mind and your brain. For a refresher on this form, see pages 16–17 and then use the SOAP progress note template below. Writing by hand has been shown to be significantly more effective for memory formation and retrieval than using digital notes,[1] so consider keeping a handwritten journal!

SOAP PROGRESS NOTE

Patient Information:

Name: Date:

Chief Complaint:

Subjective:

Objective:

Assessment:

Plan:

The Whole-System Scan Report

The Whole-System Scan is a daily or near-constant mental health checkup designed to provide a realistic analysis of your entire self. By using this technique, you can identify what you feel, diagnose the root causes, and develop a personalized treatment plan. Refer to chapter 22 for detailed guidance on the scanning procedure to help you fill in the template below.

You can include the Whole-System Scan report in the objective section of your SOAP note, complementing the subjective thoughts and feelings you've already identified with concrete insights derived from this exercise.

WHOLE-SYSTEM SCAN REPORT

Objective:

Date: **Name:**

Chief Complaint:

Relevant History:

Findings (see pages 182–183 for details on what to look for in each area below):

    Mind:

    Brain:

    Spirit:

    Body:

Impressions (see page 185 for details on what to look for in each area below):

    Areas of Cognitive Overload:

    Challenges to Emotional Regulation:

    Physiological Stress or Pain:

    Potential for Growth:

Recommendations:

    Self–Brain Surgery Operation:

    Physical Interventions:

    Emotional Training:

    Long-Term Plan:

The Thought Biopsy Report

This targeted self–brain surgery procedure is designed to help you analyze complex or recurring thoughts by assessing their nature, origin, and impact.

You can include this report in the assessment section of your SOAP note, as it provides a deeper understanding of the thoughts driving your emotions and behaviors. The insights gained here will help guide the next steps in your self–brain surgery plan.

Remember that if a thought is untrue, you are not obligated to react to it. Immediately sever the sick synapse involved in that type of thinking and do a thought transplant or other self–brain surgery operation to replace it with a true thought worthy of your response. For a refresher on how to fill in some of the details in the template below, see pages 188–192 in chapter 23.

THOUGHT BIOPSY REPORT

Assessment:

Date: **Name:**

Target Thought:

Emotional Impact of This Thought:

Cognitive Origin of This Thought:
1. Likely Source/Process:
2. Underlying Fact, Assumption, or Distortion:

Cognitive Distortions in the Thought:
1. Catastrophizing:
2. Overgeneralization:
3. All-or-Nothing Thinking:
4. Personalization:
5. Psychic Thinking/Mind Reading:

The Three Thought Tests (see pages 190–192 for guidance on how to think through each question):
1. Is it true?
2. What if the thought or feeling is *not* true?
3. What if the thought or feeling *is* true?

The Op Report

The op report is a tool to document your self–brain surgery operations. It helps you record the issue you addressed, the procedure you applied, and the outcomes you observed. You can use the template below to track your progress over time and adjust your approach if necessary.

OP REPORT

Patient Information:

Name: Date:

Diagnosis:

Procedure:

Outcome:

APPENDIX C

Pediatric Self-Brain Surgery
Helping Young People Change Their Minds

Every generation faces challenges never experienced by those who came before, but today's children and young people are under immense and unprecedented pressure. Research reveals a mental health crisis in our youth that is getting worse despite access to more resources than ever before. Kids face constant comparisons with others through social media, and they are growing up in a culture that values feelings and experiences over objective truth. Many are being raised in a "safety first" environment that implies they are inherently fragile.[1]

This reality places a responsibility on us as parents, grandparents, teachers, mental health professionals, and leaders to arm them with tools to manage their minds.[2] By teaching our youth the concepts of self-brain surgery from a young age, we can equip them to discover the truth that they have enormous internal capability to change their minds and their brains, and to manage their lives by smashing together neuroscience and faith through intentional effort. This will foster resilience, a sense of being able to endure and grow through hardship, and a strong and independent mindset.

Now that *you* have learned the approaches, principles, and procedures to refine your practice of self–brain surgery, you can pass these lessons on to the young people in your world. Pediatric self–brain surgery is a framework designed to help children and teens understand their brains and minds as tools they can actively manage. It incorporates neuroscience, psychology, and simple, actionable strategies to empower young people to make healthier choices, regulate emotions, and develop mental resilience.

Basic Principles of Self-Brain Surgery

In this book, I've gone fairly deep into the neuroscience to help you see why intentional self–brain surgery can be life-changing, but the basic tenets are quite simple. Children and teens who learn them can more confidently explore their world, identify and manage their emotions, and take reasonable risks. Here's a brief rundown of the principles you can pass on to kids:

1. **You are not just your brain.** Teaching kids from a young age that their minds have top-down control over their brains will empower them to believe that they are not obligated to listen to the voice in their heads all the time.

2. **You are not stuck with the brain you have.** Reminding children that their brains are constantly changing in response to their thinking and decisions (neuroplasticity) emphasizes the importance of thought discipline and emotional regulation, empowering them to think like self–brain surgeons. Rather than feeling powerless to behave or feel a certain way because of their genetics or experiences, they learn that they can choose how they want their brains to serve them.

3. **Feelings are not facts, and thoughts are not all true.** In a culture that encourages kids to "live their truth," we can teach them that what we think and feel is almost never true. Arming them with tools like the Thought Biopsy and showing them how this aligns with scriptural guidance to "take captive every thought" (2 Corinthians 10:5) gives them a sense of being in control of how they respond, rather than believing they must react to their impulses.

4. **People get stronger when they endure hardship.** Teaching kids not to be excessively risk averse by reminding them that they are not easily broken will give them a sense of resilience. Overparenting can lead to children believing that life is dangerous and scary, and it can promote a failure to launch. Training them to know that their brains actually get stronger when they overcome challenges—bandaging scraped knees when little, facing the tough school assignments and peer conflicts as teens—will prepare them to more successfully handle the harder things that inevitably arise later in life.

A Basic Pediatric Self-Brain Surgery Operation

You can explain to young people that they already possess everything they need to successfully operate their mind, brain, body, and life. Then be ready to provide the additional training they need to perform self–brain surgery themselves. Again, you can do so at a level they can understand and apply.

1. **Teach the patient-to-doctor switch.** From a young age, children should understand that their brains are continually running a program that is designed to keep them safe and to automate things that require less conscious thought. This is part of how we are "fearfully and wonderfully made" (Psalm 139:14), and it shows how Scripture and science align to help us.

But this automation also requires the kind of mind management that self–brain surgery creates. Knowing that the choices we make and the thoughts we allow to become real things are *within our control* is empowering and can help replace the cultural message that feelings are always real.

For example, when a child feels nervous about giving a presentation, help them recognize that their brain is trying to protect them. Teach them to reframe the nervous energy as excitement and focus on their preparation.

2. **Encourage them to build in the three-second pause.** Train the young person that it takes a little time to examine a thought or feeling and decide on a good response. Developing the discipline of pausing for a few seconds to biopsy their thoughts and consider *the best* response over the first one that "feels right" is a superpower that supports positive emotional regulation and decision-making. For example, when a child feels angry about losing a game, teach them to pause and ask themselves, *What am I really upset about? Is it fair to myself or others to lash out?*

3. **Teach them to reorder their minds.** Remember that when the pressure is on, we do not rise to the occasion; we fall to our preparation.[3] Because feelings feel so real and our internal voice sounds so trustworthy, helping kids memorize a set of family values, mottos, and Scriptures can help them choose to "believe what I believe before I believe what I feel or think."

4. **Emphasize the importance of recordkeeping.** Just like us, kids can benefit from learning to document their progress. Tracking how they change their thinking over time will give them immense confidence that they can continue to enhance their mental clarity and decision-making in the future. Train kids to use pictures or words to track how they work through their feelings and thoughts as they implement an intentional self–brain surgery practice to change their minds. When they do, they will become master self–brain surgeons. Smaller children can draw pictures of situations that provoke strong emotional reactions or confusing thoughts and how they work through them. As children get older, they can develop an age-appropriate written op report practice. (See page 289 for a template.)

The three-second pause and reordering their beliefs, thoughts, and feelings are great drills to practice with your kids. You'll be preparing them to successfully navigate whatever emotional or mental challenges life throws at them.

APPENDIX D

Guiding Others in Self-Brain Surgery
How Caregivers and Therapists Can Coach Others to Use These Tools

Coming alongside someone as they attempt to make major life changes is both an honor and a profound responsibility. Whether you're a loved one, mentor, or professional counselor, stepping into this role means investing deeply in another person's journey of transformation. Just as the family members of my patients help with their postoperative care, you've chosen to support and guide someone through their self-brain surgery—a critical role that can shape the trajectory of their healing and growth.

For counselors, therapists, and other professionals, this responsibility is magnified as you offer care to many, often under immense emotional and logistical pressure. Like surgeons wielding a scalpel to heal the body, caregivers and therapists use tools of guidance to help others navigate mental health and performance challenges and find healing. This chapter is your guide to stepping into this role—not for yourself, but for the well-being of those you serve.

As you guide others, remember this piece of ancient wisdom: "As iron sharpens iron, so one person sharpens another" (Proverbs 27:17). Whether you practice from a secular or a faith-based perspective, your work as a professor of self–brain surgery involves bringing clarity, sharpening thinking, and fostering growth. Neuroscience reinforces the value of this, showing that the brain thrives in supportive, interactive environments.

Empower your people to understand that they are responsible for making the necessary mental shifts to operate their own lives. Your role is not to change their minds for them but to convince them that they were created to take mind-down control of their thoughts and actions and that self–brain surgery *will* work if they practice from that perspective.

Your Role as a Professor of Self-Brain Surgery

Self–brain surgery isn't just about personal growth. It's a framework that caregivers, therapists, and mentors can use to accomplish several things.

1. **Teach the science.** Self–brain surgery is neither a metaphor nor a self-help trick. It is built on the solid neuroscience that our brains are constantly changing and we can direct those changes on our own behalf.

2. **Provide tools for transformation.** Teach your clients or loved ones how to identify harmful patterns and reframe thoughts—the first step in taking charge of their minds.

3. **Model healthy thinking patterns.** Practicing what you teach will reinforce the lesson and foster trust. If you do not live the message, you cannot be an effective messenger.

4. **Encourage them to question their approach.** Are they convinced that their situation is hopeless? If so, you may need to remind them that when *nothing* seems to be working, there is always *something* that can. Help them to see that experimenting with a new method is not a failure or character flaw but a strength.

5. **Help others access their internal "surgeon."** Part of your job is to empower individuals to become their own agents of change, making the patient-to-doctor switch for themselves. Your goal is to progressively shift into more of a consulting role as they develop their own practice.

Meet the Challenges by Practicing on Yourself

As you prepare for this noble yet demanding work, remember the first commandment of self–brain surgery: I must relentlessly refuse to participate in my own demise. Now this principle takes on an added dimension. While you strive to encourage your family member, friend, or client to take charge of their mental health, you must also safeguard your own. Helping people begin to practice self–brain surgery requires balance: protecting your mental health, establishing boundaries, and embodying the very principles you aim to teach. Only then can you effectively guide others without sacrificing your own well-being.

Caregiving and counseling come with their own challenges, including emotional fatigue, boundary management, and the temptation to "fix" others instead of guiding them. Understanding these pitfalls is critical to remaining an effective and empathetic professor. Before you can guide others, you must ensure your own foundation is strong.

Here are common challenges caregivers face and the self–brain surgery techniques to overcome them:

- **Emotional Exhaustion:** Use the Microsurgery for Your Mood operation (page 238) to recognize when you're feeling drained and take small steps to recharge.
- **Over-Identification:** The Filter Refocus (page 260) can help you avoid internalizing another's struggles as your own.
- **Boundary Setting:** The Offense Obliteration procedure (page 281) allows you to detach emotionally while remaining compassionate.

Adding Self-Brain Surgery to Your Practice

Mental health professionals have extensive training in a broad range of therapeutic techniques to help people improve their lives. The goal of self-brain surgery isn't to replace traditional therapy but to integrate these concepts as a lifestyle approach. This mindset empowers clients to take charge of their growth, making therapy more effective and sustainable. Once armed with the insight that our brains are changing constantly and that our minds can direct those changes positively, people can start to see themselves as empowered and capable self-brain surgeons who are *choosing to get better by whatever means necessary*. Once they make this simple mental shift, your clients can look to you as a guide who is arming them with additional tools they can use to help themselves.

Below are specific operations caregivers and therapists can employ when guiding others:

1. **The Perspective Pivot.** Help others reframe their challenges by asking questions like,

    a. What if this is happening *for* you, not *to* you?

    b. What might you learn about yourself through this struggle?

    This approach ties into neuroplasticity—helping clients shift from reactive loops to proactive rewiring.

2. **The Thought Biopsy Technique.** Train others to evaluate the accuracy of their thoughts using this structured approach:

    a. Identify the thought.

    b. Ask, "Is this true? Can I prove it?"

    c. Sever any sick synapses that led to the false or harmful thinking (limiting stories, false labels, past traumas, etc.), and transplant a true thought that fosters hope. This encourages disciplined thinking, avoiding the emotional spiral caused by unchecked thoughts.

3. **The Gratitude Graft (page 243).** Gratitude doesn't just change a person's attitude; it rewires the brain. Teach others to actively engage in small moments of gratitude each day to build resilience, conquer anxiety, and enhance reasoning and decision-making.

4. **The Suffering Substitution (page 266).** When guiding someone through grief or trauma, you can use this operation to help them reframe their suffering as part of a larger purpose, reducing the intensity of emotional pain.

How Good Professors Create Independent Surgeons

Effective caregivers and therapists are like scaffolding—essential during construction but meant to be removed when the structures (or in this case, the people) can stand on their own. Raising people to be able to practice independently is the ultimate goal of training and therapy. Here's how to foster self-reliance in those you guide:

1. **Teach principles, not dependence.** Focus on teaching operations they can use without you.

2. **Convince people that the power they need is already wired into their nervous system.** Help them understand that you are simply coming alongside them so they can take ownership of it.

3. **Celebrate small wins.** Highlight progress, no matter how minor, to reinforce their efforts.

4. **Normalize failure.** Let them know setbacks are part of the process. Use failures as teaching moments for refinement.

5. **Teach antifragility.** Disappointments and failures do not have the inherent power to destroy; rather, we can use them to strengthen ourselves.

The Most Important Thing You Bring

The most powerful instrument you have as a caregiver or therapist isn't your knowledge, skill, or advice—it's your presence. Simply walking alongside someone as they navigate their journey creates a neurochemical and emotional environment where healing becomes possible.

You may not be able to fix their problems, but you can show them that healing is always possible, growth is always attainable, and hope is always within reach.

APPENDIX E

The Self-Brain Surgery Library
Helpful Books on Neuroscience, Faith, and Where They Intersect

The following works will deepen your understanding of the ideas discussed in this book. They offer valuable insight into, as my friend Mark Batterson aptly says, "what's *really* happening when what's happening is happening."[1] This phrase perfectly sums up the quest for truth—understanding ourselves and grappling with life's profound questions like "why?" and "what now?" This curated collection will help you in that quest. It spans neuroscience, quantum physics, psychology, philosophy, and theology, offering tools to integrate science and spirituality in ways that inspire transformation, purpose, and hope.

Note that while each of these books was helpful to me, their inclusion here does not imply that I agree with everything each author has written. It's important to develop your worldview, your approach to self-brain surgery, and your faith through your own study of Scripture, engagement with science, and thoughtful observation of life.

FOUNDATIONAL NEUROSCIENCE

Doidge, Norman. *The Brain That Changes Itself: Stories of Personal Triumph from the Frontiers of Brain Science.* Penguin Books, 2007.

Newberg, Andrew and Mark Robert Waldman. *How God Changes Your Brain: Breakthrough Findings from a Leading Neuroscientist.* Ballantine Books, 2009.

Penfield, Wilder. *Mystery of the Mind: A Critical Study of Consciousness and the Human Brain.* Princeton University Press, 1975.

Schwartz, Jeffrey M. and Sharon Begley. *The Mind and the Brain: Neuroplasticity and the Power of Mental Force.* ReganBooks, 2002.

FAITH AND SCIENCE

Egnor, Michael and Denyse O'Leary. *The Immortal Mind: A Neurosurgeon's Case for the Existence of the Soul.* Worthy Books, 2025.

Guillen, Michael. *Believing Is Seeing: A Physicist Explains How Science Shattered His Atheism and Revealed the Necessity of Faith*. Tyndale Refresh, 2021.

Lennox, John C. *Cosmic Chemistry: Do God and Science Mix?* Lion Books, 2021.

Lewis, C. S. *Mere Christianity*. HarperOne, 2009.

Meyer, Stephen C. *Return of the God Hypothesis: Three Scientific Discoveries That Reveal the Mind Behind the Universe*. HarperOne, 2021.

Polkinghorne, John. *Belief in God in an Age of Science*. Yale University Press, 1998.

Strobel, Lee. *Is God Real?: Exploring the Ultimate Question of Life*. Zondervan Books, 2023.

Thompson, Curt. *The Soul of Shame: Retelling the Stories We Believe About Ourselves*. IVP Books, 2015.

APPLIED NEUROPLASTICITY, MINDSET, AND PHILOSOPHY

Dispenza, Joe. *Breaking the Habit of Being Yourself: How to Lose Your Mind and Create a New One*. Hay House, 2012.

Doidge, Norman. *The Brain's Way of Healing: Remarkable Discoveries and Recoveries from the Frontiers of Neuroplasticity*. Viking Penguin, 2015.

Schwartz, Jeffrey M. and Rebecca Gladding. *You Are Not Your Brain: The 4-Step Solution for Changing Bad Habits, Ending Unhealthy Thinking, and Taking Control of Your Life*. Penguin Publishing Group, 2011.

Seligman, Martin E. P. *Learned Optimism: How to Change Your Mind and Your Life*. Vintage Books, 2006.

Siegel, Daniel J. *Mindsight: The New Science of Personal Transformation*. Bantam Books, 2010.

Siegel, Daniel J. *Pocket Guide to Interpersonal Neurobiology: An Integrative Handbook of the Mind*. W. W. Norton & Company, 2012.

PHILOSOPHY, PSYCHOLOGY, QUANTUM PHYSICS, AND CONSCIOUSNESS

Dirckx, Sharon. *Am I Just My Brain?* The Good Book Company, 2019.

James, William. *The Principles of Psychology*. Henry Holt and Company, 1890.

Kopeikin, Kirill and Alexei V. Nesteruk, eds. *Consciousness and Matter: Mind, Brain, and Cosmos in the Dialogue between Science and Theology*. Wipf and Stock Publishers, 2024.

McGilchrist, Iain. *The Master and His Emissary: The Divided Brain and the Making of the Western World*. Yale University Press, 2009.

McGilchrist, Iain. *The Matter with Things: Our Brains, Our Delusions, and the Unmaking of the World*. Perspectiva Press, 2021.

Stapp, Henry P. *Mind, Matter and Quantum Mechanics*. Springer, 2009.

Taleb, Nassim Nicholas. *Antifragile: Things That Gain from Disorder*. Random House, 2012.

MIND-BODY CONNECTION

Amen, Daniel G. *Change Your Brain, Change Your Life: The Breakthrough Program for Conquering Anxiety, Depression, Obsessiveness, Lack of Focus, Anger, and Memory Problems* (revised). Harmony, 2015.

Amen, Daniel G. *You, Happier: The 7 Neuroscience Secrets of Feeling Good Based on Your Brain Type.* Tyndale Refresh, 2022.

Amen, Daniel G. *Your Brain Is Always Listening: Tame the Hidden Dragons That Control Your Happiness, Habits, and Hang-Ups.* Tyndale Refresh, 2021.

Church, Dawson. *Mind to Matter: The Astonishing Science of How Your Brain Creates Material Reality.* Hay House, 2018.

THE POWER OF FOCUS AND ATTENTION

Carreon, David M. *The Opposite of Depression: What My Work with Suicidal Patients Has Taught Me about Life, Hope, and How to Flourish.* Tyndale Refresh, 2024.

Haidt, Jonathan. *The Anxious Generation: How the Great Rewiring of Childhood Is Causing an Epidemic of Mental Illness.* Penguin Press, 2024.

Korb, Alex. *The Upward Spiral: Using Neuroscience to Reverse the Course of Depression, One Small Change at a Time.* New Harbinger Publications, 2015.

Shrier, Abigail. *Bad Therapy: Why the Kids Aren't Growing Up.* Sentinel, 2024.

BRAIN HEALTH

Amen, Daniel G. *Memory Rescue: Supercharge Your Brain, Reverse Memory Loss, and Remember What Matters Most.* Tyndale Refresh, 2017.

ALCOHOL AND BRAIN HEALTH

Grace, Annie. *This Naked Mind: Control Alcohol, Find Freedom, Discover Happiness & Change Your Life.* Avery, 2018.

EPIGENETICS AND MIND-DOWN INFLUENCE

Church, Dawson. *The Genie in Your Genes: Epigenetic Medicine and the New Biology of Intention.* Energy Psychology Press, 2007.

APPENDIX F

Self-Brain Surgery in the Bible

The Bible is not a science book and does not generally tell us *how* God did things but rather reveals *that* God did things. It also prescribes a way of living aimed at human flourishing so that we might achieve the abundant lives Jesus promised in John 10:10.

While Scripture predates modern science by millennia, it contains timeless wisdom that aligns remarkably with what neuroscience has taught us about the brain, mind, and human behavior. For instance, the Bible encourages renewing the mind (Romans 12:2), guarding the heart (Proverbs 4:23), and taking thoughts captive (2 Corinthians 10:5). These practices resonate with the latest findings in neuroscience regarding neuroplasticity, emotional regulation, and the powerful role attention plays in shaping reality.

In appendix A.12, which provides the Five-Minute Freeze procedure, I introduced the concept of "prehab," emphasizing that under stress, we fall to our level of preparation. Rehearsing truth and storing helpful words or beliefs in advance allows us to access them when we're struggling. Pastor and author Mark Vroegop aptly observes that "hope springs from truth rehearsed."[1] Memorizing Scripture can set up a spiritual and mental "tissue bank," providing helpful thoughts for transplantation when false or negative beliefs threaten to take over.

To that end, the following biblical passages (among many others) highlight principles from neuroscience that can guide us toward profound personal transformation. Please note that I am not attempting to reduce these rich passages only to neuroscientific principles or to imply that they were written to teach us about our brains. However, I think they illustrate how integrating faith and science empowers us to practice self-brain surgery in our daily lives—aligning our thoughts, beliefs, and actions with God's design for human flourishing.

> Do not conform to the pattern of this world, but be transformed by the renewing of your mind.
>
> ROMANS 12:2
>
> *Aligns with neuroplasticity and our ability to change thought patterns for personal transformation*

Finally, brothers and sisters, whatever is true, whatever is noble, whatever is right, whatever is pure, whatever is lovely, whatever is admirable—if anything is excellent or praiseworthy—think about such things.

PHILIPPIANS 4:8

Reflects the importance of focus and attention, aligning with Hebb's law about how we can reinforce positive neural pathways

For as he thinks in his heart, so is he.

PROVERBS 23:7, NKJV

Suggests the power of thought in shaping identity and actions, linking with how persistent thought patterns create neural structures

You will keep in perfect peace those whose minds are steadfast, because they trust in you.

ISAIAH 26:3

Highlights the role of mental focus and trust in regulating emotional and mental well-being

We demolish arguments and every pretension that sets itself up against the knowledge of God, and we take captive every thought to make it obedient to Christ.

2 CORINTHIANS 10:5

Aligns with the concept of intentional thought management for spiritual and mental health

The eye is the lamp of the body. If your eyes are healthy, your whole body will be full of light. But if your eyes are unhealthy, your whole body will be full of darkness.

MATTHEW 6:22-23

Metaphorically links focus and perspective with flourishing and mental clarity

Above all else, guard your heart, for everything you do flows from it.

PROVERBS 4:23

Reflects the importance of monitoring and shaping our inner thoughts and emotions

> The LORD is close to the brokenhearted and saves those who are crushed in spirit.
>
> **PSALM 34:18**

Links gratitude and seeking support with improved mental health during grief or hardship

> Set your minds on things above, not on earthly things.
>
> **COLOSSIANS 3:2**

Encourages perspective shifts that align with studies on optimism and resilience

> I came that they may have life and have it abundantly.
>
> **JOHN 10:10, ESV**

Shows that flourishing and abundance result from aligning with divine principles and steering our minds toward wise, positive, and grateful thoughts

> I tell you this, and insist on it in the Lord, that you must no longer live as the Gentiles do, in the futility of their thinking.
>
> **EPHESIANS 4:17**

Highlights the consequences of unproductive, aimless thought patterns and aligns with the neuroscience principle that habitual negative thinking reinforces detrimental neural pathways

> Be made new in the attitude of your minds.
>
> **EPHESIANS 4:23**

Corresponds with the idea of renewing thought patterns to reflect a healthier, more Christ-centered perspective, which parallels the neuroscience principle of neuroplasticity and the ability to reshape mental habits for greater well-being

Gratitude and Praises

My previous books were written from pain—while recovering from war, treating the sick and dying, reeling from the loss of our son. This book was written from need—my need, as both a neurosurgeon and a fellow owner of a human brain, to equip and train you to make the patient-to-doctor switch and move to a higher level of satisfaction. Please accept my praise and gratitude for the work you've done to reach this page, the changes you're making in your mind, and the impact those changes will have on your life and the lives of others. If I have contributed to helping you change to an approach that has led you to become healthier, feel better, and be happier, then I am profoundly thankful. All of the training I do in self-brain surgery is done that you may be made new by the renewing of your mind (see Ephesians 4:23).

My agent, Kathy Helmers, has guided me through four books. Along the way, with much pushing, pulling, cajoling, and shepherding, she has overseen a great transformation: I have changed from a fledgling writer with a good story to tell into a surgeon who sees words as another set of instruments to operate in the world. Kathy, I am not talented enough to write a sentence to adequately describe my gratitude for you.

To the incredible team at Tyndale Refresh, thank you for partnering with us to bring this book to life, for seeing its value, and for loving the mission.

To Daniel Amen, thank you for the beautiful foreword to this work and for your ongoing contributions to mind and brain health for so many.

To the intellectual giants who have wrestled with and sought to explain the mysteries of the mind and brain before me, I am privileged to stand upon your shoulders. I have learned much and been profoundly inspired by you. I humbly offer these pages in prayerful gratitude for your pioneering insights. I thank God for you and credit any wisdom and understanding contained herein to your groundbreaking work: William James, Henry Stapp, John Lennox, Dawson Church, Iain McGilchrist, Wilder Penfield, Jeffrey Schwartz, and Daniel Amen.

To Lisa Warren, you are my inspiration to get up every day and drive to the hospital to do my day job as a brain surgeon. There would be no teaching self-brain surgery without Lisa, as it was her insight that first opened my eyes to what was happening when people changed their minds and their brains in the MRI scanner in Auburn. She has heard every idea, read every sentence, and patiently volunteered as a test subject for every kind of self-brain surgery. Lisa, saying "Thank you" and "I love you" feels so insufficient, but thanks to our quantum entanglement, I trust you can feel the weight of those words. None of this work, this mission, or this book would have been possible without you.

Finally, to the God who has saved me—from my sins, from the bombs falling in Iraq, from the bombs life has brought through PTSD and the loss of our son—and who taught me to change my mind, and thereby my brain and my life, thank you.

Laus Deo magno medico. Praise be to God, the Great Physician.

Notes

INTRODUCTION: HOW SELF-BRAIN SURGERY WILL CHANGE—AND MAYBE SAVE—YOUR LIFE
1. W. Lee Warren, *I've Seen the End of You: A Neurosurgeon's Look at Faith, Doubt, and the Things We Think We Know* (Waterbrook, 2020).
2. W. Lee Warren, *Hope Is the First Dose: A Treatment Plan for Recovering from Trauma, Tragedy, and Other Massive Things* (Waterbrook, 2023).

CHAPTER 1: OUT OF OPTIONS?
1. Sara Lentati, "The Man Who Cut Out His Own Appendix," *BBC*, May 5, 2015, https://www.bbc.com/news/magazine-32481442; L. I. Rogozov, "Self-Operation," *Soviet Antarctic Expedition Bulletin* 4, American Geophysical Union (1964): 223–224.
2. Lentati, "The Man Who Cut Out His Own Appendix."
3. Chidinma Nwaogbe et al., "Surgeons Performing Self-Surgery: A Review from Around the World," *Translational Research in Anatomy* 10 (March 2018), 1–3.
4. According to psychology professor C. R. Snyder, hope gets you from where you are to where you want to be. I believe self–brain surgery is the vehicle to help you bridge those two points. See Snyder's book *The Psychology of Hope: You Can Get There from Here* (Free Press, 2003).

CHAPTER 2: NEW PATIENT PAPERWORK
1. Vivek Podder et al., "SOAP Notes," last updated August 28, 2023, in *StatPearls* (StatPearls Publishing, January 2025–), https://www.ncbi.nlm.nih.gov/books/NBK482263.
2. See my friend Max Lucado's excellent book *Tame Your Thoughts: Three Tools to Renew Your Mind and Transform Your Life* (Thomas Nelson, 2025).

CHAPTER 3: BUT WHAT IF I DON'T WANT TO HAVE SURGERY?
1. Iain McGilchrist, *The Master and His Emissary: The Divided Brain and the Making of the Western World* (Yale University Press, 2019), 4.
2. See appendix E, "The Self–Brain Surgery Library," for suggested reading about the power your mind has over your brain and body.
3. Jeffrey M. Schwartz and Rebecca Gladding, *You Are Not Your Brain: The 4-Step Solution for Changing Bad Habits, Ending Unhealthy Thinking, and Taking Control of Your Life* (Avery, 2011), 21.

CHAPTER 4: WHY GOOD SURGEONS CHANGE APPROACHES
1. Matthew 7:14. I realize that, in this passage, Jesus is saying that he is the only path to the Kingdom of God; however, I do think—given our brain's default to negative thinking—that this statement also applies to the difficulty of learning to use our brains to think in life-giving ways.

CHAPTER 5: APPROACH #1: NOTHING CAN HELP ME

1. To read my firsthand account of that time, see my book *I've Seen the End of You*.
2. I tell this story in greater detail in *Hope Is the First Dose* (Waterbrook, 2023), chaps. 5 and 6.
3. Trying to explain quantum superposition and the observer effect in more detail would take me too far away from the larger point of this chapter. If you're interested in learning more, here's a great article: Avery Hurt, "3 Ways You Use Quantum Physics Every Day," *Discover*, November 24, 2022, https://www.discovermagazine.com/technology/3-ways-you-use-quantum-physics-every-day.
4. See 2 Corinthians 10:5.

CHAPTER 6: APPROACH #2: MAYBE *SOMETHING* CAN HELP ME

1. Nate was my scrub tech during my time as a combat neurosurgeon in the Iraq War. He later became my son-in-law and the father of two of my grandchildren. You can read the story of how all this came to pass in my book *No Place to Hide: A Brain Surgeon's Long Journey Home from the Iraq War*.
2. Dan Harris, *10% Happier: How I Tamed the Voice in My Head, Reduced Stress Without Losing My Edge, and Found Self-Help That Actually Works* (Dey Street Books, 2014), 26.
3. Harris, *10% Happier*, xiv–xv. Italics in the original.
4. Harris, *10% Happier*, 168–169.
5. Harris, *10% Happier*, xiv.

CHAPTER 7: APPROACH #3: MAYBE SCIENCE CAN HELP ME

1. William James, *Psychology: The Briefer Course* (Dover, 2001), 2.
2. However, the atoms used to make those products were already there. In this sense, product creation/invention is just rearranging materials we neither created nor invented.
3. *Merriam-Webster* traces the English word *discover* to the fourteenth century. "Early uses of the word relate to the literal uncovering of something concealed or to revealing something unknown to others." See Merriam-Webster, "The Synonyms 'Discover' and 'Invent,'" https://www.merriam-webster.com/wordplay/word-histories-discover-and-invent.
4. There are 118 elements in the periodic table, but only 92 occur naturally on earth in appreciable amounts. There are arguments about this, and some lists include 94 or even 98 elements. The rest of the periodic table includes elements that do not occur naturally but have been created by physicists using particle accelerators. Here's a good overview: "The Nature and Organization of Elements," Exploring Our Fluid Earth, https://manoa.hawaii.edu/exploringourfluidearth/chemical/chemistry-and-seawater/nature-and-organization-elements.
5. Please don't write me to argue about who discovered neuroplasticity. William James, Santiago Ramón y Cajal, Jerzy Konorski, Donald Hebb, Bruce McEwen, Michael Merzenich, and many others made important contributions to this groundbreaking work. Who was the "first" depends on how you read their research.
6. "I praise you because I am fearfully and wonderfully made; your works are wonderful, I know that full well" (Psalm 139:14).
7. John N. Wood, "From Plant Extract to Molecular Panacea: A Commentary on Stone (1763) 'An Account of the Success of the Bark of the Willow in the Cure of the Agues,'" *Philosophical Transactions of the Royal Society of London, Series B, Biological Sciences* 370, no. 1666 (April 19, 2015), https://doi.org/10.1098/rstb.2014.0317. This is a fascinating paper examining Stone's work, the history of willow bark as medicine, and the story of aspirin's development.
8. I tell many such stories of patients finding faith and hope during hardship in my book *I've Seen the End of You*.
9. Wood, "From Plant Extract to Molecular Panacea."

CHAPTER 8: APPROACH #4: MAYBE GOD CAN HELP ME

1. God and "the Universe" are not synonymous, a point I make to prevent others from making the category error of pantheism/universalism. A logical category error occurs when a person treats two things as being in the same category when they actually belong to two different categories. This leads to confusion or false conclusions. If I say "God," and you think I am referring to a universal energy or the quantum field, but I am actually referring to a literal, living being, then we could each draw different conclusions as to what we're discussing.
2. Holmes Rolston III, *Science and Religion: A Critical Survey* (Templeton Foundation Press, 2006), 39.
3. Ruth Bancewicz, "Physics and Psalms," The Faraday Institute for Science and Religion, December 17, 2010, https://www.faraday.cam.ac.uk/churches/church-resources/posts/172/. The English Scripture inscription is quoted from the KJV.
4. James 4:17.
5. This is where training in self–brain surgery becomes a form of spiritual discipline. Romans 12:1-2 tells us that submitting our bodies—including our minds—to God's control is an essential and reasonable way to worship him: "Brothers and sisters, in light of all I have shared with you about God's mercies, I urge you to offer your bodies as a living and holy sacrifice to God, a sacred offering that brings Him pleasure; this is your reasonable, essential worship. Do not allow this world to mold you in its own image. Instead, be transformed from the inside out by renewing your mind. As a result, you will be able to discern what God wills and whatever God finds good, pleasing, and complete" (The Voice).
6. Andrew Newberg and Mark Robert Waldman, *How God Changes Your Brain: Breakthrough Findings from a Leading Neuroscientist* (Ballantine, 2010); Michelle Melis et al., "The Impact of Mindfulness-Based Interventions on Brain Functional Connectivity: A Systematic Review," *Mindfulness* 13, no. 8 (June 21, 2022): 1857–1875, https://doi.org/10.1007/s12671-022-01919-2.
7. Dawson Church, *Mind to Matter: The Astonishing Science of How Your Brain Creates Material Reality* (Hay House, 2018); Antoine Lutz et al., "Long-Term Meditators Self-Induce High-Amplitude Gamma Synchrony during Mental Practice," *Proceedings of the National Academy of Sciences* 101, no. 46 (November 8, 2004): 16369–16373, https://doi.org/10.1073/pnas.0407401101.
8. Marc G. Berman et al., "Depression, Rumination and the Default Network," *Social Cognitive and Affective Neuroscience* 6, no. 5 (October 2011): 548–555, https://doi.org/10.1093/scan/nsq080.
9. Glenn N. Levine et al., "Meditation and Cardiovascular Risk Reduction: A Scientific Statement From the American Heart Association," *Journal of the American Heart Association* 6, no. 10 (September 28, 2017), https://doi.org/10.1161/JAHA.117.002218; Madhav Goyal et al., "Meditation Programs for Psychological Stress and Well-Being: A Systematic Review and Meta-analysis," *JAMA Internal Medicine* 174, no. 3 (March 2014): 357–368, https://doi.org/10.1001/jamainternmed.2013.13018; Michaela C. Pascoe et al., "Mindfulness Mediates the Physiological Markers of Stress: Systematic Review and Meta-Analysis," *Journal of Psychiatric Research* 95 (December 2017): 156–178, https://doi.org/10.1016/j.jpsychires.2017.08.004.
10. Amy B. Wachholtz and Kenneth I. Pargament, "Is Spirituality a Critical Ingredient of Meditation? Comparing the Effects of Spiritual Meditation, Secular Meditation, and Relaxation on Spiritual, Psychological, Cardiac, and Pain Outcomes," *Journal of Behavioral Medicine* 28, no. 4 (July 28, 2005): 369–384, https://doi.org/10.1007/s10865-005-9008-5.
11. I list a host of such seeming coincidences in appendix F, "Self–Brain Surgery in the Bible."
12. See Matthew 5, for example, where Jesus teaches that hating someone or lusting after someone in our minds is the same as murder or adultery.

CHAPTER 9: YOUR ROLE IN REWIRING YOUR BRAIN

1. Chris Voss and Tahl Raz, *Never Split the Difference: Negotiating as If Your Life Depended on It* (Harper Business, 2016), 211.
2. Martin Caparrotta, "Dr. Gabor Maté on Childhood Trauma and the Real Cause of Anxiety," Human Window, January 4, 2024, https://humanwindow.com/dr-gabor-mate-interview-childhood-trauma-anxiety-culture/.
3. "So take a new grip with your tired hands and strengthen your weak knees. Mark out a straight path for your feet so that those who are weak and lame will not fall but become strong" (Hebrews 12:12-13, NLT).
4. Anne Lamott, *Almost Everything: Notes on Hope* (Riverhead, 2018), 35.
5. Nassim Nicholas Taleb, *Antifragile: Things That Gain from Disorder* (Random House, 2014).
6. Andrew Groover, "Gravitropisms and Reaction Woods of Forest Trees—Evolution, Functions, and Mechanisms," *New Phytologist* 211, no. 3 (August 2016): 790–802, https://doi.org/10.1111/nph.13968. See also Jonathan Haidt, *The Anxious Generation* (Penguin, 2024), 72.
7. The Bible said this all along! "We also glory in our sufferings, because we know that suffering produces perseverance; perseverance, character; and character, hope" (Romans 5:3-4).
8. Taleb, *Antifragile*, 3.
9. T. D. Jakes, *Disruptive Thinking: A Daring Strategy to Change How We Live, Lead, and Love* (Hachette, 2023), 3.
10. See 2 Peter 1:3.

CHAPTER 10: WHY WE NEED GUIDING PRINCIPLES

1. C. R. Snyder, *The Psychology of Hope: You Can Get There from Here* (Free Press, 2003).

CHAPTER 11: THE FIRST COMMANDMENT

1. N. S. Gill, "Is 'First Do No Harm' Part of the Hippocratic Oath?" ThoughtCo., October 20, 2019, https://www.thoughtco.com/first-do-no-harm-hippocratic-oath-118780.
2. Cedric M. Smith, "Origin and Uses of *Primum Non Nocere*—Above All, Do No Harm!" *The Journal of Clinical Pharmacology* 45, no. 4 (April 2005): 371–377, https://doi.org/10.1177/0091270004273680.
3. See James 4:17.

CHAPTER 12: THE SECOND COMMANDMENT

1. John 8:32.

CHAPTER 13: THE THIRD COMMANDMENT

1. Julie Tseng and Jordan Poppenk, "Brain Meta-State Transitions Demarcate Thoughts Across Task Contexts Exposing the Mental Noise of Trait Neuroticism," *Nature Communications* 11 (July 13, 2020): article no. 3480, https://doi.org/10.1038/s41467-020-17255-9.
2. Matthew A. Killingsworth and Daniel T. Gilbert, "A Wandering Mind Is an Unhappy Mind," *Science* 330, no. 6006 (November 12, 2010): 932, https://doi.org/10.1126/science.1192439; Roy F. Baumeister et al., "Bad Is Stronger Than Good," *Review of General Psychology* 5, no. 4 (December 2001): 323–370, https://doi.org/10.1037/1089-2680.5.4.323.
3. Jeffrey M. Schwartz and Rebecca Gladding, *You Are Not Your Brain: The 4-Step Solution for Changing Bad Habits, Ending Unhealthy Thinking, and Taking Control of Your Life* (Avery, 2011), 3.
4. Kirill Kopeikin and Alexei V. Nesteruk, eds., *Consciousness and Matter: Mind, Brain, and Cosmos in the Dialogue between Science and Theology* (Wipf and Stock, 2024).
5. Isaiah 30:21.

CHAPTER 14: THE FOURTH COMMANDMENT
1. William Shakespeare, *Macbeth*, 5.5.30–31. References are to act, scene, and line.
2. His books *The End of Mental Illness* (Tyndale Refresh, 2020) and *Memory Rescue* (Tyndale Refresh, 2017) are invaluable resources if you want to go deeper into all the ways to optimize your brain's health.
3. Alena Høye, "Bicycle Helmets—To Wear or Not to Wear? A Meta-Analyses of the Effects of Bicycle Helmets on Injuries," *Accident Analysis and Prevention* 117 (August 2018): 85–97, https://doi.org/10.1016/j.aap.2018.03.026.
4. "Alcohol Use and Burden for 195 Countries and Territories, 1990–2016: A Systematic Analysis for the Global Burden of Disease Study 2016," *The Lancet* 392, no. 10152 (September 22, 2018): 1015–1035, https://doi.org/10.1016/S0140-6736(18)31310-2.
5. "No Level of Alcohol Consumption Is Safe for Our Health," World Health Organization, January 4, 2023, https://www.who.int/europe/news/item/04-01-2023-no-level-of-alcohol-consumption-is-safe-for-our-health.
6. Natalie M. Zahr et al., "Clinical and Pathological Features of Alcohol-Related Brain Damage," *Nature Reviews Neurology* 7 (May 2011): 284–294, https://doi.org/10.1038/nrneurol.2011.42.
7. Emily M. Castro et al., "Nicotine on the Developing Brain," *Pharmacological Research* 190 (April 2023): 106716, https://doi.org/10.1016/j.phrs.2023.106716.
8. Marta Di Forti et al., "The Contribution of Cannabis Use to Variation in the Incidence of Psychotic Disorder Across Europe (EU-GEI): A Multicentre Case-Control Study," *The Lancet Psychiatry* 6, no. 5 (May 2019): 427–436, https://doi.org/10.1016/S2215-0366(19)30048-3.
9. Rita Z. Goldstein and Nora D. Volkow, "Dysfunction of the Prefrontal Cortex in Addiction: Neuroimaging Findings and Clinical Implications," *Nature Reviews Neuroscience* 12, no. 11 (October 20, 2011): 652–669, https://doi.org/10.1038/nrn3119.
10. Kathleen M. Fairfield and Robert H. Fletcher, "Vitamins for Chronic Disease Prevention in Adults: Scientific Review," *JAMA* 287, no. 23 (June 19, 2002): 3116–3126, https://doi.org/10.1001/jama.287.23.3116.
11. Karin Yurko-Mauro et al., "Beneficial Effects of Docosahexaenoic Acid on Cognition in Age-Related Cognitive Decline," *Alzheimer's & Dementia* 6, no. 6 (November 2010): 456–464, https://doi.org/10.1016/j.jalz.2010.01.013.
12. Timothy G. Dinan and John F. Cryan, "Gut Instincts: Microbiota as a Key Regulator of Brain Development, Ageing, and Neurodegeneration," *The Journal of Physiology* 595, no. 2 (January 15, 2017): 489–503, https://doi.org/10.1113/JP273106.
13. Cédric Annweiler and Olivier Beauchet, "Vitamin D-Mentia: Randomized Clinical Trials Should Be the Next Step," *Neuroepidemiology* 37, no. 3–4 (2011): 249–258, https://doi.org/10.1159/000334177.

CHAPTER 15: THE FIFTH COMMANDMENT
1. Dan Pilat and Dr. Sekoul Krastev, "Donald Hebb," The Decision Lab, https://thedecisionlab.com/thinkers/neuroscience/donald-hebb.

CHAPTER 16: THE SIXTH COMMANDMENT
1. Ephesians 5:18, NLT.
2. "Do not worry about tomorrow, for tomorrow will worry about itself. Each day has enough trouble of its own" (Matthew 6:34).

CHAPTER 17: THE SEVENTH COMMANDMENT
1. I first told this story in *Hope Is the First Dose*, pages 178–179.
2. See Psalm 103:2-5.

3. See the books listed in the "Foundational Neuroscience" section on page 297 if you want to learn more about how the Quantum Zeno effect works. I think Jeffrey Schwartz and Sharon Begley offer the best explanation in their book *The Mind and the Brain*.

CHAPTER 18: THE EIGHTH COMMANDMENT
1. University of Alberta, "Your DNA Is Not Your Destiny—or a Good Predictor of Your Health," ScienceDaily, news release, December 19, 2019, https://www.sciencedaily.com/releases/2019/12/191219142739.htm.
2. Rachel Yehuda et al., "Holocaust Exposure Induced Intergenerational Effects on FKBP5 Methylation," *Biological Psychiatry* 80, no. 5 (September 1, 2016): 372–380, https://doi.org/10.1016/j.biopsych.2015.08.005.
3. Sabrina Venditti et al., "Molecules of Silence: Effects of Meditation on Gene Expression and Epigenetics," *Frontiers in Psychology* 11 (August 11, 2020): 1767, https://doi.org/10.3389/fpsyg.2020.01767; Ivana Buric et al., "What Is the Molecular Signature of Mind-Body Interventions? A Systematic Review of Gene Expression Changes Induced by Meditation and Related Practices," *Frontiers in Immunology* 8 (June 16, 2017): 670, https://doi.org/10.3389/fimmu.2017.00670.
4. A. S. Zannas and A. E. West, "Epigenetics and the Regulation of Stress Vulnerability and Resilience," *Neuroscience* 264 (April 4, 2014): 157–170, https://doi.org/10.1016/j.neuroscience.2013.12.003.
5. Aymeric Guillot and Christian Collet, "Construction of the Motor Imagery Integrative Model in Sport: A Review and Theoretical Investigation of Motor Imagery Use," *International Review of Sport and Exercise Psychology* 1, no. 1 (March 2008): 31–44, https://doi.org/10.1080/17509840701823139.
6. Exodus 20:5-6 (NLT); Deuteronomy 5:9-10 (NLT).
7. Deuteronomy 24:16; Jeremiah 31:29; Ezekiel 18:20.

CHAPTER 20: THE TENTH COMMANDMENT
1. Kari Rusnak, "The Magic Ratio: The Key to Relationship Satisfaction," The Gottman Institute, December 7, 2020, https://www.gottman.com/blog/the-magic-ratio-the-key-to-relationship-satisfaction/.

CHAPTER 22: THE WHOLE-SYSTEM SCAN
1. Jon Kabat-Zinn, *Full Catastrophe Living: Using the Wisdom of Your Body and Mind to Face Stress, Pain, and Illness* (Bantam Books, 1990).
2. Jon Kabat-Zinn et al., "The Clinical Use of Mindfulness Meditation for the Self-Regulation of Chronic Pain," *Journal of Behavioral Medicine* 8, no. 2 (June 1985): 163–190, https://doi.org/10.1007/BF00845519.
3. Stefan G. Hofmann et al., "The Effect of Mindfulness-Based Therapy on Anxiety and Depression: A Meta-Analytic Review," *Journal of Consulting and Clinical Psychology* 78, no. 2 (April 2010): 169–183, https://doi.org/10.1037/a0018555.
4. Antoine Lutz et al., "Meditation and the Neuroscience of Consciousness: An Introduction," Philip David Zelazo, Morris Moscovitch, and Evan Thompson, eds., *The Cambridge Handbook of Consciousness* (2007), 499–554, https://doi.org/10.1017/CBO9780511816789.020; Geissy Lainny de Lima-Araújo et al., "The Impact of a Brief Mindfulness Training on Interoception: A Randomized Controlled Trial," *PLOS One* 17, no. 9 (September 7, 2022): e0273864, https://doi.org/10.1371/journal.pone.0273864.
5. Anthony P. King et al., "A Pilot Study of Group Mindfulness-Based Cognitive Therapy

(MBCT) for Combat Veterans with Posttraumatic Stress Disorder (PTSD)," *Depression and Anxiety* 30, no. 7 (July 2013): 638–645, https://doi.org/10.1002/da.22104.
6. Psalm 139:23. See also Psalm 46:10; Romans 12:1; 1 Corinthians 6:19-20; and Philippians 4:6-7.

CHAPTER 23: THE THOUGHT BIOPSY

1. Jeffrey M. Schwartz and Sharon Begley, *The Mind and the Brain: Neuroplasticity and the Power of Mental Force* (HarperCollins, 2002), 15–18.
2. Britta K. Hölzel et al., "Mindfulness Practice Leads to Increases in Regional Brain Gray Matter Density," *Psychiatry Research: Neuroimaging* 191, no. 1 (January 30, 2011): 36–43, https://doi.org/10.1016/j.pscychresns.2010.08.006.
3. John H. Flavell, "Metacognition and Cognitive Monitoring: A New Area of Cognitive–Developmental Inquiry," *American Psychologist* 34, no. 10 (1979): 906–911, https://doi.org/10.1037/0003-066X.34.10.906.
4. Max Lucado, *Anxious for Nothing: Finding Calm in a Chaotic World* (Nelson, 2017), chapter 9 title.
5. I got the idea of using three simple questions to evaluate our thoughts from author Seth Godin, who got it from writer Ursula Le Guin. See "The Le Guin Precepts," Seth's Blog, September 5, 2023, https://seths.blog/2023/09/the-leguin-precepts/.

CHAPTER 24: BASIC SELF-BRAIN SURGERY

1. From FBI hostage negotiator Chris Voss's outstanding book *Never Split the Difference: Negotiating as if Your Life Depended on It* (Harper Business, 2016), coauthored with journalist Tahl Raz. See page 211.
2. For more on the value of prehab, see chapter 25 in my book *Hope Is the First Dose: A Treatment Plan for Recovering from Trauma, Tragedy, and Other Massive Things* (Waterbrook, 2023).
3. James H. Fowler and Nicholas A. Christakis, "Dynamic Spread of Happiness in a Large Social Network: Longitudinal Analysis over 20 Years in the Framingham Heart Study," *British Medical Journal* 337 (December 5, 2008): a2338, https://doi.org/10.1136/bmj.a2338.
4. Hannah R. Snyder et al., "Advancing Understanding of Executive Function Impairments and Psychopathology: Bridging the Gap Between Clinical and Cognitive Approaches," *Frontiers in Psychology* 6, no. 328 (March 25, 2015), https://doi.org/10.3389/fpsyg.2015.00328.
5. Daniel E. Feldman, "The Spike-Timing Dependence of Plasticity," *Neuron* 75, no. 4 (August 23, 2012): 556–571, https://doi.org/10.1016/j.neuron.2012.08.001.
6. Andrew Matus, "Microtubule-Associated Proteins and Neuronal Morphogenesis," *Journal of Cell Science* 1991, suppl. 15 (February 1991): 61–67, https://doi.org/10.1242/jcs.1991.Supplement_15.9.
7. Anthony Holtmaat and Karel Svoboda, "Experience-Dependent Structural Synaptic Plasticity in the Mammalian Brain," *Nature Reviews Neuroscience* 10, no. 9 (September 2009): 647–658, https://doi.org/10.1038/nrn2699.
8. Phillippa Lally et al., "How Are Habits Formed: Modelling Habit Formation in the Real World," *European Journal of Social Psychology* 40, no. 6 (October 2010): 998–1009, https://doi.org/10.1002/ejsp.674.
9. Thomas C. Südhof, "Towards an Understanding of Synapse Formation," *Neuron* 100, no. 2 (October 24, 2018): 276–293, https://doi.org/10.1016/j.neuron.2018.09.040.
10. Christopher Vaughan, "Neural Activity Promotes Brain Plasticity Through Myelin Growth, Study Finds," Stanford Medicine News Center, April 10, 2014, https://med.stanford.edu

/news/all-news/2014/04/neural-activity-promotes-brain-plasticity-through-myelin-growth-study-finds.html.
11. For more on the critical role a good support team can play in your life, see chapter 30, "The Hard Work of Wellness," in my book *Hope Is the First Dose*.

CHAPTER 26: REWIRING FOR RADICAL TRANSFORMATION
1. Iain McGilchrist, *The Master and His Emissary: The Divided Brain and the Making of the Western World* (Yale University Press, 2009), 4.
2. Giacomo Rizzolatti and Laila Craighero, "The Mirror-Neuron System," *Annual Review of Neuroscience* 27 (July 2004): 169–192, https://doi.org/10.1146/annurev.neuro.27.070203.144230.
3. Elaine Hatfield et al., "Emotional Contagion," *Current Directions in Psychological Science* 2, no. 3 (June 1993): 96–100, https://doi.org/10.1111/1467-8721.ep10770953.
4. Avery Hurt, "When Hearts Beat as One," *Discover*, February 11, 2022, https://www.discovermagazine.com/the-sciences/when-hearts-beat-as-one.
5. Alexander Prehn-Kristensen et al., "Induction of Empathy by the Smell of Anxiety," *PLOS ONE* 4, no. 6 (June 24, 2009): e5987, https://doi.org/10.1371/journal.pone.0005987.
6. Tamara B. Franklin et al., "Epigenetic Transmission of the Impact of Early Stress Across Generations," *Biological Psychiatry* 68, no. 5 (September 1, 2010): 408–415, https://doi.org/10.1016/j.biopsych.2010.05.036.
7. Rachel Yehuda et al., "Holocaust Exposure Induced Intergenerational Effects on FKBP5 Methylation," *Biological Psychiatry* 80, no. 5 (September 1, 2016): 372–380, https://doi.org/10.1016/j.biopsych.2015.08.005.
8. Jeffrey M. Schwartz and Sharon Begley, *The Mind and the Brain: Neuroplasticity and the Power of Mental Force* (ReganBooks, 2002), 373.

EPILOGUE: HOW SELF-BRAIN SURGERY SAVED MY LIFE
1. 2 Timothy 1:7, NKJV.

APPENDIX A: TACTICAL SELF-BRAIN SURGERY PROCEDURES FOR SPECIFIC PROBLEMS
1. A good overview of major depression symptoms can be found here: "What Is Depression?" National Institute of Mental Health, https://www.nimh.nih.gov/health/topics/depression.
2. Richard J. Davidson and Sharon Begley, *The Emotional Life of Your Brain: How Its Unique Patterns Affect the Way You Think, Feel, and Live—and How You Can Change Them* (Plume, 2012); Morten L. Kringelbach and Kent C. Berridge, "Towards a Functional Neuroanatomy of Pleasure and Happiness," *Trends in Cognitive Sciences* 13, no. 11 (November 2009): 479–487, https://doi.org/10.1016/j.tics.2009.08.006.
3. Clay B. Holroyd and Nick Yeung, "Motivation of Extended Behaviors by Anterior Cingulate Cortex," *Trends in Cognitive Sciences* 16, no. 2 (February 2012): 122–128, https://doi.org/10.1016/j.tics.2011.12.008.
4. Robert Emmons and Michael McCullough, "Counting Blessings Versus Burdens: An Experimental Investigation of Gratitude and Subjective Well-Being in Daily Life," *Journal of Personality and Social Psychology* 84, no. 2 (2003): 377–389, https://doi.org/10.1037/0022-3514.84.2.377.
5. K. R. Fox, "The Influence of Physical Activity on Mental Well-Being," *Public Health Nutrition* 2, no. 3a (1999): 411–418, https://doi.org/10.1017/s1368980099000567.
6. David A. Sbarra and James A. Coan, "Relationships and Health: The Critical Role of Affective Science," *Emotion Review* 10, no. 1 (2018): 40–54, https://doi.org/10.1177

/1754073917696584; Gillian M. Sandstrom and Elizabeth W. Dunn, "Social Interactions and Well-Being: The Surprising Power of Weak Ties," *Personality and Social Psychology Bulletin* 40, no. 7 (2014): 910–922, https://doi.org/10.1177/0146167214529799.
7. Kristin Layous and Sonja Lyubomirsky, "The How, Why, What, When, and Who of Happiness: Mechanisms Underlying the Success of Positive Activity Interventions," in *Positive Emotion: Integrating the Light Sides and Dark Sides*, ed. June Gruber and Judith Tedlie Moskowitz (Oxford Academic, 2014), chapter 25.
8. Glenn R. Fox et al., "Neural Correlates of Gratitude," *Frontiers in Psychology* 6 (September 30, 2015): 1491, https://doi.org/10.3389/fpsyg.2015.01491.
9. Suzanne C. Segerstrom and Gregory E. Miller, "Psychological Stress and the Human Immune System: A Meta-Analytic Study of 30 Years of Inquiry," *Psychological Bulletin* 130, no. 4 (July 2004): 601–630, https://doi.org/10.1037/0033-2909.130.4.601.
10. Edwin A. Locke and Gary P. Latham, "Building a Practically Useful Theory of Goal Setting and Task Motivation," *American Psychologist* 57, no. 9 (2002): 705–717, https://doi.org/10.1037/0003-066X.57.9.705.
11. Jon-Kar Zubieta et al., "Placebo Effects Mediated by Endogenous Opioid Activity on Mu-Opioid Receptors," *Journal of Neuroscience* 25, no. 34 (August 24, 2005): 7754–7762, https://doi.org/10.1523/JNEUROSCI.0439-05.2005.
12. Emmons and McCullough, "Counting Blessings Versus Burdens," 377–389.
13. Simon Worrall, "The Air You Breathe Is Full of Surprises," *National Geographic*, August 12, 2017, https://www.nationalgeographic.com/science/article/air-gas-caesar-last-breath-sam-kean.
14. Mairead H. McConnell et al., "Yearning Predicts Subgenual Anterior Cingulate Activity in Bereaved Individuals," *Heliyon* 4, no. 10 (October 13, 2018): e00852, https://doi.org/10.1016/j.heliyon.2018.e00852.
15. Alexandra Touroutoglou et al., "Motivation in the Service of Allostasis: The Role of Anterior Mid-Cingulate Cortex," *Advances in Motivation Science* 6 (2019): 1–25, https://doi.org/10.1016/bs.adms.2018.09.002.
16. Amy Marschall, "The Role of the Amygdala in Human Behavior and Emotion," Verywell Mind, May 20, 2023, https://www.verywellmind.com/the-role-of-the-amygdala-in-human-behavior-and-emotion-7499223.
17. Loïc Berger, Han Bleichrodt, and Louis Eeckhoudt, "Treatment Decisions Under Ambiguity," *Journal of Health Economics* 32, no. 3 (May 2013): 559–569, https://doi.org/10.1016/j.jhealeco.2013.02.001.
18. Betsy Ng, "The Neuroscience of Growth Mindset and Intrinsic Motivation," *Brain Sciences* 8, no. 2 (January 26, 2018): 20, https://doi.org/10.3390/brainsci8020020.
19. See the second and third commandments of self–brain surgery in part 3 for a refresher on these important facts.
20. Sandy Cohen, "Training the Brain to Reconsider Troubling Thoughts Can Ease Mental Health Challenges, Says UCLA Health Research Psychiatrist," *UCLA Health*, May 9, 2023, https://www.uclahealth.org/news/article/training-brain-reconsider-troubling-thoughts-can-ease-mental.
21. Bill McCarberg and John Peppin, "Pain Pathways and Nervous System Plasticity: Learning and Memory in Pain," *Pain Medicine* 20, no. 12 (December 2019): 2421–2437, https://doi.org/10.1093/pm/pnz017.
22. A. Vania Apkarian et al., "Towards a Theory of Chronic Pain," *Progress in Neurobiology* 87, no. 2 (February 2009): 81–97, https://doi.org/10.1016/j.pneurobio.2008.09.018.
23. Ethan Kross et al., "Self-Talk as a Regulatory Mechanism: How You Do It Matters," *Journal*

of Personality and Social Psychology 106 (2014): 304–324, https://doi.org/10.1037/a0035173.
24. For incredible stories of people who've rewired their brains in this way, see Norman Doidge, *The Brain That Changes Itself: Stories of Personal Triumph from the Frontiers of Brain Science* (Viking, 2007).
25. P. Rozin and E. B. Royzman, "Negativity Bias, Negativity Dominance, and Contagion," *Personality and Social Psychology Review* 5, no. 4 (2001): 296–320, https://doi.org/10.1207/S15327957PSPR0504_2; Roy F. Baumeister et al., "Bad Is Stronger Than Good," *Review of General Psychology* 5, no. 4 (2001): 323–370, https://doi.org/10.1037/1089-2680.5.4.323.
26. Kyle Benson, "The Magic Relationship Ratio, According to Science," The Gottman Institute, October 4, 2017, https://www.gottman.com/blog/the-magic-relationship-ratio-according-science/.
27. The RAS has many functions besides gating information. See this book to learn more about the RAS: Edgar Garcia-Rill, *Waking and the Reticular Activating System in Health and Disease* (Academic Press, 2015).
28. To watch this incredible experiment, see Daniel Simons, "Selective Attention Test," https://www.youtube.com/watch?v=vJG698U2Mvo.
29. D. J. Simons and C. F. Chabris, "Gorillas in Our Midst: Sustained Inattentional Blindness for Dynamic Events," *Perception* 28, no. 9 (1999): 1059–1074, https://doi.org/10.1068/p281059.
30. Raymond S. Nickerson, "Confirmation Bias: A Ubiquitous Phenomenon in Many Guises," *Review of General Psychology* 2, no. 2 (June 1998), 175–220, https://doi.org/10.1037/1089-2680.2.2.175; Nicolas DiFonzo and Prashant Bordia, *Rumor Psychology: Social and Organizational Approaches* (American Psychological Association, 2007).
31. Ligation is a procedure in which we ligate, or tie off, something to keep it from bleeding, getting bigger, leaking, or causing other problems.
32. U.S. Department of Health and Human Services, *Our Epidemic of Loneliness and Isolation: The U.S. Surgeon General's Advisory on the Healing Effects of Social Connection and Community* (Washington, DC: Office of the U.S. Surgeon General, 2023), https://www.hhs.gov/sites/default/files/surgeon-general-social-connection-advisory.pdf.
33. Michael D. Fox et al., "The Human Brain Is Intrinsically Organized into Dynamic, Anticorrelated Functional Networks," *Proceedings of the National Academy of Sciences* 102, no. 27 (July 5, 2005): 9673–9678, https://doi.org/10.1073/pnas.0504136102.
34. Prathik Kini et al., "The Effects of Gratitude Expression on Neural Activity," *NeuroImage* 128 (March 2016): 1–10, https://doi.org/10.1016/j.neuroimage.2015.12.040.
35. D. O. Hebb, *The Organization of Behavior: A Neuropsychological Theory* (Wiley, 1949).
36. Roy A. Wise and George F. Koob, "The Development and Maintenance of Drug Addiction," *Neuropsychopharmacology* 39, no. 2 (January 2014): 254–262, https://doi.org/10.1038/npp.2013.261.
37. Rita Z. Goldstein and Nora D. Volkow, "Dysfunction of the Prefrontal Cortex in Addiction: Neuroimaging Findings and Clinical Implications," *Nature Reviews Neuroscience* 12, no. 11 (October 20, 2011): 652–669, https://doi.org/10.1038/nrn3119.
38. Doidge, *The Brain That Changes Itself.*
39. C. S. Lewis, *A Grief Observed* (Bantam, 1976), 1.
40. Psychologist Robert Neimeyer has discussed the idea of meaning-making in grief: Every experience is unique, and each of us needs to find our own path. This lines up with my experience both as a bereaved parent and a physician who cares for many families during

times of loss. For more, see Robert A. Neimeyer, ed., *Techniques of Grief Therapy: Creative Practices for Counseling the Bereaved* (Routledge, 2019).
41. Elizabeth Kübler-Ross, *On Death and Dying* (Macmillan, 1969).
42. Margaret Stroebe et al., "Cautioning Health-Care Professionals: Bereaved Persons Are Misguided Through the Stages of Grief," *Omega* 74, no. 4 (February 13, 2017): 453–473, https://doi.org/10.1177/0030222817691870.
43. Ablation is the process of purposefully destroying tissue (tumors, painful nerves, etc.) surgically. We often use heat, cold, radiofrequency probes, and other technologies for ablation procedures.
44. Stefan Hofmann et al., "The Effect of Mindfulness-Based Therapy on Anxiety and Depression: A Meta-Analytic Review," *Journal of Consulting and Clinical Psychology* 78, no. 2 (April 2010): 169–183, https://doi.org/10.1037/a0018555.
45. Ya-Xin Wang and Bin Yin, "A New Understanding of the Cognitive Reappraisal Technique: An Extension Based on the Schema Theory," *Frontiers in Behavioral Neuroscience* 17 (April 16, 2023), https://doi.org/10.3389/fnbeh.2023.1174585.

APPENDIX B: PROGRESS NOTES AND REPORTS
1. Keita Umejima et al., "Paper Notebooks Vs. Mobile Devices: Brain Activation Differences During Memory Retrieval," *Frontiers in Behavioral Neuroscience* 15 (March 19, 2021): 634158, https://doi.org/10.3389/fnbeh.2021.634158.

APPENDIX C: PEDIATRIC SELF-BRAIN SURGERY
1. Greg Lukianoff and Jonathan Haidt, *The Coddling of the American Mind: How Good Intentions and Bad Ideas Are Setting Up a Generation for Failure* (Penguin Press, 2018), chap. 1.
2. Brian K. Barber et al., "Parental Support, Psychological Control, and Behavioral Control: Assessing Relevance Across Time, Culture, and Method," *Monographs of the Society for Research in Child Development,* 70, no. 4 (2005): 1–137, https://doi.org/10.1111/j.1540-5834.2005.00365.x.
3. Chris Voss and Tahl Raz, *Never Split the Difference: Negotiating as If Your Life Depended on It* (Harper Business, 2016).

APPENDIX E: THE SELF-BRAIN SURGERY LIBRARY
1. Mark Batterson, *A Million Little Miracles: Rediscover the God Who Is Bigger than Big, Closer than Close, and Gooder than Good* (Multnomah, 2024), xiv.

APPENDIX F: SELF-BRAIN SURGERY IN THE BIBLE
1. Mark Vroegop, *Dark Clouds, Deep Mercy* (Crossway, 2019), 105.

About the Author

W. Lee Warren, MD, is a practicing neurosurgeon, award-winning author, and Iraq War veteran. Outside the operating room, his writing and teaching serve as prescriptions for connecting neuroscience to faith for radical life transformation.

He teaches the art and science of human flourishing on *The Dr. Lee Warren Podcast*, which is heard weekly in 150 countries around the world; on Substack, where he publishes the bestselling *Self-Brain Surgery* newsletter; and in his books. *No Place to Hide* was named to the 2015 US Air Force Chief of Staff Reading List. *I've Seen the End of You* was the Christian Book Award winner for Biography and Memoir in 2021. And *Hope Is the First Dose* was one of *Outreach* magazine's 2024 Resources of the Year award winners for Counseling and Relationships.

Dr. Warren lives in Nebraska with his wife, Lisa. They have four living children and a growing collection of grandkids. Learn more about Dr. Warren at drleewarren.com and on Instagram @drleewarren.

Tyndale | REFRESH

Think Well. Live Well. Be Well.

Experience the flourishing of your mind, body, and soul with Tyndale Refresh.